Re-creating Authority
in Revolutionary France

Re-creating Authority

IN

REVOLUTIONARY FRANCE

EDITED BY

Bryant T. Ragan, Jr.,
and Elizabeth A. Williams

WITH A FOREWORD BY

Lynn Hunt

Rutgers University Press
New Brunswick, New Jersey

Library of Congress Cataloging-in-Publication Data

Re-creating authority in revolutionary France
/ edited by Bryant T. Ragan, Jr., and Elizabeth A. Williams ; with a
foreword by Lynn Hunt.
    p.   cm.
  Includes bibliographical references and index.
  ISBN 0-8135-1841-5 (cloth)—ISBN 0-8135-1842-3 (pbk.)
    1. France—History—Revolution, 1789–1799—Influence—Congresses.
2. Politics and culture—France—History—19th century—Congresses.
3. France—Politics and government—Revolution, 1789–1799—Social
aspects—Congresses.   4. French language—Political aspects—France—
History—19th century—Congresses.   5. Social change—Congresses.
I. Ragan, Bryant T., 1960–   . II. Williams, Elizabeth A., 1950–
DC158.8.S88   1992
944.04—dc20   91-45492
                                                                   CIP

British Cataloging-in-Publication information available

Contents

List of Illustrations

Foreword

Commemorations of the French Revolution have a habit of coinciding with major turning points in history: the centennial in 1889 with its Eiffel Tower signaled the long-postponed success of democratic and republican government in France; the one hundred and fiftieth anniversary in 1939 came with the beginning of World War II and the imminent collapse of France as a great power; and the bicentennial in 1989 seemed to foreshadow the unraveling of communist power in Eastern Europe. Each of these anniversaries also marked, not surprisingly, a major change in the historiography of the French Revolution. After generations of bitter political and academic conflict, 1889 crowned the growing dominance of prorepublican historiography in the leading journals and university teaching. In 1939 the newly prominent socialist and communist historians wedded their celebration of the Jacobin Revolution to the need for consensus in national defense and thereby made the Marxist interpretation of the French Revolution into a kind of national catechism. Finally, 1989 saw the triumph of an anti-Marxist and anticommunist interpretation that emphasized the links between revolution and totalitarianism. It is hardly fortuitous that the changes in historiography went hand in hand with the changes in national and world politics, for the historiography of the French Revolution has served as a barometer of political opinion within France and within the ranks of international socialism.

The authors of the essays in this volume are stepping out into a terrain pockmarked by two hundred years of controversy. They make an effort to protect their flanks by aligning themselves with the recent changes in the historiography of the French Revolution, and they speak most respectfully of their elders in the field. But make no mistake: these young authors are embarked in fact on a new enterprise. Although they stop short of offering a fully elaborated alternative interpretation of the French Revolution and its long-term effects, their work opens new directions of research and interpretation. This originality becomes clearer if we look briefly at the current state of historiography about the French Revolution.

Just as the turning points of 1889 and 1939 were associated respectively with the names of Alphonse Aulard and Georges Lefebvre, both of them holders of the prestigious chair of the history of the French Revolution at the University of Paris, the historiographical turning point of 1989 was associated with the name of François Furet. Furet did not hold the chair of the history of the French Revolution; he was never a university professor and never wrote a doctoral thesis. Yet from his position as president of the Ecole des Hautes Etudes en Sciences Sociales and then as head of the Ecole's new Institut Raymond Aron, Furet wielded great power in the most important academic institution outside the university. He was able to gather around him a new school of historians and political philosophers interested in elaborating an interpretive challenge to the Marxist account that had been dominant since the 1930s in France.

Unlike his predecessors Aulard and Lefebvre, Furet's breakthrough was not based on his own research. He astutely synthesized the research of others—especially of English-speaking scholars—and combined this with a rereading of the nineteenth- and early twentieth-century historians to establish an interpretation that rivaled the Marxist one in its philosophical bent. Furet argued that the Marxist interpretation had become a hollow litany, and in its place he offered an updated Tocquevillian view: in the absence of a strong set of political institutions and a history of meaningful political participation, the French revolutionaries tried to force a democratic consensus by remaking social and political life from the top down. In the name of democracy, they developed the prototype of totalitarianism. Revolutionary political culture was decisively shaped, in this view, by the vagaries of democratic ideology, especially as formulated by Rousseau.

Although American and English historians of the French Revolution—most notably George Taylor and Alfred Cobban—had been working in a similar anti-Marxist vein long before Furet began publishing his own views, they were never able to offer an alternative account to the Marxist interpretation because they eschewed all grand theory in the name of their resistance to Marxism. They limited themselves to refuting the then dominant Marxist account, which characterized the Revolution as the triumph of the bourgeoisie as a social class and of capitalism as a mode of production. During the 1950s, 1960s, and 1970s, moreover, many English-speaking historians deliberately avoided working on the French Revolution because the subject seemed too caught up in ideological debates. In a way, then, we are indebted to Furet himself for changing this situation in the 1980s and 1990s; he validated Anglophone research by using it as his base of departure, and he opened up the interpretive field by exploding what remained of the Marxist hegemony in France.

So it is not surprising that young scholars today might take Furet as their point of departure. Yet though the authors in this collection have taken up the Furet emphasis on the political culture of revolutionary France as the heart of the story, their working definition of political culture is very different. In his eagerness to refute any materialist interpretation that might reduce politics to social interest or class struggle, Furet developed a notion of politics that was almost wholly ideological and linguistic. Revolutionary politics, in his view, was shaped by the "semiotic" struggle over who would represent the will of the people, that is, by the struggle to control revolutionary language and ideology. As a result, his account focused on Paris, on a handful of leading Jacobins (really on Robespierre), and on a few central political actions with the term *political* taken in a very narrow sense to refer to decisions at the top about national policy.

In contrast, the essays in this book open up the definition of political culture to encompass not only a broad chronological time span (a view also championed by Furet, who has written about the French Revolution as a political process reaching from 1780 to 1880) but also a capaciously defined set of cultural and social practices. Rather than concentrating exclusively on Paris, these authors include the provinces; rather than singling out the actions of a handful of male political leaders, they include groups as diverse as women, peasants, theater-goers, doctors, professors, administrators, and scientists. Political culture is not viewed here as the automatic effect of a new democratic ideology or as a set of narrowly defined political activities but rather as the fluid and ever-changing product of conflicts between different social and gender groups and of efforts to reconstruct culture along new lines. In other words, the culture is brought back into political culture, and the concept is given a variety of different and sometimes competing social meanings.

What will the reader conclude from such a diverse set of approaches and topics? What brings together essays on women who joined political clubs, peasants concerned about their taxes, revolutionary theater audiences, doctors in conflict with the clergy, hygienists interested in statistics in the 1830s and 1840s, professors of natural history, and late nineteenth-century definers of taste in furniture? In many ways, as might be expected, it is the diversity of these essays, rather than their commonalities, that matters most. In contrast to the Furet account that emphasized the deterministic, conformist effects of revolutionary ideology, the view emerging from these essays underlines the ongoing creativity of revolutionary culture, a creativity anchored in the differences of reactions to the revolution in the making. Women in political clubs and peasants in northern France, for example, shared some premises with the national leadership but had their own goals and their own means of achieving them. As a consequence, they developed new, concrete meanings for the term *equality*. Similarly, doctors, public health administrators, and professors worked out their own ways of enhancing their social and cultural authority in this time of rapid change and thereby helped increase the prestige of science and of the principle of utility. The revolutionary legacy in the nineteenth century was susceptible to the same kinds of reworking; the Revolution did not mean just one thing in the 1790s, and its meanings continued to proliferate in the generations that followed.

The Revolution offered people an unparalleled opportunity to try out new modes of action and to modify traditional repertoires for new purposes. Some of these experiences had a short half-life: women's clubs were suppressed in 1793, and Paris theater audiences soon tired of looking for direct political meaning in performances. Other developments had long-lasting cultural implications: the exclusion of women from politics, public health administration in the name of public order, utilitarian ideals in science, and the prestige of medicine all had long futures. Sometimes the future brought surprising transformations, as for instance, when the French middle classes of the late nineteenth century developed a taste for ancien régime furniture styles as a way of being up-to-date and socially in-the-know. Taken together, these essays show that the politics of culture took often surprising and always shifting forms.

The essays presented here offer more than a simple corrective to monolithic views of the workings of political culture during the French Revolution. They show, as the momentous revolutions of 1989–1991 themselves have demonstrated, that culture is always malleable and that people acting together can tap possibilities of cultural and political creativity that were previously unknown. As the implications of the revolutions of 1989 are assimilated, the historiography of their great precursor, the French Revolution of 1789, is bound to change once again. We cannot yet see clearly the direction of the general rethinking, but we can be assured that the individual essays in this collection provide much new material for the task.

Lynn Hunt
University of Pennsylvania
November 1991

Acknowledgments

This collection comes out of a conference held at Oklahoma State University on 17–18 November 1989 to celebrate the bicentennial of the French Revolution. The conference was intended to bring together historians of modern France who had recently completed their doctoral degrees to present new research assessing the impact of the Revolution on French culture and society.

The financial and intellectual support of many institutions and individuals made the conference possible. We would first like to thank the Department of History of Oklahoma State University, the Oklahoma Foundation for the Humanities, the National Endowment for the Humanities, and Fordham University for generously funding the project. In addition, we would like to extend our appreciation to the staff of Oklahoma State University for their help in planning and hosting the conference.

Many people made comments at the conference sessions that helped the contributors to this volume reconceive and rework their papers. We are especially grateful to James S. Allen, Jean Bacot, Gail Bossenga, Joseph F. Byrnes, Geraldine Friedman, Perry Gethner, John Howland, Rene Marion, Laura Mason, Anita May, Michael Mosher, Carl Strickwerda, and Kenneth L. Taylor for their active participation.

This collection would not have been possible without the careful guidance provided by Marlie Wasserman and her staff at Rutgers University Press. Their patience in dealing with the complexities stemming from a multiauthored book was unending.

Finally, we would like to thank Robert Mayer and Dennis McEnnerney for their emotional as well as intellectual support.

B.T.R.
E.A.W.
November 1991

Re-creating Authority
in Revolutionary France

Introduction

BRYANT T. RAGAN, JR.,
and ELIZABETH A. WILLIAMS

"The Revolution is over," François Furet proclaimed in *Penser la Révolution française* (1978). This seemingly simple assertion has momentous implications for the historiography of modern France.[1] Encapsulating the "revisionist" interpretation of the French Revolution, it establishes a scholarly analog to Fifth Republic politics, in which winning votes and forming coalitions have come to matter more than tracing party lineages and fighting over the "Marseillaise." From this perspective, the study of the Revolution is no longer the partisan matter it was when political legitimacy depended upon a "correct" interpretation of the origins of French republicanism. Freed from such constraints, the Revolution emerges not as the moment when the identity of modern France was established but simply as the first of several experiments in representative government that were to take place in Europe and North America. In short, the Revolution came and went. It was essential neither to the origins of modern political discourse, which had already begun to develop under the Old Regime, nor to the imposition of that discourse on political society, a process that was inevitable.[2]

Judging from the many books and essays published during the bicentennial, it seems that revisionism has come to dominate scholarship on the Revolution.[3] Although some historians still uphold elements of the long-dominant Marxist interpretation, few unequivocally defend the view that the Revolution resulted from socioeconomic conflicts and instituted a new capitalist order.[4] The attack on the Marxist interpretation, instigated some three decades ago by the work of Alfred Cobban and others, has now been powerfully reinforced by the fall of the Leninist states of Eastern Europe and the disintegration of the Soviet Union.[5] Furthermore, these political currents have dovetailed with methodological and analytical innovations that have encouraged historians to shift their attention away from the study of social and economic causation to the synchronic significance of cultural phenomena. Thus in place of the old orthodoxy, a range of revisionist perspectives has now emerged. Although they scarcely constitute a coherent new interpretation of the Revolution, these approaches do agree that what is genuinely interesting about the Revolution is the way in which a new "political culture" that was "invented" during the Old Regime was used by competing elements in the revolutionary decade 1789–1799. Both the origins and the long-term effects of the Revolution have been subordinated to study of the revolutionary "process."[6]

The historians contributing to this collection were educated at American universities while the shift away from Marxist orthodoxy was occurring. For them, the study of the Revolution has been grounded less in the concerns of the old French Left and Right than in the research undertaken by a generation of scholars dominated by Furet.[7] In some respects the historians in this collection have been decisively influenced by the methods and interpretive perspectives of the revisionists. Yet unlike much of the revisionist scholarship that appeared during the bicentennial, these essays insist that the Revolution did constitute an historical rupture essential to the development of modern France. They do so by using to powerful effect the very tool that many revisionists have employed to undercut the significance of the Revolution: the concept of a revolutionary "political culture."

As with revisionism generally, the historiography focused on political culture owes much to Furet. It was Furet who first displaced interpretive emphasis from Marx to Tocqueville, privileging the dynamic of revolutionary action rather than the socioeconomic origins or effects of the Revolution.[8] Reversing the traditionally assumed relationship between socioeconomic base and ideological superstructure, Furet described a Revolution in which "representations of power are the center of the action, and where the semiotic circle is absolute master of politics."[9] To uncover the real meaning of the Revolution, he redirected his focus from material interests to perceived interests and from social conflicts to the discourse of conflict. Furet's innovative approach encouraged other historians as well to view the Revolution as a cultural phenomenon. Particularly fruitful results came out of the Anglo-American world, where historians such as Keith Michael Baker and Lynn Hunt adapted the diverse interpretive tools of literary criticism, contemporary political theory, and cultural analysis to redefine the central problematics of the Revolution. Accenting discursive formations and the process of symbolization, Baker defined political culture as "the set of discourses or symbolic practices by which . . . competing claims are made by individuals and groups in any society."[10] In a definition that put more stress on collective attitudes and behavior, Lynn Hunt characterized political culture as "the values, expectations, and implicit rules that expressed and shaped collective intentions and actions."[11] Such studies have had the combined effect, as Hunt observed, of "rehabilitat[ing] the politics of revolution."[12] They have done so by conceiving the language and action of the Revolution not as familiar expressions of easily recognized class interests but instead as representations of passions, aspirations, and intentions whose inner, contemporary logic can be retrieved only by intensive cultural contextualization.

Yet until now, investigations of political culture have stressed either the political processes at the level of actual governance or the political ideologies of social elites. Furet, for example, defined revolutionary politics as "a matter of establishing *who* represented the people, or equality, or the nation," and he was interested chiefly in analyzing the "victory [that] was in the hands of those who were capable of occupying and keeping that symbolic position."[13] Thus for Furet, research should focus on political success stories: influential political theorists, lawmakers, leaders of Parisian clubs, and the like. Exploring how revolutionary symbols and rhetoric were invented, contested, and used, Hunt also concentrated on governmental elites, even though she found that political leaders came from "outsider" backgrounds. Baker too explored the creation of revolutionary discourse by examining the political language of intellectual elites during the Enlightenment.

In this collection, the authors conceive of political culture in a broader, more synthetic and inclusive sense than that previously employed by historians of the Revolution. They direct their attention not to political leaders or elites but to participants in the Revolution who were engaged in myriad micro-struggles for legitimacy, authority, or power that accompanied but did not always intersect the central contest for dominance over the state apparatus. The essays examine how these revolutionary actors consciously or unconsciously constructed and adapted new political language and forms to achieve highly specific ends—an enhanced political voice, economic relief, control of scientific institutions or standards of taste. Using diverse archival and other primary materials, as well as a range of historical and analytic methods, the authors shift the focus of investigation away from Parisian to local and provincial politics and from politics as such to struggles for the control of knowledge and cultural production.[14] And rather than focusing upon whether particular actors actually "won" their struggles, the articles explore how revolutionary political culture was created, assimilated, and transformed.

These investigations do reinforce the revisionist view that little is to be gained by perceiving the Revolution strictly as a struggle over the objective social and economic interests of supposedly monolithic classes—aristocrats, bourgeois, sansculottes—but they also argue that the events after 1789 provided an unprecedented opportunity for diverse revolutionary actors to forge group identification, achieve social empowerment, and even, in some cases, bid for political power in the ordinary sense. So although the essays in this collection do not advocate a return to a strict Marxist interpretation of the Revolution, they do show the importance of anchoring explorations of political culture in concrete social contexts.

This collection also marks a departure from much of current revolutionary historiography in its attention to the connections between the Revolution and the nineteenth century. Apart from some rather obvious comments made by political historians about the "revolutionary tradition" of 1789, 1830, 1848, and 1870–1871, surprisingly little in-depth work has been done on the relationship of the Revolution to the nineteenth century.[15] This neglect is especially puzzling given the primacy of Marxist historiography in France for so many generations. After all, it was Marx who characterized the French Revolution as the first "bourgeois" revolution. Yet despite long-standing claims that a new social order was created by the bourgeois Revolution of 1789, Marxist historians have proven more interested in analyzing the origins of the Revolution than in examining how that revolutionary class came to dominate the nineteenth century. Nor have revisionists shown much interest in exploring the relationship of the Revolution to the nineteenth century. Instead revisionist scholarship has looked back to the eighteenth century, when the political culture of revolutionaries is said to have been created. Hence we have studies of Enlightenment political theory, the social environment of Grub Street, and concrete political struggles between the Crown and increasingly disaffected elites. We still know little about the concrete and endlessly multiplying meanings the Revolution assumed in French culture and society in succeeding decades.

Some historians have even implicitly suggested that research into the long-term effects of the Revolution is not particularly worthwhile. Furet argues, for example, that the unfolding of events after 1789 entailed only the working out of the internal logic of revolutionary discourse, which "bequeathed to France conflicts between legitimacies and a virtually inexhaustible stock of political debates: 1830 was 1789 all over; 1848 re-enacted the First Republic; and the Commune echoed the Jacobin dream."[16] In this analysis, there is little point in studying the actual developments of the nineteenth century in the light of the Revolution: circumstances may have changed, but revolutionary discourse did not.

The essays in this collection do not assume that the history of nineteenth-century France was simply the history of a revolutionary discourse continually replayed. Rather, they demonstrate that in a world in which power had been delegitimized, the political culture of the Revolution was constantly being reshaped in the changing contexts of new struggles. They suggest, moreover, that the most volatile, intense, and consequential of the struggles of the nineteenth century were not necessarily those waged at what has always been assumed to be the "center" of political action. These articles do not focus on the Parisian barricades, clubs, and assemblies of 1830, 1848, or 1871. Instead they examine "decentered" struggles of diverse cultural elements, such as medical practitioners, natural historians, and "taste professionals," to continually readapt revolutionary political culture in order to extend a cultural authority first established during the Revolution itself.

One of the most valuable insights of these essays lies in their recognition that in the nineteenth century the political culture created by the Revolution was often manipulated to achieve objectives different from—in some cases even antithetical to—those of the revolutionaries of 1789–1799. To take but one example: when doctors in the revolutionary era argued for the creation of a new "medical authority" to supplant clerical dominance over questions of body, mind, and morals, they articulated their claims in the revolutionary discourse of utility and meritocracy. Yet a generation later, specialists in the medical field of hygiene, whose authority derived from the events of the Revolution, turned revolutionary discourse on its head to argue against the political and social demands of the urban poor. Such a perspective on the political culture created by the Revolution is wholly at odds with the view that nineteenth-century actors merely "replayed" past struggles. It insists rather on the protean potential of discourses and symbols drawn from ever-altering memories and constructions of the Great Revolution.

The opening essays in this collection focus on struggles for power that developed in the highly volatile circumstances of the revolutionary decade itself. Although they do not ignore the political events unfolding among the leaders, factions, and crowds emphasized in older historiography, they focus on participants in the Revolution who previously had lacked a discursive or organizational vehicle for their political ambitions (villagers, women's clubs) or whose arena of action was not overtly political (medical discourse and institutions, theatrical performances). Suzanne Desan's article draws together dispersed and previously unused archival material on revolutionary women's clubs. Desan demonstrates that during the Revolution there was a broad movement for women's political mobilization in the provinces, encompassing some sixty women's clubs. Steeped in the political culture of the Revolution, these clubs appropriated republican language and institutions not only to demand a greater political voice for women, but also to influence government decisions on issues ranging from the dismantling of the Constitutional church to the regulation of the price of grain. Challenging recent scholarship, Desan argues that the women's movement of the early Revolution was suppressed both because male revolutionaries were seeking to legitimize their own quest for power by excluding women from the revolutionary process and because the women's actions threatened the stability of gender roles in both the public and the private sphere. Opening a fruitful line for further research, Desan argues that although the women's clubs of 1791–1793 were suppressed, their legacy shaped the continuing nineteenth-century struggle between ideologies of empowerment versus domesticity.

In his study of the rural Somme from 1789 to 1793, Bryant T. Ragan, Jr., argues that although rigid Marxist categories cannot alone explain provincial power struggles, class conflict must still be viewed as a key element in village politics during the Revolution. He suggests, however, that the concept of class should be redefined to encompass the interrelationships between social and discursive circumstances. This definition moves away, then, from fixed socio-economic variables, such as landownership, seigneurial rights, and corporate ties, toward the dynamics of particular moments of social action. Ragan shows how villagers conceived of themselves and their political alliances by focusing on how they advocated a new national tax program based on the revolutionary principle of equality. He argues that the political allegiances of rural inhabitants shifted depending on whether villagers perceived other actors—the central government, bourgeois elites, the urban lower classes—as potential allies or enemies. Class is thus reintroduced as a category of analysis but as one dependent on the discursive framework of "equality" rather than "objective" economic relationships.

Although Desan and Ragan analyze groups—women, villagers—who employed overtly political language and institutions to press their claims, other essays in this volume consider struggles that unfolded outside the realm of political contestation proper, cultural domains that are not often treated as arenas for political conflict. In his essay on revolutionary audiences, for example, James H. Johnson explores the ways in which theatergoers insisted on an absolute congruence between the political *vrai* and the theatrical *vraisemblable*, between the real and the represented. In this study, Johnson moves beyond traditional studies of art and the Revolution that tended to catalogue the themes of revolutionary plays, paintings, and sculptures. Instead he looks at the dialectic between actors, who continued to regard plays as representations, and audiences, who collapsed the distinction between theatrical language and political reality in keeping with the revolutionary discourse of "transparency." Johnson's work suggests that although the radical Revolution failed in a lasting way to collapse aesthetics into politics, it established dimensions for the politicization of art that in subsequent years could neither be forgotten nor discounted.

In her article treating the creation of medical authority during the revolutionary decade, Elizabeth A. Williams explores the ways in which physicians of the revolutionary era used a vitalist-inspired conception of holistic or "anthropological" medicine to claim authority in cultural spheres previously dominated by the clergy. She argues that the claims of the physicians were part of a general cultural shift away from the sacral authority of monarch and church toward a "usufructory" authority based on efficacy and social utility. Williams shows that these claims were disdained by the popular revolution, which attempted to establish consensualism as an alternative to the authority of traditional or new elites, but that they were sufficiently validated by succeeding revolutionary governments to bequeath a legacy of intense clerical-medical conflict to the nineteenth century.

The last three essays in the volume move from the revolutionary decade 1789–1799 to the survival and transformation of revolutionary political culture in the nineteenth century. They take as their common point of departure the view that the Revolution constituted a rupture in areas of French cultural life hitherto little examined (if at all) by students of the "revolutionary tradition." These articles demonstrate how various cultural arbiters (hygienists, natural historians, taste-professionals) employed elements of revolutionary discourse to construct positions of cultural authority. Catherine J. Kudlick explores the enhanced development of what she calls the "culture of statistics" amid the cholera epidemics of 1832 and 1849, focusing especially on the visual representation of mortality statistics in the daily press. Kudlick shows that statistics gathered by the government, in conjunction with specialists in the new field of hygiene, were used to represent the "truth" of cholera and thereby to strengthen governmental and medical authority in an urban setting where disease and revolution were viewed as dangers emanating from the lower classes. Kudlick goes on to explore the paradox that although medical authority derived from the Revolution of 1789, hygienists later generated a counterrevolutionary discourse intended to control the Parisian "dangerous classes" by intruding into the urban space of cholera victims.

In his article on the development of "applied natural history," Michael A. Osborne also addresses the link between revolutionary discourse and cultural authority. Osborne shows that when in 1793 the National Convention abolished most scholarly institutions and corporate bodies, the Museum of Natural History avoided dissolution and indeed gained new official support by presenting its research agenda in the Jacobin language of utility. Osborne argues further that even after Jacobinism was widely discredited in the nineteenth century, the language of "utility" continued to be an essential element of the self-justification and public presentation of applied natural history.

Whereas the papers of Kudlick and Osborne consider the uses made of revolutionary discourse in efforts to control and legitimize fields of knowledge, Leora Auslander deals with the political semiology of artistic productions. She explains how the destruction of courtly society by the Revolution had some important unexpected side effects in the arbitration of taste. Examining "historicism" in the nineteenth century decorative arts, Auslander analyzes the way historical "narratives" are constituted in material objects such as furniture. She shows in respect to furniture styles that it was the Revolution that "created" the Old Regime and transformed it into a symbolic repertoire. Tracing nineteenth-century struggles over who should define good taste, Auslander maintains that taste professionals dictated to both producers and consumers by encoding furniture styles with the politicized oppositions—Old Regime/Revolution and masculine/feminine—that had been charged with new intensity by the conflicts of the Revolution.

As this discussion of the contents should indicate, this book contests the increasingly widespread view that the French Revolution had little importance in the development of French history.[17] It reasserts, as Eric Hobsbawm recently put it, "what was obvious to all educated persons in the nineteenth century, and is still obvious: the Revolution's centrality and relevance."[18] The essays included here explore not only particular moments of the Revolution itself but also ways in which the Revolution had profound and lasting effects on French culture in the nineteenth century. Collectively the essays indicate that the Revolution did constitute a rupture in French history because it created a new set of vocabularies for expressing and shaping political conflicts, values, and ambitions. This does not mean that the political language and symbols created by the Revolution subsequently enjoyed universal, or even widespread, assent. It means rather that they became persistent and often bitterly controversial elements of the language of politics. The concept of equality that undergirded the fiscal struggle of Somme villagers became a permanent feature of the landscape of nineteenth-century republicanism, rural and urban. In contrast, the articulation of women's political rights was drowned by a chorus of voices celebrating women's peculiar physico-moral constitution and the virtues and joys of domesticity. If in the case of "equality" the survival of the Revolution's vocabulary was assured, and its significance patently demonstrable, nevertheless the importance of the statement of women's political claims was no less great since the rhetoric and ideology of domesticity developed in dialectical antagonism with the discourse of women's political mobilization created by the Revolution. Similarly, the revolutionary construct of utility persisted throughout the nineteenth century, if in many different guises, while the revolutionaries' insistence on the absolute transparency of language did not outlast Thermidor. But again it would be misleading to describe as "significant" only the discursive element that continued to enjoy ritual approbation and to consign to oblivion the revolutionary virtue of "transparency." Although in the nineteenth century there were no Robespierres to assault the boundary between the political and the private, still the creation of that very problematic influenced all later discourse treating the necessity to reconcile private wills and public exigencies in democratic politics. It is precisely the creation of this kind of enduring discursive feature or cultural element, whatever its subsequent valuation or manipulation by actors whose own struggles necessarily evolved in myriad directions, that the historiographical perspective of this collection is intended to illuminate.

Although the contributors to this volume have been influenced in important ways by the revisionist perspective on the Revolution, they are not prepared to conclude, with Furet, that "the Revolution is over." It may be that the bitterly divergent interpretations of the Revolution that so long fueled the politics of the French Left and Right are moribund, but the political legacy of the Revolution certainly is not. The perspective adopted in this book, with its emphasis on the ramifying trajectories followed by revolutionary political culture in the nineteenth century, indicates that the language and symbols of the Revolution will continue to shape and be shaped by political action in diverse new settings. For the moment at least, it is inconceivable that the language of equality, representation, and utility forged or remade in the struggles of the Revolution will become obsolete. That such an assertion even has to be made—at a moment when another generation of European revolutionaries is retrieving and remolding the language of the Revolution to new ends—indicates that it is not revolutionary discourse that is ossified but the political and academic traditions confining it. The essays in this book argue that even in the era when the Revolution supposedly had its clearest, if wholly conflicting, significance for Left and Right, the meanings given revolutionary culture in lived struggles over gender and class constructions, professional and cultural authority, were diverse, unstable, and subject to rapid transformations of circumstance. So much the more will the uses to which the Revolution may be put in our time be unrecognizable to anyone anticipating another replay of the traditional Left-Right conflict. But if the conclusions of this book are correct, it would seem that as our politics alter, so too will our memory and construction of the Revolution. In this view the Revolution is not over; it is simply changing.

1

"Constitutional Amazons":
Jacobin Women's Clubs in the French Revolution

SUZANNE DESAN

In 1792 in the town of Besançon, a group of women founded a new patriotic club, the "Société des amies de la liberté et de l'égalité." Under the energetic leadership of the *citoyenne* Maugras, the club members studied revolutionary politics, orchestrated municipal festivals, set up programs of patriotic education for their children, and founded a workshop to employ needy women and to produce clothes and blankets for soldiers. Eager to participate in local and national politics, they lobbied the municipality for market price controls, backed the Constitutional clergy, petitioned the National Convention on a variety of political issues, and even demanded early in 1793 that the new constitution extend the vote to women.

At first, the Jacobin men's club of Besançon offered enthusiastic, if somewhat condescending, support for their sister society. But in January 1793 its journal, the *Vedette*, accused the women of allowing "hermaphrodite patriots, unctuous and fawning men" to attend their workshop to ogle and leer at the women workers. Warning that these men of dubious "feuillantin" politics might seduce the women by "usurping the reputation of being patriots," the Jacobin men insisted that the women should draw "a line of distinction between vice and virtue, . . . between the honest woman and the woman who sells herself." But when the women attempted to exclude all men from their work space, the male Jacobins protested that the husbands, sons, and fathers of the women should be allowed to come. As time passed, the relationship between the two clubs only deteriorated. When the citoyenne

Maugras spoke out against several male Jacobins for wasting the hard-earned funds for volunteers on a patriotic banquet, the Jacobin leadership and the *Vedette* denounced "the scandalous scenes in the Société des amies," vilified Maugras's personal reputation, and ultimately claimed that she had taken advantage of her gullible sisters to turn the society into "an instrument of her hatred and her ambition." "Women, women, show us that you are worthy of governing yourselves by yourselves, and that you don't need masters to do good," admonished the *Vedette* in March 1793. Maugras resigned in April, and despite her return in July, the society never regained its former spark and independence before being definitively closed in November 1793.[1]

The activism of these women, and the reception that it met, was not so unusual in the early years of the Revolution, for especially between 1791 and 1793, women in various parts of France founded political clubs to voice their own support for the Revolution, to educate themselves and their families in revolutionary ideology, and to lend a hand in the war effort. Although most women's clubs did not come as directly into conflict with local male Jacobins as the Besançon society did, they invariably met with an ambivalent reception and were subject to mockery and satire, if not to outright attack. As in the Besançon case, this critique of women's societies frequently questioned the members' morality, emphasized the susceptible and irrational nature of the feminine, and recommended the control of husbands and fathers over the disorderly women. Ultimately, the National Convention banned women's political societies altogether in October 1793.

These provincial women's clubs provide a window into a little-explored aspect of the French Revolution—the developing political consciousness and actions of ordinary provincial women far from Paris and the national legislature. For even their short-lived independent existence bore testimony to public female participation in the Revolution and contributed over the long term to the political education of French women. Yet, as the opening scenario suggests, the study of provincial women's societies offers the opportunity not only to ask how the Revolution politicized women, but also to examine how this era cast gender dynamics and the role of women into question. For although certain activities of women's clubs met with a warm reception, in other ways the public political participation of women, their assimilation of certain revolutionary ideals, and their attempt to bring politics into the private space of the home seemed to challenge gender roles, threaten the power of male Jacobins, and throw into disarray the sexual and social order. Male revolutionary leaders ridiculed and eventually suppressed women's societies in part because the exclusion of women from the public political sphere helped to create space and legitimacy for male democratic politics.[2]

Yet the definition of the private sphere and its relationship to the public was also a matter of debate, uncertainty, and conflict in the morally charged atmosphere of the 1790s. The French Revolution altered and obscured the line between public allegiances and private life: private choices were loaded with public political meaning and each individual's public legitimacy became dependent on his or her private morality.[3] This invasion of the "public" and "publicity" into what had formerly been considered "private" awakened fundamental unease and turmoil, which became intertwined with anxiety over gender roles and over the relationship between men and women. This paper will examine the political development of provincial Jacobin women's clubs and analyze their reception by local male Jacobins. I will argue that the suppression of women's political associations was an attempt by male revolutionaries not only to exclude women from the public sphere, but also to delineate the boundaries of feminine *sensibilité* and to redefine and clarify the nature of the private sphere as well.

The Founding and Functioning of Women's Clubs

Women's clubs flowered in about sixty towns throughout France. The cities of Bordeaux, Dijon, Lyon, and Besançon boasted the most active clubs outside of Paris. By and large, Jacobin women's clubs were an urban phenomenon, although they were also founded in some smaller towns or villages, especially in the southwest.[4] The clubs ranged in size from the tiny society of twenty-two girls in Civray in Poitou to the largest Jacobin women's organization of Bordeaux, which claimed "seven hundred to eight hundred citoyennes" as members in 1793. On a regular basis, membership of most clubs seems to have hovered between about thirty and seventy, with a handful of especially dedicated and zealous members. Higher numbers of women—often several hundred—participated in the clubs' revolutionary festivals or founding ceremonies. Indeed, this same club in Bordeaux drew a crowd of thirty-five hundred women to one of its early dedication ceremonies in 1791, while "two to three thousand women all decorated in the national colors," carrying flags and shouting "vive la nation, vive la liberté," flocked from the villages around Gevrey in the Côte-d'Or to take part in the initial oath-taking festival.[5]

Members came primarily from bourgeois backgrounds, although women of shopkeeping or artisanal classes also participated. Not surprisingly, leaders and founders tended to be slightly better off and better educated than most of their followers. The pattern in Dijon, Grenoble, and Besançon may well have been typical: many of the leading women were bourgeois wives of active members of the men's clubs. In Pau, however, a laundress founded the club, and the women of one club in Bordeaux emphasized their lack of wealth, describing themselves as "citoyennes peu fortunées." In Ruffec the 236 members of the "Amies des vrais amis de la Constitution" had a wide range of occupations and identities: they included a schoolteacher, a curé's sister, a midwife, a baker, several seamstresses and laundresses, two cabaret owners, two wigmakers, as well as the wife of the *procureur syndic*.[6]

As the title of the society at Ruffec suggests, many of these women's clubs began as offshoots or auxiliaries to men's clubs. While the Jacobin men's clubs in many towns throughout France allowed women to attend meetings, almost invariably the women were relegated to galleries or back benches and deprived of any right to speak officially, let alone vote.[7] As they founded independent societies, the women repeatedly expressed their desire to mount the podium with more autonomy, to voice particular support for the Constitutional church, to combine charitable efforts with political education, and above all, to manifest and enkindle the patriotic spirit that they shared with their husbands and that they hoped to pass on to their children. In 1791 for example, anxious to prove that women were not "tranquil spectators . . . [who] had fallen behind in the Revolution," Madame Masuyer urged the "Dames patriotes" of Dijon to promote a vast network of female Jacobins in every department. When they appealed to men's clubs throughout France to foster sister societies, the "Amies de la Constitution" of Dijon proclaimed, "It is in uniting in societies that we can help the *patrie* by forming the younger sisters of our modern Spartans and inspiring them with the love of liberty. . . . We invite [the women of France] to join us in establishing through correspondence the basis of this public spirit that should animate us all and assure the success of our armies. . . . Impatiently, we await the moment when we can communicate directly with [these new women's clubs.]"[8]

The idea of founding a club frequently seems to have been spontaneous and indigenous. One or two particularly fiery and articulate women often provided the impetus behind the initial founding. Pauline Siro of Pau, Madame Sta of Lille, Madame Maugras of Besançon, and Madame Normand of Dijon all acted as soul and spirit behind the initiation of their clubs. Yet support for the notion of women's clubs was in the air nationally among patriotic circles. In December 1790 the journalist Carra published two articles in his *Annales patriotiques* lauding new women's associations in Alès and Bordeaux; his praise may have helped inspire the spread of new clubs early in 1791.[9] In the spring of 1791, when the Jacobins of Brest sent their fellow societies a circular with a speech by Madame Pradier proclaiming that "Nature" had endowed women with crucial "influence over morals . . . [and] stability," the women of Dijon, Grenoble, and Lille seem to have drawn inspiration from her words to create their own societies. The activist Etta Palm d'Aelders in Paris and the women's club of Dijon each proposed in 1791 that networks of women's clubs should be founded throughout France. Finally, smaller towns and villages undoubtedly found models in the major clubs in Paris, Dijon, and Bordeaux.[10]

Many men's clubs supported the formation of sister organizations. In Provence in the summer of 1792, the republican Representatives on Mission even made it a policy to foster new women's clubs, to be supported by local male Jacobins.[11] The relationship between men's and women's societies was frequently affable, but it was invariably hierarchical and could become contested and problematic. In most towns, the men's and women's clubs got along best in the early stages. The men often sent envoys to instruct the women in the fundamentals of revolutionary ideology or to help them establish the format of their meetings. Occasionally, they took even more initiative and control: in an unusual case, Monsieur Sobry of Lyon not only founded the "Association des citoyennes dévouées à la patrie," but also appointed himself and his wife as the first presidents.[12] In some cities, the two societies collaborated on festivals or sent occasional joint petitions to the local municipality or the National Convention. In general, however, despite the support from men's clubs, the women by and large ran their own show and provided the initiative behind the founding and functioning of their clubs.

As the women laid the groundwork for their new clubs, they frequently took as a partial model the primary form of women's organization already familiar to them: the religious confraternity of the Old Regime. The early women's clubs fused patriotic politics with religious devotion and charitable activity. Support of the Constitutional church and clergy generally stood at or near the top of the political agenda of the societies in 1791, and most clubs pledged themselves to ceremonial and charitable functions that grew directly out of the prerevolutionary roles of Catholic confraternities.

Nonetheless, the lessons learned from these religious groups were over-laid and fused with new political structures, purpose, and consciousness. For example, the "demoiselles" who founded the "Sisters of the Constitution" in Bréteuil in 1790 sounded like members of an Old Regime confraternity as they outlined the appropriate ceremonies to commemorate the eventual marriage of any of their members, uttered promises of filial submission, and set up in their bylaws the moral conditions of repentance and contrition for those who broke these sworn promises of obedience and virtue. Yet these *filles citoyennes*, as they called themselves, also displayed remarkable politi-cal consciousness as they anxiously pronounced the revolutionary ideal of equality among all the sisters/members, swore an oath of loyalty to the laws in typical revolutionary fashion, and set up bylaws to be sent to the local municipality and even to the National Assembly.[13]

In fact, during the period 1791–1792 local authorities and male club members often initially approved of the women's clubs because they viewed them as a useful bulwark against the power of the nonjuring clergy. Male revolutionary speakers repeatedly echoed the appeal of Citizen Pille, who entreated the "dames patriotes" of Dijon on the day of their inauguration in 1791 to combat "all the intrigues, the sly maneuvers, the libels of the refrac-tory priests."[14] Female Jacobins embraced this task, often clinging to their defense of the state church well into 1793, when many of their husbands sought its suppression.[15] In a ceremony that differed from those in other towns only in size and pomp, the "Amies de la Constitution" of the Saint-André parish in Bordeaux initiated their society, and inspired the founding of several others, with a Te Deum in honor of the Constitutional bishop and an elaborate oath to the nation, Constitution, and Constitutional church. In a similar spirit, Mademoiselle Mantegués told the local men's club in 1791 that the "Constitutional Amazons" of Grasse were outraged by the conflicts leading many to "abandon the religion consecrated by the laws of the State" and had dedicated themselves first and foremost to fighting these "enemies of the Constitution." In an even more colorful fashion the following spring, Elisabeth Lé wrote to the president of Bordeaux's powerful Surveillants Club suggesting that France sell the refractory clergy to the king of Mo-rocco: "This king buys all the scoundrels of Europe; we couldn't sell him better merchandise."[16]

Women's clubs opposed the refractory church in action as well as words. In the midst of the religious troubles in Arles in the fall of 1792, citoyenne Philippeau, the housekeeper of a Constitutional clergyman, founded a club of 602 women of varied backgrounds to defend the Constitutional church

and the new republic. Likewise, the prorevolutionary women of Dijon originated their club in the late spring of 1791 partially in express reaction
against female supporters of the refractory clergy. During the next few
months, they provoked repeated violent confrontations by conducting chari-
varis at nonjuring masses and petitioned the Legislative Assembly to reduce
the number of nuns' communities, which they dubbed "asylums of fanaticism, lairs of hypocrisy." In the summer of 1792 they gained a certain
notoriety by joining their male counterparts in a massive and unruly attempt
to force refractory nuns out of their convents. In a more positive vein, the
women of Dijon, like the female club members in many other cities, took
over as much as possible the charitable and educational duties formerly
performed by nuns.[17]

Popular conceptions about female psychology supported women's particular prerogative in the realm of religion and morals. For in the late
eighteenth century most French men and women shared the belief that
women were particularly *sensible*—that is, sensitive, impressionable, susceptible, and compassionate. This characteristic *sensibilité* had two sides: it
made women especially gullible, malleable, and open to influence (of "fa-
naticizing" nonjuror priests, for example); on the brighter side, it also gave
women peculiar power over morals and special ability to touch and evoke
the emotions of others. In the context of a battle over religious allegiance
and cultural "regeneration," women played a crucial role because, in the
words of Monsieur Sobry of Lyon, "the people have as much need to be
moved as to be regulated."[18] Thus many revolutionary men and women
alike assumed that the women's clubs, more than the men's, should be able
to win over others, especially their fellow women, who had been led astray
by fanaticism. "The power of women," asserted Françoise Sanson of Caen
in her 1791 speech against women deceived by counterrevolution, "is in
their sensibilité; let us use this valuable arm." Madame Brillat of Bordeaux
concluded her long speech about the value of popular societies with an
appeal to female supporters of the refractory church: "You French women
who are kept far apart from us by the error of your ways, tear away your
blindfolds. . . . Come into our midst, you will find tender sisters worthy of
friendship; leave behind your fanatic priests who fool you. . . . Listen to a
citizen who prefers the sweetness of liberty to vile slavery. Tear off your
chains and save yourselves in the bosom of free women."[19]

As forces for moral regeneration and as descendants of religious confraternities, the women's clubs frequently focused their energy on the organization of festivals and charitable activities. From Grenoble to Lille to

Cognac, women's clubs promoted and participated in myriad festivals to celebrate revolutionary unity, Te Deums to bless the Constitution, balls and banquets to launch the nation's volunteers, and funerary ceremonies to honor Mirabeau, Le Peletier, and Marat.[20] The nature of the festivals reflected the radicalizing turns of the Revolution, but two recurring themes stand out. First, the festivals repeatedly proclaimed the capacity of women to inspire male valor and patriotism. Solemn send-offs of volunteers by women's clubs invariably included reminders that women's praise and love would be the reward of fearless struggle on behalf of the *patrie en danger*.[21] Second, the festivals often reinforced the maternal and pedagogical role of women. In their exclusively female initiation ceremony, the citoyennes of Marseille embraced their maternal role with oaths and with the solemn baptism of newborns—one young girl was named "Bienvenue Désirée Liberté." The women of Lorient prepared their children for the ritual recitation of a new set of Ten Commandments, swearing to "chase all tyrants far beyond Hindustan," and in a ceremony reiterated across France, the "Amies de la liberté et de l'égalité" of Lyon bestowed awards on their patriotic offspring for reciting the Declaration of the Rights of Man, the seventh chapter of Rousseau's *Social Contract*, and a longer series of revolutionary prayers, oaths, and songs.[22]

As long as the women did not try to hold autonomous festivals or to carry arms, male Jacobins, politicians, club members, and journalists appreciated these ceremonial and educational actions as "natural" and useful.[23] Women's vibrant and colorful presence at revolutionary festivals "crowned the success of the Revolution," according to the *Journal patriotique de la Côte-d'Or*, and "stirred up everyone's courage," according to Claude Hollier of Bordeaux. Women's role was not to change the political course of the Revolution, but rather to decorate and inspire, to crown and to animate. Some men clearly took delight in the possibility of orchestrating this ornamental role of women. Citizen Sobry jubilantly announced that the principal "practices" of the "Citoyennes dévouées à la patrie" would be "ceremonies and works of benevolence"; sounding like a frustrated fashion designer, he outlined in detail the appropriate patriotic attire of white dress, red belt, blue jacket, tricolor ribbon, and gilt bronze medallion to be worn by Lyon's women as they "represented the interior of the patrie."[24] Moreover, women often portrayed philosophical or political concepts, such as Liberty, Reason, or Marianne as the Republic. The very abstractness of these ceremonial roles distanced women from involvement in the pragmatic, everyday workings of politics and set up a model of femininity that was aloof, moral, and abstract.

Representations of abstract ideals, chaste young women, and patriotic mothers did little to validate the political activism of women in clubs, streets, or assemblies.[25]

In a similar vein, men's clubs endorsed the extensive benevolent activities of the women's societies. Echoing the functions of Old Regime confraternities, these charitable actions became especially widespread and crucial once France had entered war. Workshops in Dijon as well as Besançon, for example, employed poor women, especially the needy wives of volunteers, and produced clothes, bandages, and blankets for the armies. The men's clubs of Bordeaux repeatedly honored the various local women's clubs for their patriotic donations, bureaus of poor relief, aid to war widows, education of schoolchildren, and above all, for their replacement of the nuns at local hospitals. The male "Amis de la Constitution" early in 1792 implored all the unmarried or widowed women to staff hospitals and oust counterrevolutionary nuns: their published appeal claimed that nature had given men the "physical and moral forces needed to run the machine of government, . . . she [nature] has given you women . . . more empathetic hearts, . . . patience, . . . and the discernment to know, foresee, and care for the patients' needs and desires better than we ever could." In Dijon and Besançon as well, the male Jacobins supported their sister societies in conflicts against the religious administrators of hospitals and endorsed the women's attempts to set up schools.[26]

Undoubtedly, the revolutionary attack on the church led to confusion over education, poor relief, and care of the sick that opened up these spheres for greater initiative and activism by lay women. This expansion of lay women's roles was possible in part because women's participation in socially beneficial work was seen as a natural extension of female maternal instincts and skills, transferred from the family to the society at large. Not only did the role of caring women fit well with dominant perceptions of female character, but also women's willingness to step in for nuns had political as well as pragmatic significance: they became crucial in the revolutionary battle against the remnant Roman Catholic church.[27]

For the most part, these benevolent, didactic, and ritualistic functions gave rise to little discussion or resistance from male Jacobins. The women's actions bore a resemblance in spirit and function to their roles in Old Regime religious confraternities, but they were harnessed to new revolutionary causes and programs. Moreover, they seemed to complement the belief shared by both men and women that women should act as moral guardians and forces of regeneration within the new revolutionary society. But as they stepped into the political arena beyond these roles, the women's clubs stirred up controversy and opposition. Their actions offered implicit challenges to traditional gender roles and to the newly developing image of the ideal republican woman as mother and moral educator, because women held an unusual position on the hinge between public politics and private morality. The journalist Carra, who favored women's societies, pointed out this dual role of women: "if they exist partly [*de moitié*] for the domestic consolation and enjoyment of men, they also exist in part for the progress and advancement of virtue and social prosperity." Public clubs, he argued, would facilitate this social role.[28] The relationship between the domestic role and the more public social and political role, which Carra envisioned as simple and natural, in fact quickly became problematic.

Public Structures and Political Agendas of Clubs

In this era when the nature of the relationship between public politics and private morality was under such close scrutiny and redefinition, the women's clubs provoked three major troubling challenges. First, although virtually all patriots agreed that women should act as cultural missionaries and patriotic educators, not all revolutionaries agreed about the extent to which women's role as moral regenerators required public meetings and sessions of clubs. Second, the clubs taught their members to politicize their private lives as well, thus awakening unease about the power of women over men within the private realm. Third, the women's societies seemed at times to suggest that revolutionary education would change the interior nature of women. Their actions, speeches, and meetings suggested directions that many men found troubling: could women set aside their softness, their frivolity, even their sensibilité, in favor of rationality and "transparency" to serve the public realm of the new republic? For a woman to be "transparent," she would not only have to express her political opinions openly and without machination as a transparent revolutionary man would, she would also have to set aside her "natural" tendency toward mystery, seduction, and deception.[29] In short, women's clubs were public institutions that posed disturbing questions about the public role of women, as Joan Landes in particular has stressed.[30] But it is crucial to recognize that they also aroused pervasive unease and in some places intense controversy by attempting to reformulate the private roles and character of women and by raising ambiguity about the relationship of the public to the private and of men to women.

A look at the structure and political programs of these clubs not only provides insights into the politicization of revolutionary women, but also helps us to understand why women's clubs faced mockery and finally were suppressed. These women sought to create public political structures having official rules of behavior and a definitively political agenda. First, let us turn to the structure and functioning of these clubs. The "Amies des vrais amis de la Constitution" at Ruffec provide an example. The minutes of their sessions from 7 August 1791 through 13 May 1792 betray their self-conscious effort to learn and execute the new rules of public politics. Week by week, the members of this fledgling club invented and enacted new procedures, divisions of political labor, and uses of the vote. They began by electing a president, swearing an oath of loyalty, legislating that their sessions would be public and that small children should not attend and distract members from the serious issues at hand. Gradually, like the men's clubs, they added additional elected offices—a bureau of correspondence, a male adjunct to the secretary, a bureau of surveillance, a treasurer (who later was caught trying to return paper money for the coin money collected earlier as dues). It is striking to watch the studied progress of these women who had little experience in nonreligious public life, let alone in the running of a democratic organization. They had trouble with voting at first, for example. They held secret ballots to admit new members, but one of the early scrutiny votes for admission had to be redone because "several sisters" had voted with red beans, thinking these granted admission, when in fact they cast negative votes. Gradually, the women of Ruffec, like women in other political clubs across France, mastered the art of public meeting—petitioning, voting, negotiating with the men's clubs, debating, and taking the floor to make a point.[31] Although the women clearly learned much from their male colleagues, who offered advice and sent speakers, and in some cases notetakers, the women nonetheless took charge of their organizations.

They were self-consciously aware not only of the procedural rules of sessions, but also of the need to be public. In part, they sought like their husbands or brothers to transact the factionless, transparent politics that Rousseau had called for; they also knew that to be public could help protect the organization from accusations of back-room machinations and slander. To be public was to be more serious as well. The women of Dijon, for example, began by meeting in private, but then chose to make their meetings public as of August 1792. A male Jacobin commented, "So much the better, you will be more emulated and calumny will have less power over you." The public and collective structure of the clubs would facilitate their moral, charitable, and didactic goals, argued the leaders of women's societies. How could women learn the laws and values of the Revolution without meeting? They needed this education to teach their children patriotism in turn. In her response to the journalist Prudhomme's attack on women's clubs, the citoyenne Charton of Lyon commented about her sisters: "the goal of their association is to learn the decrees of the Convention, . . . to help their unfortunate brothers, to teach their children about the new order of things." Public meetings, in short, would help form private patriotism.[32]

Above all, the development of official public sessions was meant to create a framework that would enable Jacobin women's clubs to take part in the *bien public* and influence local and national politics. In this era emphasizing popular participation and the creation of institutions to voice popular political viewpoints, female club members recognized that public structure gave them official voice. As the citoyenne Blandin-Desmoulins wrote to the journalist Prudhomme in the winter of 1793, a republican government called on each individual to cooperate on behalf of the bien public. Citoyennes too "should make themselves useful to the public good. . . . To contribute in the surest and most advantageous fashion, we had to meet together; for what can individuals do if they remain isolated from each other? . . . We do not limit ourselves to singing hymns to liberty, as you advise us; we want also to partake in civic acts."[33]

Indeed, especially in the hopeful mood of 1791, the early leaders of the women's clubs expressed their confidence that women, too, should participate in the creation and expression of public opinion. In 1791 Madame Masuyer, one of the Dijonnaise leaders, commented overoptimistically, "Messieurs, you have no doubt been waiting for French women to manifest a *public opinion* about the great interests that consume you" (my emphasis). As Madame la présidente Chedaneau of Ruffec put it at the outset of her inaugural speech, "Although women seem to take little part in public affairs, in all times their feeble hands have held the destiny of the universe; their wishes, desires, and caprices have made war and peace." She then went on to proclaim naively that the new Constitution of 1791 "would never be established until women *publicly* adopted it" (my emphasis).[34]

Within the newly established structure of the Jacobin women's clubs, the members developed a political agenda that became radicalized over the course of the Revolution. Like their male counterparts, some women's societies chose new names to reflect this changing political commitment. Many groups changed their 1791 name, "Amies de la Constitution," to "Amies de la liberté et l'égalité" in the fall of 1792; and some chose the more radical "Amies de la République" in 1793.[35] Their early support for the constitutional monarchy and the Constitutional church transformed into broad-based support for the democratic republic and popular sovereignty, yet the women's clubs also developed their own points of emphasis and their own demands.

Sometimes the women's clubs gave opinions on the political behavior or the needs of women. The women of Besançon, for example, petitioned the National Convention in January 1793 to judge Marie-Antoinette as well as Louis XVI, and the women's club of Orléans sent the citoyenne Baudry to address the men's club of Rouen on the issues of female education and female participation in public club life.[36] And just as they had embraced the defense of Constitutional Catholicism, Jacobin women rushed to influence local economic policy, especially with regard to subsistence matters. In Besançon, the women's club acted as a forceful lobby for market price controls, while the women's club of Dijon joined the local men's club in petitioning the national legislature on the use of sugar and coffee. Because of the centrality of subsistence issues, Jacobin women's agitation in this domain had a decisive impact on municipal politics. When the revolutionary women in Dijon rioted against a newly elected mayor who satirized their demand for cheaper grain and other goods, the incident mushroomed into a broad-scale attack on the mayor, including a march on the municipality to free the imprisoned ex-mayor. Their activism eventually resulted in the election of a third compromise candidate as the new mayor.[37] When the price of grain, oil, soap, wood, cheese, meat, and other goods soared out of control in Lyon in September 1792, members of the women's club led their fellow citoyennes to march on the municipality and then to draw up a manifesto denouncing hoarders and monopolists, setting the prices of sixty essential foods and goods, and articulating a revolutionary economic vision of just price based on "the will of the people, justice, equity, and equality." The women posted these price lists all over Lyon and delegated female patrols to enforce them. Faced by empty markets, continual rioting, the desertion of the National Guard, and the bewildering emergence of self-appointed "female police commissioners," the municipal and departmental authorities finally agreed to set low price controls and to seek out counterrevolutionary agitators.[38]

But Jacobin women did not hesitate to express their opinions on a variety of issues beyond bread, religion, and the behavior of their fellow women.[39]

Often the women's clubs tried to persuade male politicians to take particular political stances on other major issues, including the various constitutions, the guilt of the king, and the nature of popular sovereignty. The women's club of Besançon, for example, sent the "administrators and people" of the neighboring department of the Jura an address in August 1793 urging them not to persist in their federalist stance against the National Convention. Likewise, the two major women's clubs of Bordeaux both sought to make peace with the Montagnard Representatives on Mission, sent to Bordeaux in the summer of 1793 to put down the Girondin federalist revolt there. The women's clubs, especially the large one based in the Saint-André parish, corresponded with the deputies Ysabeau and Baudot and then sent them delegates in order to survive the political downfall of the Girondins and avoid suppression. But clearly the women sought above all to win sympathy and grain from the deputies so that Bordeaux could recover from its disastrous revolt. The exchanges betray the acute political savvy of the Bordelaise women. This same women's club in Bordeaux actively sought to influence the sections to endorse the new Constitution of 1793. In fact, women's clubs of Damazan, Clermont-Ferrand, Le Mans, Nancy, and Beaumont all voted to accept the Constitution and sent their endorsements to the National Convention in the summer of 1793.[40]

As women publicly expressed their political opinions on crucial matters, they raised the feminist issue of greater formal political participation for women. Their endorsements of the Constitution of 1793, for example, sometimes contained a demand for a greater political voice and role for women. The clubs of Nancy, Le Mans, and Beaumont reproached the Convention for denying them the "right to express their vote" or "ratify the act" that, in the words of the Beaumont women, they had so "effectively supported." The Besançon club too had appealed for the vote in February 1793. In 1791 Elisabeth Lafaurie, a twenty-two-year-old mother of four, gave a speech to the Jacobin men's club of Saint-Sever-Cap, entitled *Discourse on the State of Nothingness in which Women are Held, Relative to Politics*. She argued that the denial of a political voice to women was "unjust, because the total mass of women is subject to Laws, which they have not been able to refuse or approve, which is contrary to their liberty and to the idea that we should have of social conventions." Likewise, the women of Bordeaux complained in 1793 to the National Convention that "because of prejudices that it would be easy to destroy, . . . our sex is deprived of both political administration and of the glory of dying in defense of liberty." Resolving to accept their limited role as wives and mothers for the moment, these women nonetheless expressed the "hope that necessity, like Reason, would make [this prejudice] disappear."[41] Explicit demands for female suffrage or direct female political representation did not dominate the agenda of the women's clubs. But their attempt to influence national and local politics, their requests to bear arms, their appropriation of revolutionary ideology, and above all their entry into the public political sphere beyond ceremony, riot, or charity recurrently raised the question of how women could fully be "citoyennes," active participants in popular sovereignty.[42]

Female Patriotism: Sensibilité, Seduction, and the Challenge of "Feminine" Politics

As women entered the public sphere of politics, their peculiar position on the hinge between public and private inevitably affected the nature of their revolutionary politicization and education. The feminine character of sensibilité, with all its moral power, became the basis of their political strength. Paradoxically, this same sensibilité became the source of their downfall as well.

Even as they sought to influence public politics, the women's clubs never denied that their primary role was within the home. They embraced their maternal role above all: Women should promote revolutionary ideology and patriotism by inspiring their children to be "useful to the patrie" and by "teaching them at a young age to speak the male language of liberty," in the gendered language of one male speaker in Orléans.[43] The promotion of patriotic motherhood grew out of the war effort and the revolutionary emphasis on education and moral reform. The American Revolution had witnessed very similar appeals.[44]

But what is more striking in the case of the French Revolution is the call to women to *politicize their relationships* with their husbands and lovers, to bring political judgment as well as moral lessons to the bedroom. In the revolutionary context where public and private became increasingly inseparable, the sensibilité that gave women a unique power to influence others and to mold morals should be put to use for the patrie. The women of Ruffec, for example, took an oath "to be loyal to nation and laws, to maintain the Constitution"—nothing new—but the unmarried women also swore "to give hand and heart only to him who conforms to the true principles of the Constitution." This same women's club heard an exhortation from one of their male colleagues: "If it is necessary, let a prudent and friendly refusal of your caresses be the punishment of traitors [to the cause]; use the irresistible force of your insinuations to weaken the heart of stone that the sweet name of liberty cannot move." He comments, "Sisters and friends, you form opinion. . . . It is before your tribunal that politics must submit its operations and the warrior his triumphs." Likewise, the young women of Neubourg (Eure) took an oath that they would marry only young men who had served in the army, and in 1791 the "Jeunes citoyennes patriotiques" of Nantes imitated the Parisian "Société fraternelle des deux sexes" by promising never to marry aristocrats.[45]

As women urged one another to politicize their love lives, to use their peculiar prerogative over morals to bring political issues into the private realm, they raised questions both about the nature of male-female relations and also about the changing quality of the female character. For example, in a 1792 speech to the "Amies de la Constitution" of Bordeaux, Marie Dorbe praised the late Mirabeau for freeing women from being "forgotten, reduced to housework and the education of our children; deprived of the benefits of the law, we lived in abject obscurity, painfully enduring our degradation." She then urged the unmarried members "to form ties only with those men who have shown the most ardor for the defense of liberty and the most love for this dear patrie. . . . Tell them that the *language of flattery and romance no longer pleases you*, and that now you only love frankness and truth" (my emphasis). In this discourse on how to be a "citoyenne libre" and "chercher l'homme patriote," Dorbe suggested that the revolutionary context transformed women in a striking fashion: they would no longer be so gullible and easily duped by pretty words with no meaning, and like male citizens, they could and should develop public, political allegiances that transcended private ties.[46]

Male and female republicans believed that women should act on this new fidelity to the nation and the Revolution. In the ideal revolutionary vision, public loyalty to the patrie was meant to reinforce the bonds of family and certainly to cement the maternal role, but this new allegiance could also disrupt bonds to one's family, husband, or friends in a disturbing conflict between public and private loyalties. When the daughter of an émigré, Emilie Tardy of Besançon, abandoned the counterrevolutionary politics of her family in 1793 and joined the women's club, she proclaimed: "Citoyennes, sisters, friends, . . . I have raised myself as much as I possibly can to the heights of the national spirit; family affections, the ties of friendship have never and never will make me deviate from the principles of liberty and equality. . . . Please accept, sisters and friends, this *public testimony* of my gratitude" (my emphasis). This alternative of a different, transcendent loyalty was most directly expressed by the citoyenne Maugras of Besançon: "Raised to the heights of the Revolution, we prefer liberty and equality to all the platitudes of love."[47]

This politicizing of the private realm conformed to prevalent images of women as moral regenerators, and it attributed a certain amount of power to women. But it was nonetheless problematic in the context of the Revolution. First, it opened women to even closer sexual and moral scrutiny, for they themselves had to be morally upstanding and politically pure in order to influence male morality and make judgments about men's valor and patriotism. Second, this politicization of the bedroom awakened male resentment about women's power and allegiance to forces outside the home. Third, it endowed women with a form of power that was dangerously close to the mysterious, seductive—and therefore dubious and evil—influence that some elite women had exercised in court politics in the Old Regime.[48] Male revolutionaries frequently used the language of seduction when they spoke of women's sway over their hearts and morals. As Grosjean of Besançon commented, "If the patrie is well loved by you, you will seduce us all by defending its rights."[49]

The appeal to women to reinforce and spread public values through their intimate relationships was set within a discourse that also sought to reform women's traditional methods of attracting and influencing men. Throughout France, male and female speakers in the clubs asserted that women should set aside their frivolous and capricious ways from the days of the Old Regime. This discourse took place in a number of registers. In part, it grew out of the revolutionary attack on the luxurious and wasteful life-style of the aristocracy and the parallel appeal for austerity so necessary because of the war effort. For example, when the women's club of Dijon presented their contributions for weapons and offered to arm themselves as well, they declared, "Women who are free and animated with love of country know how to scorn frivolous adornment . . . and generously make the sacrifices that the dangers of the country demand." But the turn away from frivolity would also bring women closer to the transparent and orderly politics that the revolutionaries valued: the citoyenne Guillemet of Besançon appealed for club meetings that were "peaceful, . . . without outbursts. . . . Let us avoid caprices." Many club women clearly saw that they had to dissociate themselves from the fickle and frothy images of the Old Regime that not only linked them to aristocratic and deceitful backroom politics, but also denied them the rationality and status of public actors. Blandin-Desmoulins of Dijon asked, "Do you wish to hold women forever in a state of childhood or of frivolity? . . . It is time to bring about a revolution in the customs of women; it is time to reestablish their natural dignity." Citoyenne Challan of Meulan proclaimed in 1790 that women who were "for too long given over to frivolity by their faulty education, had at last come to deserve the rank assigned to them by the Creator."[50]

It was clear to men and women alike that the nonfrivolous woman would be a better republican mother and would be far removed from the pernicious and immoral qualities of an Old Regime aristocrat. "Republicans are frank in their speech and faithful to their promises. . . . You [women] will not be coquettish with us. . . . *You can continue the club in the heart of your home*" (my emphasis), pronounced one male speaker in the Puy-de-Dôme. But the attack on feminine caprice was riddled with ambiguity, coupled as it often was with an appeal to women to exercise private influence on their men through seduction for the patrie. When the president of the men's club of Ruffec appealed to the female club members to set aside the ways of a "frivolous century" and to turn their homes into "schools of patriotism," he also reminded them of the power of their "tears, . . . flattery, and re-proaches" to win over patriots.[51] In short, the appeal to women to exercise political influence in their private relationships and simultaneously to set aside their capricious ways only contributed further to building an ever higher moral standard for female behavior. One source of women's private political power and influence was also a source of their weakness. Male ambivalence about the political and moral power of women in the private realm would expose women to attack.

In a parallel fashion, women's clubs stirred up much uncertainty about the nature of female sensibilité. How should this quality best be put to work for the Revolution, and how would the revolutionary context and education transform female sensibilité? While many women and men alike agreed on its importance in the make-up of the republican mother, some women none-theless sharply recognized the limiting qualities of female sensibilité and questioned the usefulness of the softer side of this characteristic for the bien public. In 1791 Madame Peutat, as leader of the patriotic women of Avallon, proclaimed: "Sensibilité, gentleness, moderation are without a doubt the precious attributes of our sex; but citizens, if the fury of enemies exposes us to the violent shock they threaten, don't you think we ought to make an effort ourselves to suspend for a moment these gentle affections before more sublime sentiments, *the love of Liberty and the patrie*? This sensibilité, this gentleness, this moderation would be only weakness and would become criminal if it became a question of sparing men who want to massacre our children, our husbands, our fellow citizens, our brothers" (my emphasis). While still embracing the role of patriotic mother, she appealed for women to move beyond the home and to take up arms if necessary in defense of the country. She tried, apparently without success, to win the sympathy of male Jacobins by aligning her views with revolutionary radicalism: "We hear *cowardly moderates* say that other cares keep us busy at home; that our hands are made to wield the spindle, and not the sword!" (original emphasis).[52]

The women's clubs began to challenge traditional conceptions of female sensibilité in yet another way. Although Jacobin women often referred to themselves as the weaker sex and sometimes admitted that they were easily led astray, by 1792 and 1793 the women's speeches began to express the certainty that women were being transformed by revolutionary rationalism. They declared that women, too, were becoming more rational and less easily deceived because of the education brought by the Revolution. Second, they implied that the twists and turns of revolutionary politics indicated that men, for their part, were often *trompés*, tricked, fooled, duped. In November 1792 the members of the largest women's club of Bordeaux, keenly aware of women's reputation for credulity, were quick to denounce Marat's attempt to flood them with pamphlets and infiltrate their society. "He thought [it] was weak and easy to corrupt. He was fooled," wrote the women. By April of the next year this same women's club had become more forthcoming in its assertions of female constancy. Declaring boldly that they were not taken in by factional intrigue, the members wrote to the "Recollets" men's club, "We are women and do not turn like some men do at the mercy of their passions and their interests, basely sacrificing the interests of the country." As these women saw, the factionalism and emotional turmoil of revolutionary politics had called into question men's ability to detach themselves rationally from political interest and passion. A similar case arose in the summer of 1793 in the Rouen men's club, when the citoyenne Mabon denounced the return of Girondin members who had been "fooled." She proclaimed, "But let them be on guard, women are not so easily fooled. Even though they treat us as spies, stool pigeons, factionalists, we will be on surveillance while they sleep."[53]

Not only did revolutionary politics seem to become less "rational," it also became increasingly entangled with definitions of personal virtue and morality. The investment of political motivations and choices with such heavy moral ramifications conceivably lessened the gap between men's and women's ability to see politics clearly—at least in the eyes of some female Jacobins. Women sometimes implied that they could draw integrity and resolution from aligning their moral sensibilité with reason. Earlier in the Revolution, the citoyenne Vigoureux assured the men's society of Rouen that the women who had assembled on their own to read political papers were protected from counterrevolutionary or aristocratic infiltration by their own "shield of reason, uprightness, and love of country." As the journalist Carra put it succinctly in his endorsement of women's clubs in 1791, "The reign of their [women's] reason has also arrived."[54] Not all male revolutionaries shared Carra's positive assessment of women's clubs. On the contrary, the recurring suggestion that women could exercise political judgment as well as men and could perhaps overcome the handicaps of sensibilité without losing its moral force threatened to overturn the sexual and social order. This fear became especially acute in the turbulent politics of 1793 when male revolutionaries themselves became increasingly open to the charge of having been either trompés or morally corrupted.

The Attack on Women's Clubs

On 30 October 1793 the National Convention outlawed all "clubs and popular societies of women." Two weeks later the Paris Commune upheld Chaumette's proposal to bar women from its sessions as well. This repression of women's clubs was influenced by the particular Parisian context of violent confrontation between the "Citoyennes républicaines révolutionnaires" and the market women over price controls and the tricolor cockade. Moreover, as Dominique Godineau has argued, Jacobin leaders, such as Fabre d'Eglantine, Amar, and Chabot, sought to suppress the Parisian women's club in part because the women's political appeal for direct democracy was too radical for the Jacobin deputies, who preferred representative democracy and who would move next to take power away from male sansculottes.[55] But although the political and economic dynamics of the fall of 1793 certainly influenced the repression of women's organizations by the National Convention and the Paris Commune, clearly this move was part of a broader attempt to draw a clear-cut line between public and private and to reestablish order in male and female roles and character. Order between the sexes was necessary to reestablish some social order within the republic.

Analysis of the reception of the provincial women's clubs helps to explain the Jacobin move to exclude women from political power. For even the most docile women's provincial clubs, which got along quite well with their male Jacobin compatriots, faced a marked ambivalence, more than occasional satire, and the continual suggestions of possible impropriety. Women's participation in public politics, their appeal for the politicization of intimate relationships, and their questioning of "natural" female characteristics provoked corresponding critiques of female disorder and irrationality, an appeal for women's return to domesticity, and bitter attacks on female sexuality and morality. Paradoxically, the moral power and sensibilité attributed to women were both their strength and the source of the vulnerability that led to their downfall.

Generally, the assault on provincial women's clubs contained several dominant characteristics. First, many men, and some women as well, viewed with mistrust the public role of women and argued that women had no need or ability to participate in the official creation of the republic. Rather they should stay at home and raise their children as patriots, particularly since their apparent proclivity for hysteria made them too irrational to be public political actors. The left-wing journalist Prudhomme, for example, in his *Révolutions de Paris* attacked the Jacobin women's clubs of Lyon and Dijon in this way: "Why did they give themselves a president? Why hold sessions according to proper procedures? Why keep a register of their deliberations in these sessions? . . . Why have they asked the departmental, district, and municipal administrators to witness the holding of these sessions?" Calling the clubs a "plague to the mothers of good families," he urged women to stay home, otherwise "there will be clubs everywhere, and soon there will be no good housekeeping anywhere."[56]

Prudhomme's oft-quoted attack was prefigured and reiterated in other forms in the provinces, particularly when women club members requested the right to bear arms or to exercise institutional political power. In that same winter of 1793, shortly after the women's society of Besançon petitioned the National Convention for the vote, the Jacobin journal, the *Vedette*, published a letter ridiculing the "delirium" and "vanity" of these women who "are ignorant of the difficulties of domination." After an angry outburst blaming women for starting wars that made men victims, the letter-writer admonished the club women, "Women, don't think about sharing our work; our children who can do without their fathers have an essential need for their mothers. Guard our hearths; let us fight for the public prosperity on which you depend. Watch over your distaffs, and they will help spin your happiness; do not envy us the pen and the sword by which we reign. . . . On your behalf we are the slaves of our power." Likewise, when Peutat and her feisty followers in Avallon appealed for the right to bear arms and set aside their feminine softness, they quickly found themselves prey to satirical attack and advice in verse: "Abandon rather all these pikes, / Take up more civil arms, / Less terrible than those. / I know one which tickles. / Seize it, it's the distaff / With which Eve spun." (Abandonnez pourtant ces piques / Prenez les armes plus civiques / Moins terribles que celles-là. / J'en connais une qui chatouille / Empoignez-la, c'est la quenouille / Avec laquelle Eve fila.) Private domesticity, not public defense, was the appropriate role for women in the new nation.[57]

Male Jacobins also satirized or attacked the speeches and meetings of the women's societies in another vein. In language ranging in tone from mild rebuke to artful satire or angry denunciation, male Jacobins from the Pyré-nées to the Rhine were quick to proclaim that the Revolution had not in fact changed the "natural" characteristics of irrational, flighty, and credulous women. Wary of their own exposure to accusations of irrationality, incon-stancy, or immorality, male Jacobins anxiously reasserted the lines of sexual difference. In one exchange with the "Amies de la liberté et de l'égalité," the Surveillants of Bordeaux rebuked the women for their "credulity"; the male Jacobins commented to them, "your sex is different from ours."[58]

The perceived female tendency toward loquacity, irrationality, and chaos became recurring themes in male Jacobin discourse. The men of Saint-Servan excluded women from private sessions because they feared women's "proverbial incontinence of language." In a more biting fashion, an anony-mous pamphlet entitled *La Déclaration des droits de la femme*, which ap-peared in Lyon in 1791, proclaimed satirically, "The art of talking nonsense [déraisonner] is an inherent and imprescriptible right of women; no woman can be deprived of this right." In this same town, the male leader of the first women's society explicitly noted that the women "should not be permitted to deliberate on the public good" and that any potential member needed the written permission of her husband or father to join because "particular institutions should support general institutions . . . and never go against the laws of family." The regulations of the society stated that the male president should allow only one woman to speak at once; he had the power to fine or suspend any members who "spoke all at once and created tumult in the assembly." In case of "impossible discord," he could close the session. Al-though the Lyon club was unusual in having male officers, the issue of male control was pervasive.[59]

Often implications of female gullibility and fickleness were combined with warnings about the power of fanaticism to entice women to abandon the republic in favor of their old superstitious ways. "It is in the weakness of their mind that fanaticism grows," warned Besançon's *Vedette* in 1792 with an appeal for greater patriotic education for the women club members. Jacques Boileau of Avallon cautioned the men's popular society about the "feeble souls and especially the consciences of women," who should be under the control of good republican husbands rather than priests. In his 30 October 1793 speech against women's clubs, the deputy Amar emphasized the brawls and chaos excited by the Parisian "Citoyennes républicaines révolutionnaires." The examples could be multiplied, as male Jacobins repeatedly reiterated the seventeenth-century notion that women's internal nature made them "dissimulating, . . . changeable, light, unfaithful, impatient, credulous, and subject to babbling."[60]

The assault on women's clubs combined the discourse on female disorder and irrationality with repeated questioning of the morality and virtue of the leading women. In this age of the all-pervasive Rousseauist notion that politics must be founded on pure morality, such an attack was not unusual. From Brissot to Marat to Robespierre, myriad male politicians called for a democratic republic built on the virtue of its citizens. But in the case of women's clubs, the scrutiny and mockery of female politics most often took on a sexual tone. Fairly typical was the satirical song mocking the young women in Bréteuil who met to create a white flag for the municipality. "Where are you running so foolishly after this white flag, fickle young women?" asked the anonymous songwriter. In lyrics laden with sexual innuendo, he warned the young women of the "traitorous and nasty" powers of love and smirked that a "soldier can easily strip you, kind young girls, . . . in the front and in the back of your white flag." When the women's club of Lyon patrolled the city in the grain uprising of 1792, the *procureur général* Laussel denounced the rioters as "the dregs, hussies, . . . prostitutes." In Besançon, as we have seen, the women's club, especially its leader Maugras, was subject to suggestions of sexual misconduct, and the male Jacobins who took their side were denounced as effeminate "hermaphrodites" with feminine powers of dissimulation and seduction. Boileau of Avallon warned that the presence of women in popular assemblies or men's clubs threatened to corrupt men: "The podium is becoming a musk-scented area; the women are seated in the front, the speakers aim only to win them over." Even in Dijon, where the women's and men's clubs seem to have gotten along well, the men warned the women vaguely about the dangers of scandal and "calumny." The sensibilité that gave women the power to politicize their

intimate relationships was quickly undercut by a male discourse emphasizing both the sexual susceptibility of women and their dangerous, corrupting
power as seductresses.[61]

In some cases critics of the women's societies warned that women were
becoming masculinized. In 1791 Pauline Siro of Pau organized an all-female
festival against the wishes of the municipality, which pointed out the "anom-
aly of such a ceremony" and denounced its potential "danger . . . as cause
and occasion for disorder." When the "open war [between] the respectable
amazons and municipality of Pau," as one journalist put it, escalated into a
pamphlet battle raging as far away as Paris, Pauline Siro was subjected to
endless sexually loaded attacks about her illicit union with the Constitutional bishop. But one anonymous pamphleteer in particular denounced this
female "grenadier" and proclaimed that if all women followed Pauline Siro,
"there will be no more women; and in this case what will become of us?"
The women of Pau, attacked by local authorities and undermined by popular opinion, disbanded their club. At least in the revolutionary archives, the
women remained silent. But the questioning of female virtue, with its threatening implication that women had become masculinized, would be forcefully echoed two years later: Chaumette proclaimed in the Paris Commune
in November 1793, "It is contrary to all the laws of nature for a woman to
want to make herself a man. The Council must recall that some time ago
these denatured women, these *viragos*, wandered through the markets with
the red cap to sully that badge of liberty. . . . Since when is it permitted to
give up one's sex?"[62]

In the eyes of male Jacobins, women's clubs had done more than enter the
public sphere of politics; they had questioned the nature of the feminine,
created contesting discourses about the strengths and weaknesses of sensibilité, and claimed that public political participation increased their moral
and intellectual ability to wield political influence in private relationships.
Certainly, the male revolutionaries who suppressed women's clubs sought to
exclude women from the public political sphere in order to stake out space
and legitimacy for the emergence of male republican politics. But at the
heart of the attacks on the immorality and disorder of women's clubs was
more than an attempt to exclude women from the fledgling male political
sphere and more than a wariness about the most radical feminist demands.
Male Jacobins found women's clubs threatening in part because the invasive

politicization of the private posed a threat to men in the home as well as at the public tribunal or assembly hall.

Particularly in the turbulent politics of 1793 when the definition of morality was hotly contested and integrally related to the exercise of public power, leading men felt a profound ambivalence about surrendering moral power to women even in the private realm of the family and the marriage. To attack women's morality was to impugn and to limit their private as well as their public political power. As the deputy Amar commented in his devastating and successful call for outlawing women's clubs in 1793: "If we consider that the political education of men is at its beginning, that all its principles are not developed, and that we are still stammering over the word 'liberty,' then how much less enlightened are women, whose moral education has been practically non-existent." In sum, republicans such as Amar suppressed women's clubs because they sought not only to undermine the public role of women, but also to curtail their traditional moral dominion over the private as well. In the context of a revolution that demanded the virtually total subordination of the private, or at least the invasion of the public into the private sphere, to reiterate the lines of sexual difference, emphasize the domestic role of women as republican mothers, and delineate the limits and characteristics of female sensibilité was to reconstitute social order and to clarify the muddled relationship of the public to the private as well. Many male Jacobins shared the view of Amar when he stated, "The social order results from the differences between men and women."[63]

The Jacobin women's clubs, then, leave a mixed legacy. On the one hand, their widespread success and activism bear tribute to the power of revolutionary ideology to politicize and educate French women in many cities and towns. On the other hand, the optimistic vision of the "Dames citoyennes" of Montcenis—who promised in 1791 that "proud and courageous like amazons, we will conserve our liberty"—would not be fulfilled.[64] The suppression of women's clubs in the fall of 1793 would lay the groundwork for the continued exclusion of women from official politics and for the fuller development of the domestic ideology of the nineteenth century.

2

Rural Political Activism and Fiscal Equality in the Revolutionary Somme

BRYANT T. RAGAN, JR.

Article 13: A common tax is indispensable to maintain the public force and support the expenses of administration. It must be shared equally among all the citizens of administration. It must be shared equally among all the citizens in proportion to their means.

Article 14: All citizens have the right to ascertain, personally or through their representatives, the necessity of the public tax, to consent to it freely, to know how it is spent, and to determine its amount, basis, mode of collection, and duration.

Declaration of the Rights of Man and Citizen, 26 August 1789[1]

On 23 March 1790 the municipal councilors of the village of Roye-sur-le-Matz (pop. 800) petitioned the Constituent Assembly for tax relief.[2] An epidemic was raging through their small community in the southern Somme: four hundred men and women had already fallen ill, and as many as five were dying each day. Friends who had come from neighboring communities to care for the sick were beginning to catch the disease themselves. To make matters worse, the previous year's harvest had been so meager that the storehouses were almost empty. Moreover, the village leaders were afraid to grind the remaining grain because they thought that the flour might spread the disease further. Famine and disease combined to create a crisis so severe that the very existence of the community was threatened. The village councilors admitted that there was little the Constituent Assembly could do to alleviate the suffering caused by the epidemic or the famine, but they believed that the Assembly could provide some relief in the form of "the remittance of the remaining tax obligation from 1788 and 1789, an obligation that is impossible for us to pay."

The petition from Roye-sur-le-Matz demonstrates how acute the economic situation had become during the early years of the Revolution in the rural Somme, the heart of the ancient province of Picardy, and it suggests that the question of impositions was of vital importance to villagers. By focusing on such crucial fiscal issues in the Somme countryside from 1789 to 1792, this essay shows villagers to have set and pursued political goals in an active, self-directed manner. Rural inhabitants seized on the opportunities created by the Revolution and utilized revolutionary ideology to help define their role in the new nation.

Two types of documents in particular provide the basis for this exploration of rural political *mentalités*: riot reports and petitions. Scores of communal disturbances broke out across the Somme during the revolutionary decade, and the departmental Directory, the highest local administrative body governing the Somme, worked hard to suppress them. The departmental archives contain a large number of investigative reports stemming from these disturbances, as well as correspondence between plaintiffs, municipal officers, and departmental administrators involved in disputes. The archives of the Committees of Feudal Rights and Finance stored in the National Archives also contain hundreds of petitions that rural inhabitants and village councilors sent to Paris in the belief that national representatives should know about the myriad of difficulties confronting their communities.[3] People wrote to the Assembly for a host of reasons, such as to request a tax break because of a bad harvest or to ask for a son's release from military duty. The communal petitions, signed by municipal councilors and often by dozens of villagers, provide the clearest articulation of rural public opinion on fiscal matters. When seen in combination, the petitions and the police reports on disturbances reveal that rural politics had become in the revolutionary context a dynamic blend of old and new forms of political expression.

Most interpretations of rural France during the Revolution overlook the dynamism of rural politics, in part because they rely on one of two models designed to explain peasant unrest under the Old Regime. Influenced by the Annales school, historians such as Yves-Marie Bercé and Charles Tilly stress the "antistate" characteristics of the revolutionary tax revolt. In this view, villagers did not really have a coherent "proactive" political ideology; rather the countryside was reenacting its historical antipathy to the centralizing tendencies of the nation-state.[4] Rural revolts during the Revolution, then, resoundingly echoed their seventeenth-century *croquant* ancestors, exhibiting the following traits: village solidarity, the desire to return to a better past, the strong resentment of fiscal innovation by national authorities, xenophobia, the tocsin ringing, the crowd assembled, the festive revolt turned violent, the tax collector run out of the district or killed. And according to Eugen Weber, the peasantry was not particularly interested in politics, except when it was threatened by the state, well into the nineteenth century.[5]

The other interpretation, which owes much to Marxism, suggests that peasant activism resulted from the socioeconomic cleavage between the seigneurial class and the peasantry. According to the traditional Marxist explanation, the peasantry rose up against the exploitative aristocratic class in 1789.[6] Once feudalism had been dismantled by bourgeois revolutionaries, however, rural inhabitants sank back into their "natural" apolitical state. Georges Lefebvre and Pierre de Saint-Jacob greatly refined this model by arguing that rural activism in the 1780s and 1790s stemmed not from an antifeudal impulse but rather from anticapitalist sentiment. In the eighteenth century, seigneurs began to impose a new form of production on the countryside, agrarian capitalism.[7] They resurrected long-forgotten feudal rights to make more money in the growing capitalist economy. Some lords, for example, reasserted their ownership over village commons and then enclosed the land to raise sheep made more valuable by the growing national and international cloth markets. Others used feudal prerogatives to claim title to local streams. By redirecting streams through their own croplands, they improved their net agricultural production, while depriving peasant farmers of vital water resources. The resulting economic deprivation and social dislocations caused by agrarian capitalism and growing state taxes in the eighteenth century enraged villagers. Because the punishment for revolt was so severe, rural communities often fought their seigneurs in court, even though their chances of winning were slim and the court costs high.[8] The downturn in the economy in the 1780s, however, left desperate rural inhabitants with little choice but to take more drastic action; in hundreds of violent uprisings throughout France, villagers attacked châteaux, burned legal records, and brutalized aristocrats.

Both of these models portray rural communities as inherently reactive before and during the Revolution. They draw a triangular relationship of state/seigneur/villager in which villagers acted *only* when new impositions (taxes, feudal dues) were levied and when the innovating exploiter (administrator, seigneur) was perceived to be vulnerable.

At first glance, the case of the Somme seems to support the view that rural inhabitants were generally apolitical, reacting only when they felt threatened by aristocrats, the rural bourgeoisie, or the state. Northern France did have a long history of antistate and antifeudal animus. From the jacqueries of the late Middle Ages through the antinoble disturbances of late July 1789, villagers in the northeastern province of Picardy exhibited a strong determination to fight the exploitation of Parisian bureaucrats and local elites during periods of great economic crisis. And the Picard economy was starting to exhibit some important structural weaknesses on the eve of the Revolution. Although the province was relatively wealthy in terms of overall agricultural production, most people did not benefit from its wealth. It has been estimated that three-quarters of the rural population of southern Picardy owned less than ten percent of the land.[9] In addition, agrarian capitalism, firmly entrenched in the Somme valley by the 1770s, had exacerbated cleavages in the countryside. Out of some sixty households in a typical village, only two or three would have been classified as *laboureur* households, farmholdings that were sufficiently large to benefit from the new capitalist forms of agricultural exploitation. The typical village comprised ten to twenty middling peasant households and from twenty to forty *manouvrier* or salaried agricultural worker households.[10] Thus although overall village productivity may have been increasing in the eighteenth century, it only enriched a few members of each rural community.

On the eve of the Revolution, taxes and seigneurial dues remained high in northern France while the cost of living was rising. Fewer rural families could subsist by farming alone and agrarian capitalism was taking away badly needed jobs. So villagers began to engage in cottage industry in ever greater numbers. The inhabitants of the Amiénois, the region around the Picard capital of Amiens, had traditionally specialized in wool manufacture; they began to diversify into satin, linen, and silk production.[11] Cottage workers in the Ponthieu, the lowlands along the English Channel, were moving into the locksmith trade, while important paper and leather manufactures were springing up throughout the south and the east.[12] Although rural families looked to these new sources of income to maintain their standard of living, their attempts were rendered largely unsuccessful by their inability to compete with English producers and by a series of catastrophic harvests. The commerce treaty with England in 1786 led to the closing of approximately eighty percent of the cloth manufactures in the rural Somme, forcing male and female villagers to rely more heavily on their traditional mode of production, agriculture.[13] The mediocre harvests of 1787, 1788, and 1789, however, dashed any hopes of maintaining their standard of living. In short, the economic climate of the Picard countryside by the outbreak of the Revolution was in dire straits. Rural inhabitants were being forced to decide which financial obligations they were going to pay when the Revolution gave them an opportunity to question the fairness of the entire system of fiscal impositions.[14]

Reports of tax revolts and community petitions indicate that during the Revolution the rural inhabitants of the Somme were not merely reactive and that their collective actions cannot be categorized simply as antifeudal, anticapitalist, or even antistate. Rather villagers believed that they had a vital stake in the new nation and consequently were prepared to pay their *fair* share of the new revolutionary tax burden. They tried to create a new relationship between the countryside and the nation based upon the revolutionary virtue of equality. Standing between them and their goal were three fiscal impediments: the persistence of seigneurialism, onerous indirect taxes, and inequities in direct taxation.

Rural inhabitants had called for the abolition of feudal privileges long before the fateful night of 4 August 1789, when the National Assembly promised to abolish feudal impositions. Villagers quickly found out, however, that the complete dismantling of the seigneurial system was going to be long and torturous because of stiff resistance from some of the national representatives. Nevertheless, they continued resolutely to challenge seigneurialism until the very last feudal privilege was abolished. Meanwhile villagers in the Somme consistently advocated a national taxation system based on equality. They especially resented excise taxes, because these taxes were most heavily borne by the lower and middle classes. Despite the tension between town and country, townspeople and villagers allied to fight against sales taxes and import/export duties. Villagers fought on their own, however, for the reform of direct taxation. They did not question the obligation to pay direct taxes to the national government, but they wanted to ensure that every citizen who owned land pay a fair share of the burden. Largely due to pressure from the countryside, most of these inequities—seigneurial impositions, a number of important excise taxes, and unfair direct taxation—were eliminated by 1793. Thus the Assembly finally put in place a national tax program that met the demands of rural inhabitants.

Fighting Seigneurialism in the Somme

When the Revolution erupted in the summer of 1789, the most obvious fiscal inequality in the French countryside was the persistence of seigneurial dues. Villagers immediately targeted "feudalism" as having no legitimacy in the new revolutionary order, and communal actions against seigneurs occurred throughout Picardy and indeed throughout the whole nation in late July and early August 1789.[15] The young Constituent Assembly realized immediately that if these events, called the "Great Fear," continued unabated, France might well fall into anarchy.[16] The representatives met and decided to put an end to feudalism in an emotional meeting on the night of 4 August, a true watershed as François Furet has argued. According to Furet, this evening witnessed the destruction of an ancient legal system based on orders and privileges and left in its stead "a social world conceived in a new way as a collection of free and equal individuals subject to the universal authority of the law."[17] After heatedly debating how to make this momentous social and legal change, the representatives decreed on 11 August that "The National Assembly entirely destroys the feudal regime."[18]

In spite of the best intentions of the national representatives, it quickly became clear that it was going to take months, if not years, to eliminate feudalism. The resolution of 11 August decreed that those rights and dues "deriving from personal serfdom, and those that represent them, are abolished without compensation; all others are declared redeemable, and the price and manner of redemption will be determined by the National Assembly." A great deal of time and energy was necessary for the legislators to specify which rights were redeemable, for the administration and the courts to settle on prices, and for the villages themselves to come up with the money. Villagers were impatient for fundamental change and could not help but be very disappointed by the way things were turning out.[19] But they refused simply to wait passively for seigneurial privilege to come to an end and instead exerted even more pressure on the Assembly. They participated in numerous collective actions (riots and petitions) until legislation had eliminated the last vestiges of feudal privilege in the summers of 1792 and 1793.

A riot at the château of the countess de la Myre in Davenescourt (pop. 700) demonstrates how serious the rural inhabitants of the Somme were about ending feudalism. It attracted national attention because of its size and because François-Noël Babeuf (1760–1797), better known as Gracchus Babeuf, used the occasion to highlight his role as a rural leader. The disturbance did not really come as a surprise to the countess. In a letter dated 3 June 1790, she said that she was afraid of her "ex-vassals." They resented her because in 1785 they had been forced "to consent to the alienation of one third of the [common] marshland in my favor, according to a judgment [based on a law from 1669] made by the sovereign." In his in-depth analysis of the confrontation at Davenescourt, R. B. Rose finds that the dispute over land was in actuality but one of many conflicts between the villagers and the countess over seigneurial privileges.[20]

De la Myre was unmoved by the misfortune caused by a disastrous hailstorm in 1788. The village's entire crop had been wiped out, and the community had still not recovered by 1790.[21] That spring many of the inhabitants of Davenescourt decided to take the law into their own hands; after arming themselves, they went to work the lands they had lost to de la Myre in the court case. The irate countess petitioned the Assembly for help, reporting: "The village council refuses me any type of help and warns me that it will be even more dangerous if I ask for [help from] the mounted police force, which is too weak to dissipate the seditious mobs. [The people in the mob] are scared by the spirit of anarchy in neighboring villages, and they threaten to kill the municipal officers as well as the officers of justice if [the officers] take even the smallest step [to stop] the invasion of my proper-ties." De la Myre asserted that her only recourse was to appeal to the national government. Meanwhile the village councilors also wrote to tell their side of the story. In their letter they denounced the countess, accusing her of having usurped their land and having "impoverished the inhabitants of Davenescourt through court costs." They ended by appealing to the Assembly for help.[22]

When Paris failed to support them, the village council decided on 24 February 1791 that it was time to settle the dispute with the countess once and for all.[23] Apparently the rest of the village had come to the same conclu-sion: the next morning, while the councilors were talking to de la Myre about the conflict, the tocsin rang out, and several hundred villagers gath-ered and attacked her château. As a few armed men forced open the grill of the tower, the prescient municipal officers withdrew from the scene. In the following fracas some of the rioters shot at the château's defenders, and the countess's valet Monceaux was wounded in the arm. Next the villagers stormed the house and ran to the master bedroom, where smashing open the door, they found de la Myre and her two children. They put a noose around her neck and threatened to hang her; then they forced her to renounce her claim to the local marshland. While the family's private archives were being destroyed, the countess and her entourage were allowed to flee the scene of destruction. Although her life had been spared, de la Myre had been wounded by a saber. Because the local mounted force was too frightened to come to Davenescourt, a detachment from the bourg of Roye came and suppressed the riot. Later the leaders of the riot were thrown in jail in the district capital of Montdidier, where by chance they met another prisoner, Gracchus Babeuf. Babeuf agreed to undertake their legal defense, and after a great deal of publicity, he succeeded in getting them acquitted.

The riot at Davenescourt has attracted considerable attention from historians because of the role played by Babeuf in defending the community's actions and the impact this episode had on his political formation. The Marxist historian Victor Dalin insists that it was "Picardy, one of the most economically sophisticated provinces in France, that provided Babeuf with abundant material to critique not only feudal relations but also capitalist ones."[24] Dalin argues that Babeuf embodied the as yet unarticulated socioeconomic aspirations of villagers who were already well on their way to participating in a capitalist economy. In a very different vein, R. B. Rose maintains that class cleavages alone cannot explain Babeuf's radicalism. Instead Rose believes that Babeuf's attack on the philosophic basis of feudalism was "a complex process in which private misfortunes, national politics, and the ripening of a personal ideology all played a part."[25] Yet despite their differences, Rose and Dalin agree that Babeuf was essential to the movement against seigneurial privilege in the Somme: "Thanks to the intervention of a popular leader of a new type, making inspired use of new opportunities, the Davenescourt Affair was thus transformed from a purely parochial conflict about particular grievances to an exemplary episode in a far wider and ongoing political struggle."[26]

Because Babeuf became such an important figure in the Revolution, it is of course important to explore how the socioeconomic relations of Picardy, as well as his participation in the Davenescourt affair, led him to develop his protocommunist political ideology. Yet although Babeuf did help make this particular event a cause célèbre, uprisings like the one at Davenescourt also provide an opportunity to look at how "ordinary" villagers themselves conceived of revolutionary politics and ideology.

Popular activism in the Somme predated Babeuf's participation and did not require in later instances his personal leadership. The riot at the de la Myre château may have been one of the more well-known demonstrations against seigneurial privilege, but it was only one of a long litany of calls by villagers to abolish the last traces of feudalism. Although the August 1789 decrees had promised them the complete dismantling of feudalism, some seigneurial privileges were still very much in evidence in 1791. And villagers were not going to rest until the last of these gross inequalities had ceased to exist.

Rural inhabitants understood the basic premises of the new laws against feudalism as well as the revolutionary spirit underlying them. In addition to rioting, villagers in the Somme valley also used formal channels—petitions— to contest feudal impositions, and the rhetoric and political strategies used in some of these petitions reveal a high level of political sophistication. Some villagers, for example, tried to play elites off against one another in order to achieve their political aims. The inhabitants of Mailly and Raineval (pop. 295), Thory (pop. 350), Louvrechies (pop. 240), and Sauvilles (pop. 340), for instance, protested various seigneurial exactions by asking their national representatives to correct the many "abuses" they had long been forced to endure from their lord, the duke of Mailly.[27] They were particularly angry about the destruction wrought on their crops by the duke's game birds, which were protected by feudal law. They wanted "each landholder to be *equally* authorized according to the terms of the national decree to hunt and kill destructive game birds on his *private property*, the only way of putting every-one in a position to pay the taxes that will be assessed on each of their lands according to the orders that have been received" (my emphasis). By using legal expressions and referring to national laws, the petitioners were able to make their argument more credible. In addition, they stressed the relationship between the persistence of feudal dues and their inability to pay national taxes, subtly indicating their willingness to ally with central authority in order to challenge local elites. Finally, they highlighted two of the major concerns of revolutionaries—equality and private property—to make their demands even more compelling. They ended the petition by asking the government to make the duke pay them for all the damage done to their lands.

Because of a concern to protect private property, the Constituent Assem-bly was wary of abolishing seigneurial privileges without having some kind of compensation paid to lords. Yet despite the ambivalence of the national government toward abolishing seigneurial rights once and for all, villagers still appealed to the Assembly to end the feudal system, as in the case of Mailly. In their petitions villagers were quick to note that determining the amount of the compensation was going to be very costly in terms of both time and money. On 19 May 1790, the municipal councilors of Saint-Aubin (pop. 450) wrote that "Articles 2 and 3 of Title 3 of the decree relating to the redemption of seigneurial rights make for an infinite number of court cases, because as jurisprudence has always varied in this subject, the resulting trials will be neither less frequent, nor less rigorous."[28] In their particular case, they explained, the seigneur de la Haye had only recently claimed the seigneurial right of harvest dues (*champart*). No matter how the village responded, it would be ruined, either by paying the unjust dues or the court fees. They asked for the enforcement of Article 29, which they claimed mandated the privileged members of the Old Regime to prove they had owned a contested privilege for at least thirty or forty years.

A number of other communities also wrote the Assembly about seigneurial dues. The municipality of Moliens-le-Vidame (pop. 796) complained about the difficulties of implementing the law governing the redemption of seigneurial rights.[29] The village councilors began by saying that they did not know how to determine the value of the champart so that they could buy it. What kind of evidence was needed to evaluate its worth? More to the point, they did not understand why they had to pay anything for it since the right had been acquired so recently by the seigneurs. They wrote that although they wanted to take their case to court, they could not afford a lengthy juridical battle. In the petition, the municipality made it clear that the community felt it had borne the brunt of the financial burden of the region long enough and that it was time for the *aisés* and the *riches* to give up their unfair privileges. In another petition dated 29 October 1790, the inhabitants of the village of Boismont (pop. 410), near the port town of Saint-Valéry, denounced their ex-seigneur to the Assembly's Committee on Feudal Rights.[30] Since the opening of the canal of Saint-Valéry, farmers in Boismont had enjoyed the right of using it to water their pastures. The seigneur of Boismont, however, arbitrarily decided in 1790 that they could no longer use the canal water for irrigation. When the villagers wrote to Amiens for support, the departmental Directory backed up the lord's claims, leaving the villagers with the dilemma of giving in or fighting a long, expensive court battle. The Directory's policies must have infuriated residents of Boismont. On the one hand, the bourgeois administration claimed that the traditional rights of seigneurs were private property rights and must therefore be protected in some way (i.e., reimbursed by the village community). On the other hand, the community's use of precedent did not carry any weight whatsoever.

The confusion over the redemption of seigneurial dues continued for more than a year. In a letter dated early June 1791, the curé of Rincheval (pop. 512) wrote to the Committee of Feudal Rights to report that the Directory of the Somme was misinterpreting national laws to serve the interests of seigneurs.[31] He said that by the law of 15 May 1790, the Assembly had declared that nobles wishing to be reimbursed for a particular feudal right had to prove that they had possessed that right for at least forty years. The departmental administrators, the priest claimed, interpreted the law differently: the Directory "pretends today that the presentation of one of those titles is only necessary when it is a question of a privilege suppressed without compensation." The departmental administrators, then, really wanted feudal dues reimbursed regardless of the letter of the law. The priest continued, saying, "Our country inhabitants are furious about this declaration. They feel deeply the falseness and attribute it to the interest of the majority of the Directory. They feel very energetically that it is in the natural order that the presenter have a title." He asked the Assembly to state clearly that it was not necessary to pay the redemption unless a title was provided. Time was of the essence, he ended, because violent disturbances were starting to break out in the canton.

The directors of the Somme refused to back off from this policy and made it clear to their constituents on numerous occasions that they supported the Assembly's program requiring the redemption of feudal dues.[32] In a circular to the department on 29 June 1791, the administrators stated that feudalism must be dismantled only by "justice, moderation, firmness." They criticized the communal actions of Somme villagers: "How could a spirit of dizziness have led a people who are naturally just and sweet to such excesses? Why this turbulent agitation of spirits, these threats, realized in a few places where the consequences could be very grave? Why these plots refusing the payment of these rights and charges of the property that you defend?"[33] The departmental administrators rightly argued that when the Constituent Assembly had voted to abolish feudalism, it had not meant to attack property itself.

In spite of their desire to safeguard property rights by strictly enforcing the redemption of seigneurial dues, the Somme's administrators sometimes found it difficult to make villages buy the rights. In early August 1791, most of the inhabitants of Hallivillers (pop. 341) gathered, saying that they intended to "put an end to the payment of the champart and force the other landholders to unite with them to refuse the tax."[34] Led by the farmer Jean-Baptiste Morel and the salaried day-laborers Jean Berenger and François Pisson, the angry men and women insulted and threatened the communal assessors. Then they turned their wrath on several wealthy peasants, who had already paid their allotted share of the champart. This turn of events suggests that the community was beset with internal conflicts that may have run along class lines. It is not surprising that the members of the community who had the most interest in preserving property rights and could afford to pay the seigneurial dues, the wealthier peasants, that is, would have done so. The following day the unruly crowd again threatened the men entrusted with the collection of the champart. When the departmental directors heard of the riot, they ordered the mayor to report immediately to Amiens and they sent in a detachment of soldiers to put down the disorder. After a similar protest against the champart broke out the same month in Hornoy (pop. 1180), the Directory decided that perhaps the best way to maintain order was by punishing village councilors, who should be "pursued as troublemakers of the public order."[35] Yet even this measure failed to produce the desired compliance in some of the recalcitrant communities.

While the departmental Directory continued to press for the redemption of seigneurial dues, representatives in Paris slowly began to change course.[36] The Legislative Assembly passed a law on 18 June 1792 that abolished many minor seigneurial rights without compensation unless a title could be presented. Another series of laws passed on 25–28 August 1792 required lords to show a title if they wanted to claim the necessity of redemption for any seigneurial imposition. The burden of proof now lay on the formerly privileged property owners.

By 1793, representatives in the National Convention were talking less about protecting feudal prerogatives as property rights and more about the injustice of perpetuating the feudal order. Communities that acted to end the last vestiges of feudalism now met with less resistance at the national level. On 6 February, after reviewing the petitions of Pont-Noyelle (pop. 501) and Saint-Vast (pop. 475) that asked for the return of their old common lands, the minister of the interior wrote, "Feudal power has not yet been demolished. In 1790, after legal proceedings of thirty years, the ex-seigneur of the aforementioned communes was given the possession of . . . one hundred *journaux* of marshland by a decree of the ex-parlement. From this decree that has stripped the inhabitants of more than six hundred years of use, it is enough to observe that the unhappy and never ending proceedings took place . . . in a time when the law . . . against weak people was the law of the day."[37] He called for this injustice to be remedied immediately.

On 17 July 1793, the National Convention abolished all seigneurial dues without compensation.[38] Rural inhabitants had finally won the struggle they had begun in the summer of 1789. They had not been merely reacting against an onerous system of privilege; rather they had realized that the basic inequities of seigneurialism were illegitimate and contrary to revolutionary principles. Nor did they have to be led; instead they were the leaders

of the rural political movement. In some cases they vented their anger by
rioting, while at other times they thought it more appropriate to work
through legal channels. They proved that they were conversant with revolutionary ideology and national legislation, and it was only when the national
representatives realized the inconsistencies between revolutionary principles
and the persistence of inequality in the countryside that the goals of villagers
were achieved.

The Struggle for Fair Taxation

National legislators knew that the government needed tax monies to function; after all, the Revolution had happened to a large extent because of a
fiscal crisis. Putting the new state on a sound financial footing was consequently one of their prime concerns, and on 19 September 1789, on the
recommendation of the duke d'Aiguillon, the representatives decided to
reserve each Friday and Saturday to deal with budgetary matters, even at the
expense of their constitution-writing activities.[39] The charged debates over
taxation reveal a wide range of motives, from lofty idealism to profound
cynicism. In a memoir addressed to the Constituent Assembly (17 December
1789), the first minister of finance advised: "The public, in surrendering
itself to great uneasiness, does not notice that a number of dues that you are
thinking about suppressing . . . could be replaced by others of the same type,
only under the care of each provincial administration. [This] condition
would suffice to calm [the public], either in reality or in imagination." He
then stated that it was imperative to "fix opinion and stop the course of
baleful forebodings to which people abandon themselves."[40] Whether cyni-
cal or idealistic, one thing was obvious: the state had to think about ways to
collect money without pushing the citizenry to revolt.

It was not at all clear how to establish a new tax assessment system. At
times it seemed as if everyone in France—wealthy merchants and salaried
workers, townspeople and peasants—was clamoring for lower taxes, and
legislators knew that people were going to feel ill-treated no matter how the
burden was to fall.[41] Before the Revolution, the countryside had paid a
disproportionately large share of the national tax burden, and in general
legislators thought that the best policy, at least in the short term, was for
rural inhabitants to continue financing a large percentage of the national
budget. The representatives knew, however, that they had to approach the
whole issue with great care. At a time when Paris and many other cities were

so volatile, they could not afford to have significant strife in the countryside. Yet despite the best efforts of their representatives, villagers were not willing to allow the status quo ante to continue without a fight. In the summer of 1789, tax revolts broke out around France, from Normandy in the north to Roussillon in the south, from Lorraine in the east to Touraine in the west.[42] Some of the largest political actions took place in Picardy.

It is not surprising that villagers from the Somme were passionately interested in fiscal matters as the Old Regime came to an end.[43] Before the Revolution, rural inhabitants had to pay a plethora of seigneurial dues and religious tithes. Moreover, Picardy figured among the most heavily taxed provinces of France. It was subject to numerous impositions, most notably the onerous salt tax (*grande gabelle*) and the hated excise tax on wine (*augmentation*), which was levied on the quality as well as the quantity of the product.[44] Picards also had to pay numerous import/export duties (*octrois*), the direct tax on land (*taille*), and various sales taxes (*aides*).[45] Because of the impossibility of paying all of these heavy impositions during a period of great economic crisis, villagers believed that tax reform was necessary. The village *cahiers de doléances*, the grievance lists compiled in early 1789, railed against burdensome taxes.

Coinciding with the Great Fear, the first major tax revolt in the Somme took place in the bourg of Péronne (pop. 3680), where peasants and townspeople ransacked two guardhouses and the customhouse on 18 July 1789.[46] On the same day townspeople pillaged the customhouses at Roye (pop. 3174). Then, taking advantage of the mayhem, villagers brought dutiable products into Roye to sell tax-free. Similar insurrections broke out all over the Somme during the next month. On 16 August 1789, in one of the more destructive riots, a large crowd in Doullens (pop. 3000) devastated the residence of the local sales-tax collector, M. Morillot.[47] Subsequently the rioters burned all of his business records in a "joyous fire" in the middle of the street. Excited by such a vivid display, the crowd continued to demonstrate; the next day it converged on the administrative office of customs duties, salt taxes, and tobacco and burned the records there too. The rioters then tried to occupy the offices of the court clerk and the salt storehouse, retreating only after severe warnings were made by M. Dusevel, the chief administrator of these two institutions.

In the most comprehensive study of the "tax rebellion of the Somme," R. B. Rose explains that this kind of rioting was not limited to towns; similar collective violence also broke out in smaller communities throughout the department, from Fins (pop. 426) in the east to Moreuil (pop. 826) in the west.[48] In these riots villagers typically attacked and burned the houses of tax collectors. The movement only intensified when the Assembly voted to "establish equality for all citizens with respect to taxes and public charges" on 7 October 1789, and it lasted through the end of the year.[49] An important challenge to excise taxes, for example, occurred in the western bourg of Crécy (pop. 1207), the site of one of the most important battles of the Hundred Years' War.[50] D'Agay de Mutigny, intendant of the *généralité* of Amiens, reported on 23 November that villagers in Crécy had refused to pay the sales taxes on alcohol and farm animals since early October. When he ordered a militia force into the community to put an end to the buying and selling of animals in the marketplace, some villagers wanted to give in and pay their taxes. Their more radical neighbors, however, threatened to harm them if they surrendered to governmental pressure. Most of the community continued to resist, and on 2 November an unarmed crowd declared publicly the abolition of market taxes and then ordered the two officials in charge of excise taxes to leave Crécy. The intransigent villagers gave one of the officials eight days to leave the community, while his colleague was given only twenty-four hours. The intendant ordered twenty-five soldiers into the village to end the insurrection. When the detachment threatened to fire on the assembled villagers, the crowd went home. But the villagers still refused to pay their taxes.

The case of Crécy indicates how badly villagers of the Somme wanted fiscal reform. Their opposition to the heavy tax load grew once the rhetoric of the Revolution had explicitly promised them equality.[51] In the middle of these department-wide struggles entered Gracchus Babeuf; in January 1790 he joined the tax rebellion and became one of its leading proponents. A struggle in Roye between the grocers and cafe-owners, who were unwilling to pay the high sales taxes on alcohol, and the municipal council, which was trying to force them to pay, had turned incendiary: "We will perish," the rebellious townspeople said, "before yielding the fruit of our labor to nourish the revolting idleness of these vampires of the people."[52] The opposing parties in Roye hardened their positions. Babeuf then appeared, making a stirring address in which he encouraged the townspeople and villagers not to pay their taxes.[53] Following this speech he began to travel around the department to garner support for a widespread tax revolt. For the next four months, the national government attempted to suppress the revolt peaceably, ordering Babeuf on numerous occasions to stop causing trouble. Babeuf refused to back down, and on 18 May the Cour des Aides, the administrative body regulating taxes on alcohol, arrested him and brought him to Paris.

Many historians assume that this movement was politically effective only because Babeuf was one of the leaders of the revolt.[54] But as in the case of seigneurial dues, the popular movement toward tax reform had clearly started *before* Babeuf joined it. Villagers did not shy away from political action nor did they need Babeuf to articulate their demands. The numerous tax protests in the Somme continued through 1790 and into 1791 while Babeuf was in jail and caused the national administration more and more concern. On 21 August 1790 the minister of finance wrote to the Directory of the Somme, saying that "it is time that the French people of this department fulfill their duties to the country. . . . The true citizens, the French people submitting to the law, only await our orders to join themselves to us and ensure the payment of taxes. . . . We are responsible like you. We would be weak and criminal if we did not demand that you use all of the means of the Constitution placed in your hands for the reestablishment of taxes."[55] The departmental government, however, was too weak to collect tax revenues from the restless countryside.

Villagers and townspeople, who worked together to fight against the salt tax, customs duties, and sales tax on alcohol, ultimately succeeded in convincing the Constituent Assembly that the new revolutionary tax code should not be based on indirect taxes. Abolishing these excise taxes was a risky proposition for the government; at a moment when it was going to ask for new types of taxes, it was difficult to propose eliminating older forms of revenue. Yet any hesitancy that legislators may have felt over abolishing indirect taxes seemed insignificant when compared with the growing militancy of the provinces. On 21 and 22 March 1790, the Constituent Assembly voted to abolish the much-hated salt tax, as well as the excise taxes on leather, iron, starches, oil, and soap; and on 30 October of the same year, it suppressed all internal import and export taxes.[56] Finally, on 2 March 1791, the national legislators decided to end the detested sales tax on alcohol, as well as various taxes on paper and playing cards.[57] Although the inhabitants of villages, bourgs, and small towns cannot be given exclusive credit for the complete reform of the national tax code, they were key players in the ending of some of the most onerous indirect taxes in the nation.

Villagers pursued a very different path in moving beyond opposition to indirect taxes toward demanding the reform of direct taxes. In the case of property tax reform, rural inhabitants and townspeople did not share the same concerns. Although many villagers participated in riots to demand the abolition of what they considered to be illegitimate indirect taxes, their petitions suggest that direct taxes, if equitably distributed, were reasonable.

Before the Revolution two major direct taxes were imposed on property in the Picard countryside: the *taille d'exploitation*, a tax based on the productivity of the land, and the *taille de propriété*, a tax levied only on the property where the principal residence was located. Both of these taxes pitted rural inhabitants against wealthy townspeople who owned land in the countryside. Absentee landlords could pass their productivity tax on to their lessees through rents, while a bourgeois who owned a farm in a village community but claimed a town house as his or her chief residence did not have to contribute to the community's tax assessment.[58] On 26 September 1789 the Constituent Assembly passed a new law requiring people who had been tax-exempt under the Old Regime to start paying national taxes. The law also stipulated that the tax would be retroactive to July 1789. On 16 October the king consented to the law and ordered the tax to be collected according to the old guidelines; thus the exploitation and propriété distinction was maintained.[59]

Although the new law was a step in the right direction insofar as it eliminated the class of tax-exempt men and women, rural inhabitants were nevertheless disappointed because it perpetuated some of the inequalities of the prerevolutionary tax assessment system. M. Anginer, a farmer from Acheux-en-Vimeu (pop. 821), wrote the Assembly to criticize the new revolutionary tax law.[60] He maintained that although "les bons citoyens" in the region were extremely patriotic, they had "seen with pain" the king's proclamations of 14 and 16 October continuing the assessment of taxes according to the location of the principal residence. This practice, he maintained, would prove especially disastrous in an area where most of the rural land was owned either by the privileged of the Old Regime or by townspeople. According to Anginer, "the odious regime of the financial hydra" rested on the backs of poor village laborers. The only solution to this intolerable situation, he asserted, was to make all landholders contribute to the local tax burden no matter where they lived.[61]

The inhabitants of the village of Moliens-le-Vidame were also angry about the inequalities embedded in the tax system. In a petition dated 22 November 1789, they pointed out that during the Old Regime "the apportionment [of taxes] was vicious," and even the nonprivileged wealthy landholders, "who had professions in different parishes, escaped the tax for the most part, because the tax assessors could not know what possessions they had in their households."[62] They had hoped that the Revolution would initiate a new fiscal policy in which individuals would pay a share of the tax burden on all property owned. By abolishing the fiscal privileges of bourgeois landowners, the tax burden of ordinary rural inhabitants would be lessened and revolutionary principles realized. Like Anginer, the signatories from Moliens pointed out that whereas the intention of the revolutionaries had been to collect revenue from people who had once been exempt from direct taxes, the way in which the ex-privileged were going to be taxed under the new system perpetuated gross inequities. The root of the problem, they maintained, lay with Articles 17 and 18, which demanded that "the assessment of the ex-privileged be made for the exploitation tax according to the location of their property and for the propriété tax according to the location of the owner's residence."[63]

The citizens of Moliens-le-Vidame claimed (and their articulate plea merits quoting at some length) that the new tax law would lead to the following negative results:

1. [Preparing] the tax rolls of each parish is going to double (or more) the amount of . . . work, because the rural inhabitants also farm in neighboring lands. Each person will be assessed a property tax in his parish . . . which was not done before and which is going to increase the work and confusion.
2. The individuals of each place will be placed on the tax roll of their residence, reducing the propriété tax on the property that they cultivate in neighboring lands and leaving to the assessors of the neighboring villages the task of assessing the rate of exploitation if they can. How can the assessors of the neighboring villages know about [these properties]? Thus these properties are going to escape half of the tax.
3. The landowners who have professions in far-away places and who cannot be surveyed by the assessors of their parishes will escape at least one-half [of their direct taxes].

These villagers strongly resented the financial privileges of bourgeois men and women and the concomitant tax benefits allotted to them as absentee landlords. This nascent class hatred, pitting the peasantry against the rural bourgeoisie, is made explicit by the inhabitants of Moliens in the following point:

4. The bourgeois of the large cities (like Amiens) who have not been taxable until the present [combined with others who have been tax exempt like] the clergy and charitable institutions [and who] possess from three-quarters to seven-eighths of the property in the countryside will pay through their farmers the exploitation tax where their properties are situated; but in the case of the propriété tax they will pay on the tax rolls of the [location] of their residences. . . . The religious houses, the Order of Malta, the great seigneurs, the rich landowners, who have great property . . . will pay their propriété tax on the tax roll of the [location] of their residence. . . . Three thousand bourgeois from Amiens, who have never been taxable, possess property in thirty to forty parishes, . . . [and] pay the exploitation tax through their farmers. . . . By this simple device the great apportionment . . . will always be disproportionate and the small properties in the countryside will always bear the tax burden while the bourgeois of the large cities and the large properties will escape from paying the tax.[64]

The only remedy, according to the petitioners, was to assess taxes in each parish by the amount of property owned, and perhaps by the total income generated from that property.

Whereas the inhabitants of Moliens may have struggled more tenaciously than did other communities in the Somme against what they perceived to be unfair taxation, they were by no means alone in the battle. Many other municipalities sent similar petitions complaining about national impositions. At the end of November 1789, for example, the municipal councilors of Acheux, the home of farmer Anginer, reported that most of the villagers in their community strongly resented the fact that such a large percentage of the land was owned by bourgeois landlords, who by virtue of their absenteeism were exempt from contributing to the tax burden of the community.[65] The poor farmers were consequently forced to assume the entire tax burden. The municipal councilors argued that all landowners, regardless of where their principal residence was located, should contribute to the village's tax obligation. Other village councils throughout the valley of the Somme, including the municipalities of Chepy (pop. 780), Hérissart (pop. 850), Tœufles (pop. 565), Tours (pop. 906), and Vaux (pop. 199), sent in similar petitions stating the necessity of assessing taxes on the basis of property rather than of residence.[66]

The Constituent Assembly finally resolved the issue in late November and December 1789. The representatives from Champagne drew up a proposal stipulating that the ex-privileged pay taxes on the basis of property, not residence. When the proposal was first brought before the Assembly, it was sent to the Committee of Finance for study.[67] After stalling, the committee finally discussed and recommended against the proposal on 25 November. Some members argued that it was a parochial matter, of interest only to the inhabitants of Champagne. Others maintained that it was unfair to people who owned property in different communities. In any case, on 28 November the legislators voted against the committee report. The Assembly decreed that the issue was of importance for the entire country and that the principle underlying the September legislation had been violated. Henceforth the ex-privileged were to pay "for the last six months of 1789 and [for the entire year] 1790, not according to the location of their residence, but according to the location of their property."[68] Less than one month later, on 17 December, the Assembly extended the law to cover all property owners. Due in part to pressure from the countryside, by the end of 1789 the principle of fair taxation was no longer simply a dream, but was becoming a reality.

Fiscal Equality in the Countryside

It is somewhat ironic that villagers in the Somme were so committed to the principles of the Revolution when the revolutionary government—in Paris and in Amiens—was so reluctant to help them implement equality in actuality. But as villagers knew, the Revolution had enshrined in law the fundamental principle of equality, thereby adding legitimacy to their claims. The antifeudal laws of August 1789 and the Declaration of the Rights of Man and Citizen had given villagers—as citizens—the legal right to participate in shaping the new fiscal order in revolutionary France, and the example of the Somme shows that villagers took advantage of this right.[69]

Rural inhabitants had long struggled for equality. They understood that feudalism, which had for centuries caused them so much hardship, was contrary to the basic principles of the Revolution, but their efforts to dismantle feudalism were impeded by national and departmental legislators who did not want to set a precedent for violating the principle of private property. Yet villagers persevered in demanding the establishment of real equality in the countryside. Thus in a political context in which villagers used riots and petitions to point out the disparity between the revolutionary commitment to equality and the reality of the legal perpetuation of privilege, national legislators finally abolished feudalism once and for all.

Villagers also understood the necessity of creating a revolutionary tax system based on equality. Indirect taxes, in their view, were inherently unfair, and they worked to end them. These taxes stifled commerce and hit villagers and lower and middling townspeople disproportionately. In the Somme these two groups of people worked together—or perhaps more accurately, rioted together—to show that they would no longer pay excise taxes. Once again they achieved their goal, when the Assembly voted to suppress all indirect taxation.

The debate over direct taxes perhaps tells the most about the way rural inhabitants viewed the state. In their petitions, villagers from the Somme did not oppose paying a fair share of the tax burden. They were clearly not antistate in the same way as prerevolutionary rural revolts are purported to have been. Whereas seigneurial privileges and indirect taxes were obviously inegalitarian, direct taxes were in principle reasonable, and rural inhabitants appeared willing to help finance the revolutionary government. But they wanted the taxes apportioned in a fair manner; they did not want to subsidize wealthy landowners any longer. In the fight over indirect taxes, rural inhabitants and townspeople worked together. But they did not share the same concerns about direct taxation, so villagers worked alone to change the policy of direct tax assessment. Village communities in the Somme sent numerous petitions to the Constituent Assembly, not only complaining about the inequities of the system of direct taxation, but also giving advice about how to make it more equitable. And in the end the government once again made the law consistent with the principle of equality.

The case of the Somme suggests new lines of analysis for rural political movements in the Old Regime and in the nineteenth and twentieth centuries. During the Revolution, Picard villagers drew on both traditional and new forms of political activism to think about their role in the revolutionary state. What were the early modern antecedents of progressive rural political activism? Historians have pointed out the antistate and anticentralization components of the prerevolutionary rural revolt, but do they alone characterize rural politics? Similarly, rural politics in the modern period cannot be characterized simply as apolitical, conservative, or antistate. Rather the progressive trends within rural politics—for example, the interwar rural communist movement or mid-twentieth-century rural collectivist movements—have a genealogy dating back at least to the Revolution.[70]

Revolutionary Audiences and the Impossible Imperatives of Fraternity

JAMES H. JOHNSON

In early 1794 a resident of Bordeaux was guillotined for having shouted out, "Long live our noble King!" some months before. The charge of royalism was nothing new for the time, but the circumstances certainly were. Arouch was an actor, and he had called out the words, just as the script instructed, during a performance of Pedro Calderón's *Life Is a Dream* at the Grand Théâtre. Angry spectators had denounced the company for the lines, the Military Commission of Bordeaux had arrested all eighty-six members of its cast, and after a month of imprisonment and hearings, it was determined who had spoken the phrase. All were eventually released except Arouch, who reportedly went to the scaffold desperately repeating, "But it was in my part!"[1]

Arouch was the only actor of the Revolution to pay the ultimate punishment for the crimes of his character, but he was neither the first nor the last to be denounced by spectators demanding political purity on the stage. An officer on leave from Lyon was shocked to see actors depicting British aristocrats at the Comédie-Française in a 1793 production of *Pamela* and rushed from the hall to the Jacobin Club in midperformance to denounce the cast as counterrevolutionaries. The aristocratic manners, black cockades, and lofty titles were offensive in their own right, he explained to the Jacobins present, but an actor's plea for political pluralism—"The persecutors are the guiltiest," his lines ran, "and the tolerant most forgivable"—was unacceptable. (Several spectators had protested to the officer without effect that the lines in the fiction of the play referred to *religious* and not political toleration.) By the next day the theater had been shut down, and all its cast but three were in prison as accused traitors, where the majority remained until the fall of Robespierre ten months later.[2]

Perhaps the most bizarre arrest of a performer during the Revolution involved an actor denounced for having brilliantly played the role of a moderate—opposed to the war, indifferent to the Revolution, in short, a counterrevolutionary—in a heavy-handed farce called *Le Modéré* at the Théâtre de la République. The actor Dugazon was hauled from the stage to the local revolutionary committee, where he was interrogated and asked to make an "expiation" by admitting his mistake and declaring himself fully committed to the Revolution. The twist here was that the play, which the Parisian press universally described as patriotic above reproach, was written by Dugazon himself.[3]

Coddled by kings and steeped in luxury in the Old Regime, performers entered the revolutionary era under a cloud of suspicion. The skepticism was not easily dispelled, moreover, because many performers and their aristocratic patrons maintained their earlier associations. In the early years of the Revolution, aristocrats still gathered in theaters—most notably the Paris Opera—to show their political colors by shouting, singing, and occasionally fighting.[4] But the popular tendency to view performers as hidden royalists was more than simple guilt by association. Many actors and actresses openly showed their sympathies for royalty. A singer at the Comédie-Italienne braved a storm of insults from the pit in 1792 when she turned toward Marie-Antoinette to sing the otherwise innocent lines, "I love my master tenderly; oh, how I love my mistress!" and an actor at the Opéra-Comique provoked pandemonium in 1791 when he substituted 'Louis' for 'Richard' in a passage from Grétry's *Richard, Cœur de Lion* that lamented the fate of the kidnapped Richard the Lionhearted.[5]

The accusers of Arouch, Dugazon, and the Comédie-Française were quick to cite this connection between the stage and the nobility. Robespierre, who happened to be present at the Jacobin Club the night Jullien de Carentin stormed in to denounce *Pamela*, improvised a speech condemning the Comédie as "a disgusting den of every sort of aristocrat" and demanding that it be closed.[6] The radical *Feuille du salut public* gleefully reported the demise of the theater, "an impure seraglio," it wrote, where "Prussian and Austrian croaking has always dominated."[7] Likewise, the military commission that conducted the arrest and trial of the Bordeaux troupe announced in its report to the Interior Ministry that it had destroyed "a foyer of the aristocracy" and claimed that performers there had maintained "close relations with counterrevolutionaries and correspondence with émigrés."[8]

But if the long, nefarious association between the theater and elites seemed to justify an overall mistrust of performers, it cannot fully explain certain fascinating ambiguities surrounding the denunciations of Arouch, Dugazon, and the performers in *Pamela*. Why would spectators doubt the patriotism of Dugazon when his play so clearly showed the dangers of political indifference? Why could Arouch not convince his accusers that his lines referred to an unreal king in a fictitious kingdom? And why did Carentin and his fellow Jacobins see seditious political content in lines counseling religious understanding between a Catholic and a Protestant in a story about England?

The answers to such questions extend well beyond the traditional ties between actors and aristocrats and involve issues of dramatic form and the artistic perceptions of audiences. These denunciations reveal the fusion of categories, a collapse of dramatic fiction into political reality. As a result of their own understanding of the Revolution and its principles, coupled with a particular dramatic experience that new political works for the stage seemed to produce, spectators during the Terror refused to suspend their disbelief for the sake of drama. Traditionally, spectators had accepted stage illusion— and with it a healthy share of crimes and turpitudes—as *the* necessary condition for drama. As for performers charged with portraying evil, audiences tacitly recognized the paradox most fully explored by Diderot that the best actors necessarily remained detached from the passions and convictions they conveyed on the stage.[9] One of Talma's greatest personal triumphs, in fact, was his portrayal of the malicious and inept king in Chénier's *Charles IX* in 1789.

For audiences during the Revolution, however, this dramatic distance that distinguished the part from the player gradually disappeared. By the autumn of 1793 a triumphant Jacobin ideology had found its aesthetic embodiment in a fundamentally new set of dramatic standards that purified plots and performers so that not only princes and secret conspirators were eliminated from the stage but so, too, were the actors who portrayed them. In the service of revolutionary fraternity, which united performer and spectator in the higher unity of citizenship, stage fiction gradually disappeared and "drama" became the public re-creation of everyday scenes.

Yet if the repertoires reflected a thoroughgoing revolution in theater, the ideal of transparency that determined its course—transparency between stage and street, transparency among spectators, and transparency between performer and his part—remained elusive. Indeed the distrust among audiences that led to the denunciations of Arouch, Dugazon, and the Comédie-Française intensified even as spectators reported a closer bond with the performers and with one another; a truly unanimous dramatic experience seemed perpetually attainable but never quite attained. In truth this revolutionary vision of experience, which vigilantly identified and exposed all obstacles to genuine fraternity, would never be satisfied: in the end, its imagined ideal of transparency was impossible.

From Accustomed Plots to a School for Virtue

Although the popular sentiments that led to the fusion of stage and street developed gradually, it was only with the onset of the Terror that these long-simmering suspicions produced actual denunciations. The arrest of the Comédie-Française cast occurred in early September 1793, just two days before terror was officially imposed as the order of the day. Dugazon was denounced in October, and the Bordeaux arrests came in late November. Autumn 1793 was clearly a turning point, as dramatic experience subtly shifted from passive reception to engaged participation and as vague misgivings about performers were focused into sharp scrutiny. Audiences had previously lacked the sort of unified revolutionary enthusiasm that would produce arrests, as one nervous teenager discovered in the summer of 1793 at the Opéra-Comique when he jumped onto the stage after the final curtain to sing a patriotic song and was quickly silenced by laughter and derision.[10]

Before 1793, audiences were largely resistant to the *scènes patriotiques* and dramatic reenactments of events of the Revolution that would later encourage such close identification between spectator and performer. Although the steady but comparatively small supply of works with revolutionary references certainly elicited loud responses from spectators, critics of the period were very clear in asserting that from a dramatic point of view, audiences still believed that efforts to weave actual events into fictitious plots compromised the action.[11] Press descriptions of the period drew a careful distinction between the dramatic content of the pieces and their relationship to current events. *La Chêne patriotique*, an opéra-comique by

Jacques-Marie Boutet, *dit* Monvel, and Nicolas Dalyrac produced at the Comédie-Italienne four days before the Festival of Federation in 1790, sought to present "a faithful portrait of what will occur all over France on 14 July."[12] Two young lovers, the son of a former seigneur "without prejudices" and the daughter of an honest villager, carve their initials into a tree that is to be replanted in the village festival on the fourteenth. The initials are discovered as the festival begins. The fathers embrace, soldiers fire cannons to announce the fête, the civic oath is repeated by all, and the play ends with happy songs about fraternity among the orders.[13]

According to the *Chronique de Paris*, the success of *La Chêne patriotique* did not lie in its contemporary references but rather in its "light and lively pace" and "happy episodes."[14] The *Journal de Paris* was yet more circumspect in appraising the work's merit: "We won't say anything about what makes up the action here; these sorts of plays should be regarded less as literary works than as patriotic tributes."[15] The critic nevertheless went on to evaluate the work by customary standards, omitting all mention of its patriotic content. "We will be content to say that the work had wit, some cute couplets that the audience demanded to hear again, and the kind of music that M. Dalyrac so often furnishes for the stage."[16]

The public reportedly showed similar skepticism about the dramatic elements of *La Journée de Marathon*. This five-act play ostensibly portrayed the heroic defense of Athens against the invading Persians, who hoped to reinstate a descendant of the tyrant-king Pisistratus in the city. Its many contemporary allusions made it an elaborate allegory of the wars of the Republic. Premiered in August 1793, it was quickly recognized as the most important effort thus far to incorporate the events of the Revolution into a dramatic work. The *Journal de Paris* listed the main events of its action: "A tyranny overturned; the exiled family of the tyrant now leading armies against Athens; supporters of the ancient despotism scattered throughout the towns of Greece, ready to betray their homeland; its partisans in Athens itself, trying to divide the people for their own gain."[17] But despite the transparent references to contemporary events—or, more likely, because of them—*La Journée de Marathon* was a virtual failure. "*La Journée de Marathon* was received rather coldly," reported the *Moniteur universel*; "two days ago it was welcomed with a sort of coolness," the *Journal des spectacles* read.[18]

The press attributed the play's lukewarm public reception to its dramatic weaknesses, specifically its imposition of modern scenes onto an ancient subject. "The parallel between this moment in history and our present war is without doubt of great interest, but there is little action and consequently little dramatic interest. The subject itself does not suffice."[19] Too close a correspondence between reality and action on the stage, in other words, risked sapping the drama of its own dynamic. The analogies between the plot of *La Journée de Marathon* and France's current state were "superb," commented the *Journal des spectacles*, "but this is not enough for a play. There must be interest and action, without which the scene dies, however much heroism there is."[20]

The plays and operas with political references that enjoyed the greatest popularity in these years of the Revolution therefore worked their contemporary allusions into traditional plots dependent upon uncertainty, suspense, love, and psychological conflict—in short, the basic elements of stage fiction. *Les Rigueurs du cloître*, which appeared at the Théâtre-Italien in 1790, demonstrates how clever playwrights could be in using political events to supplement and even resolve the contretemps of the plot while still keeping them secondary. This play is the story of two lovers who are separated when the girl is forced into a convent against her will. The girl's hidden cache of love-letters is discovered by her tyrannical abbess, who decrees that her charge will spend the rest of her days on rations of bread and water in the darkest cell of the compound. But hardly is the sentence pronounced when the young man bursts on the scene in his new National Guard uniform to announce the dissolution of monasteries and convents and freedom for all inmates![21] Such passing references to the Revolution were undoubtedly amusing, but according to the reigning conception of drama, these events shared the stage awkwardly with a dramatic fiction that had its own internal coherence. This dominant view of drama is undoubtedly a principal reason why the overwhelming majority of plays and operas performed before 1793 were still drawn from Old Regime repertoires. Theaters followed the basic rule of presenting what their audiences liked; it was simply not profitable to stage works with aggressively political content.[22] Like their Old Regime political counterparts, most spectators before 1793 still wanted diversion.

Yet even as audiences sought an evening's entertainment watching an opera of Gluck or a play of Molière, revolutionary leaders were questioning the value of theater as mere diversion. What began as isolated calls for the reshaping of theater into an institution of national education gradually grew into an explicit revolutionary goal. One of the earliest such appeals came in an anonymous pamphlet circulated at the Comédie-Française that spoke of the stage as "a school of morals and liberty." Arguing for the abolition of censorship in theaters in 1791, Le Chapelier asserted that spectacles must "purify morals, give lessons in citizenship . . . and be schools of patriotism and virtue."[23] In late summer 1793, the Jacobin government made it an official priority to transform the theater so that instead of offering mere entertainment, it would teach civic virtue. By a decree of 4 August 1793, particular theaters were instructed to perform *Brutus, William Tell, Caïus Gracchus*, and other works "that retrace the glorious events of liberty." Such plays were to be presented at least three times weekly, with one of the performances given to the public free of charge at the government's expense. As Georges Couthon reasoned in presenting the decree, "[theaters have] served tyranny too long; they must also serve liberty."[24]

Under official pressure, but also as a result of the changing climate of public opinion that the decree itself reflected, larger numbers of dramatic works with explicit political content began to appear. Unlike the earlier dramatic works that contained only passing references to the Revolution, these new works had particular lessons to impart; their entertainment value, though still present, clearly took second place. In *L'Heureuse décade*, a virtuous family devotes each of the ten days of the revolutionary week to a particular civic act such as donating fabric for soldiers' uniforms or selling crops at a loss to help fight the steep inflation.[25] *Le Vous et le toi* was a popular vaudeville that showed citizens of all ages effortlessly tutoi-ing one another in their songs and conversation. "We invite all citizens who are still reluctant to pronounce *toi*—which should be the common tie of universal fraternity—to go to the Théâtre de la Cité and applaud *Le Vous et le toi*," recommended the *Moniteur*. "As did all those who were present at the premiere, without a doubt, they will leave tutoi-ing their neighbors."[26] *La Plaque retournée*, a rather darker lesson in revolutionary goodness, was well suited to the climate of suspicion that prevailed in the winter of 1793–1794. In the play, a virtuous mason discovers a stash of hidden money while repairing a fireplace and immediately denounces the owner of the house as an aristocrat. "I'm not in the home of a patriot," he reasons. "You don't hide money when you believe in the Republic."[27]

In addition to these loose fictions that offered models for the daily lives of citizens, reenactments of great patriotic events also began appearing regularly in 1793 and 1794. *La Réunion du 10 août, La Prise de la Bastille, L'Offrande à la Liberté, La Fête de la Raison*, and *La Fête de l'Etre Suprême* were among the many works that reproduced actual events of the Revolution. *La Réunion du 10 août*, an opera in five acts and one of the longest-running patriotic pieces, consisted of "stations" of the Revolution: a scene at the Bastille, a scene at the Place de la Révolution, a scene at the Champs de Mars, and so on. Each act was a static tableau in which actors dressed as citizens sang patriotic songs and made speeches or recited poetry appropriate to the setting.[28] Performers crowded the stage for these reenactments. One spectator at the Opéra describes three hundred men, women, and children waving bonnets and banners in an elaborate send-off to troops in *L'Offrande à la Liberté*.[29] In *La Prise de Toulon*, which appeared in five different versions in the winter of 1794, and in *Le Siège de Thionville*, performers hauled guns and cannons onto the stage to fight mock battles that were punctuated with rousing speeches and enthusiastic singing. (After the Terror at least one theater director would complain about the enormous damage to his sets caused by the smoke.) Rather less destructive were the reenactments of festivals: the Opéra re-created the great Festival of Reason at Nôtre Dame for its own *Fête de la Raison* in December 1793, the Cité Variétés gave a version of the Festival of the Supreme Being, and the Festival of Equality appeared in two different re-creations for the stage.[30] Under the rubric of commemoration, these reenactments fundamentally altered the rules of dramatic representation by offering scenes that corresponded more or less faithfully to actual events. As with the explicit didacticism of the scènes patriotiques, commemoration necessarily reduced the fiction in drama and consequently narrowed the dramatic distance between audience and actor.

As the nature of drama changed, so too did the attitudes of spectators toward the earlier repertoires. By the spring and summer of 1793, audiences were showing unprecedented enthusiasm for dramatic works with contemporary allusions. Part of this evolving public taste was no doubt a reflection of the changing composition of audiences themselves, as crowds sympathetic to republican principles now filled the seats formerly occupied by royalists. If the range of opinion had narrowed to bring a greater enthusiasm for political content in drama, however, there was still sufficient division among audiences to provoke disorder; indeed, if anything, the battles inside theaters were growing more violent. A particularly brutal riot erupted in February 1792 when the Théâtre de la Vaudeville mounted a short comedy that mocked Chénier's *Caïus Gracchus*.[31] The press carefully avoided calling for imposed censorship since liberty of dramatic expression, granted in 1791 after decades of royal censorship, was held virtually sacrosanct. But it nevertheless urged theaters to exercise voluntary control over their productions. The *Chronique* justified such self-censorship as a decision "not to fight public opinion."[32]

This popular preference for the politically unifying over the politically divisive mirrors the phenomenon of gradual political radicalization that was now underway in virtually all sectors of public life: it was the policies and parties, the dress and speech of the past that bred dissension, the logic ran; achieving genuine revolutionary fraternity was merely a question of cleansing the present of all divisive remnants of the past. Once accomplished, the smooth reign of unanimity would begin. In the perpetual revolution, however, the past could as easily refer to the previous year as to the previous monarch, and one season's drama of popular virtue became the next season's threat to public order.

As the clashes continued, the public showed less and less tolerance for the former classics, which they increasingly blamed for prompting reactionary outbursts. Employing the rhetoric that would later condemn actors like Dugazon and Arouch, the public now began to link particular works to seditious designs against the Revolution. In May 1792 the *Chronique* wrote that Grétry's *Richard, Cœur de Lion*, Gluck's *Iphigénie en Aulide*, and Piccini's *Didon*—all standards of the Old Regime operatic literature—brought "delirious applause of aristocrats," whose enthusiasm showed "signs of revolt and the desire to see France devastated by foreign armies."[33] Still insisting that these classics ought not to be "distorted" by censorship, the paper nevertheless recommended the production of patriotic operas and the discreet omission of works from the Old Regime that were apt to trouble true republicans. The ideal operas, it imagined, would promote the views of "neither Feuillants, *ministériels*, moderates, *impartiaux*, independents, nor Jacobins." "But," it urged, "they must be patriotic, they must represent nothing contrary to the laws that govern France."[34]

Those who argued with such confidence in 1791 that the abolition of censorship would free the theater to become a school for civic virtue probably never imagined the two ideals working at cross-purposes, but by the summer of 1793 the opinion of many both in and out of government was that dramatic liberty had degenerated into a vicious license whose excesses blocked genuine instruction. The Jacobin deputy Jérôme Pétion, hoping to finesse the issue, proposed that magistrates issue "invitations" expressing the "imprudence" of mounting certain works, an expedient that the Committee of Public Instruction used for a time in attempting to keep works "tending to corrupt the public spirit" out of production.[35] Others called for stronger action. Alexandre Sévère, who frequented the Comédie-Française, wrote to the *Feuille du salut public* to express his disgust that the theater still showed counts and princes on the stage, "with all the haughty insignificance of their blood and manners."[36] According to Sévère, the comedy *L'Amant bourru* contained an especially offensive scene in which an aristocrat slaps his valet, an affront "calmly observed by the spectators and suffered with resignation by the actor." Unthinkable in the Republic, the insult was inexcusable on the stage. Sévère was sure the actor—not his dramatic persona but his personal, republican self—suffered deep humiliation in the scene. "He was only playing his role, I know as well as you; but God! is this the time to show us such habits? Can the French people really think . . . we were made to be slapped by nobles?"[37]

Sévère's letter opened a new line of attack against traditional repertoires, with their self-enclosed fictions and humiliating demands on republican actors. Unlike earlier calls for changes in programs that were based upon threats to public order, Sévère's rested upon threats to the public spirit. Moreover, the particular way Sévère described this threat—identifying with the actor, asserting "we" were not made to be slapped by nobles—illustrates the mentality that welcomed republican plots and revolutionary reenactments while denouncing the fictions of the past. A month later Sacchini's *Œdipe à Colonne* at the Opéra provoked a noisy outburst from one livid spectator, who made roughly the same point. Leaping from his seat during the singing, he shouted that it was "shameful for republicans to continue tolerating works with kings, princes, and the like" and that it was "time to forget these old mistakes of our fathers."[38]

Under this combined popular and official pressure, *Roland*, *Iphigénie en Aulide*, and *Œdipe à Colonne* were withdrawn from the repertoire of the Opéra as irrelevant to most republicans and positively dangerous for the weaker in spirit among them.[39] Jacobin censors, who as a part of the decree of 4 August 1793 previewed all dramatic works before they could be staged, made changes in scenes and settings where minor revisions might salvage a script; otherwise, they forbade its production. (They had, incidentally, cleared the version of François de Neufchâteau's *Pamela* that precipitated the arrests.) In *Le Déserteur*, "le Roi passait" became "la Loi passait"; in *Tartuffe*, "nous vivons sous un prince ennemi de la fraude" became "ils sont passés les jours consacrés à la fraude"; in *Le Cid*, the king became a general of revolutionary armies in Spain; and the action of *Alceste* was moved from the kingdom of Thessaly to a republic commanded by military officers.[40] In dramatic terms these changes in the older works had the same effect as the staging of republican scenes and reenactments: by putting citizens in the primary roles and setting the action in the present they effectively reduced the distance between fantasy and truth.

As the stage became a mirror of the present even in its retouched production from the past, spectators gradually came to judge plays by the standards of revolutionary gospel. "Good art" was that which was true; "bad art" that which transgressed. "Such a living tableau clings to none of the dramatic rules," wrote the *Abréviateur universel* in 1794 about *Toute la Grèce*, a historical piece filled with republican sentiments, "and this only proves that one can produce grand effects on the stage by explicitly renouncing all theatrical illusion."[41] When *La Journée de Marathon* reappeared in November and December after having earlier foundered for its belabored analogies to the present, the reception was nothing short of ecstatic: the public cheered when the Athenians vowed to kill the usurper-king and reacted with "inexpressible transport" to the play's "analogies to [our own] liberty."[42] The enthusiastic and apparently unified displays of audiences that erupted during the Terror at the slightest reference to revolutionary principles stood in sharp contrast to the earlier, tepid reception of plots based upon political events. "Is there anyone in France or in Europe," a police spy wrote to his superior after seeing *Le Siège de Thionville*, "who still doubts how dear the Republic is to the French? They should hear the singing of the couplet that follows the news . . . that there is no longer a king in France. . . . At these words the hall, pierced by bravos, fell into a single burst of applause that was so loud that one would have thought the roof would rise to the heavens!"[43] Spectators of *La Discipline républicaine* "proved by their applause that they shared the generous sentiments of citizens who were dying for their country."[44]

With stage action justified inasmuch as its events and characters were recognizable, the definition of dramatic truth shifted from embracing the plausible in some abstract sense to the actual in the most concrete terms. According to this logic, fiction was tantamount to falsehood, so that ultimately even dramas without the objectionable cast of aristocrats were considered unacceptable if they were not "true." Such was the flaw of Dalyrac's opéra-comique *Merlin et Ugande*, according to the *Feuille du salut public*. Set in the time of Amadis de Gaul, the newspaper reported, this "fairy tale" sought to please by illusion and fantasy instead of by drawing analogies to the glorious present. "Why should we stay in the realm of dreams and trinkets," the journal asked, "when reality surrounds us? Why look outside ourselves for pleasure when the republican finds it within himself and in everything around him?"[45] This was no doubt why *Révolutions de Paris* had nothing but praise for a new opera that was "without dances, without ballets, without love, without fairy scenes."[46] Not that plays and operas no longer entertained, however: one spectator eagerly looked forward to seeing tragedies from the Old Regime *for their comic value.* "Once simplicity and republican decency have replaced the luxury and absurdity of the Old Regime, our children will laugh at the stupidities of their forefathers."[47]

The disappearance of fiction from the stage in 1793–1794 took on a momentum of its own as audiences conditioned by republican analogies and reenactments began to see references to the present even in dramatic works with no intended relevance. Several spectators denounced *Adèle de Sacy* at the Lycée des Arts, for instance, and its director found himself at the Jacobin Club trying to explain that the pantomime, which told the simple story of a kidnapped woman who was saved by her husband and his brother, was *not* a hidden analogy to Marie-Antoinette.[48] This was the same literal-mindedness that had led Jullien de Carentin to denounce the cast of *Pamela* for advocating political toleration when the context of the drama so clearly specified that the issue was religious. There are few more eloquent examples of the fusion of state and society achieved by Jacobinism during the Terror. By autumn 1793, the onrush of politics into every sphere had politicized all things to such a degree that nothing, not even stage fiction, was innocent of political meaning.[49]

Transparency and the Problem of Representation

The pressures and suspicions that produced the gradual disappearance of fiction from the stage may make the denunciations of performers playing aristocrats more understandable in a general way, but they fall short of fully explaining the loss of dramatic distance among audiences. Alexandre Sévère found it highly offensive, after all, that a noble should slap his servant on the stage even while he recognized that the actor "was only playing his part." The detractor of *Merlin et Ugande* likewise understood that the work, however inappropriate, was in the realm of "dreams and trinkets." To fault fiction for giving a bad civic example, in other words, was not the same as losing the ability to recognize it as fiction.

The blurring of distinctions between stage and street by the autumn of 1793 can be understood in part as an effect of the Terror and its premises. The purge of the Convention's Girondins by revolutionary crowds the previous May was intended to ensure that the locus of power would rest in local committees—the nation assembled—and not in its representatives. The triumph of this Rousseauist conception of sovereignty over the rival vision of Feuillants and Monarchists promised inalienable and indivisible power to the nation and excluded particular interests to the point of rendering private experience not so much inadmissible as obsolete. The general will in the Jacobins' view was not only unified, it was unanimous; and with all division gone, privacy was superfluous.[50]

The slow evolution of drama and its audiences since 1789 created a space for the national will that was eminently suited to the Jacobin rhetoric that labeled private experience divisive and suspect. By replacing dramatic ambiguity with clear lessons and morals, the new productions reduced the risk that spectators would find their own private meanings in the works. With the Revolution the subject, audiences became participants rather than passive observers; reports describing spectators singing with the singers or dancing the Carmagnole in the pit when it was danced onstage are eloquent testimony of this participation.[51]

In addition, the very nature of the new stage works promoted a correlation between the actor and the role. In reducing the distance between art and life, these works did not so much *represent*—understood in both senses as performance before passive observers and as "actors" expressing the will of the people by proxy—as encourage a radically democratic participation in the drama. By dressing in ordinary street clothes and singing the songs of the people, performers became citizens. As the closing lines of *L'Heureuse décade* amiably stated in a direct address to the audience: "We wanted to offer with these couplets, some pleasant scenes for all good patriots. If you have enjoyed yourself, applaud the author and the actors; they are all sansculottes."[52] But citizens, too, became performers as they watched the inspiring spectacles. A police spy wrote that during patriotic scenes the audience "is yet more citizen than spectator. . . . Everyone was an actor as the masculine voices of the hall supported those on the stage."[53] This fluidity between actor and audience made citizens realize that the drama—that is, the Revolution itself—was still unfinished when the final curtain had fallen. This was how theater without "dramatic" action so effectively inspired its revolutionary audiences. "We whipped the English buggers at Toulon," a young man was heard saying after he saw *Le Siège de Toulon*, "but we'll whip 'em even better next spring when we go to London."[54]

At its highest moments the dramatic experience of the Terror truly seemed to achieve the transparency that Rousseau had dreamed of for the theater but ultimately believed impossible. The fault line of fiction that divided spectator from actor and made performance always inauthentic, the weakened human bond as spectators forgot one another in the darkened hall but found pity for unreal characters, the lack of moral instruction that could lead to sympathy for villains and a distaste for the upright: each of these obstacles to true communion of sentiment in the theater outlined by Rousseau seemed to be overcome in the dramatic experience of the Terror.[55] The sentimental openness this transparency involved took on Rousseauist political associations as well, for it implied the sacrifice of particular wills for the sake of the indivisible whole. What better place for viewing the nation assembled than the theater? How better could the sovereign people express its general will than in collective enthusiasm? In this grand illusion to end all illusion, the spectators became the spectacle, and the division between audience and actor was transcended in their common identity in the nation.[56]

The evident success of achieving a transparency between spectator and spectacle, between audience and actor, saddled performers with the precarious burden of actually being their roles. The category "character" disappeared in the minds of spectators who witnessed their own struggles and achievements before them. In a spectacle of common celebration, the task of the citizens/actors was nothing other than to declare their own patriotic sentiments before others in public. It followed that insufficient zeal was the fault of the citizen/actor. This reasoning led one critic to charge that an actor in *Le Quaker en France* was not forceful enough in his defense of war against pacifist arguments: "When one actor mentions peace, if another actor with him on the stage does not reply: 'No peace as long as our enemies are sullying our soil; no peace as long as there are still tyrants who haven't given homage to the Republic; no peace until the Republic is avenged,' then the actor is wrong and can be accused of being a moderate."[57] Patriots offstage, these actors were patriots onstage. Did it not follow that aristocrats, British agents, or moderates onstage were aristocrats, British agents, or moderates offstage? This was the logic that doomed Arouch, Dugazon, and the Comédie-Française.

Performers were particularly vulnerable during the Terror for a second reason, one that is closely tied to the Jacobin ideal of transparency that transformed performers into spectators and spectators into performers: because they had spent their lives perfecting the art of deception, how could one be sure that actors sincerely felt the solidarity they seemed to share with the audience?[58] As François Furet has so perceptively discussed, one engine of Jacobin ideology was the drive to unmask, to denounce, to expose hidden conspirators who disguised themselves as friends of the Revolution the better to subvert it.[59] Secret plots were, as Furet writes, the "anti-principle" of the Revolution, and, like an episode of Rousseau's paranoia writ large, they seemed to loom ever larger as citizens opened their souls to the gaze of others.

As the Jacobin drive to unmask set the popular suspicion of deception on a hair trigger, the very talent that defined actors—the "absolute lack of sensitivity" that Diderot had so admired—was suddenly politically threatening. "Only actors enjoy the surprising privilege of being perfect monarchists in the very bosom of the Republic," one spectator warned of the insidious gift for deception performers possessed.[60] Similarly, just after the arrest of the Comédie-Française troupe, the *Feuille du salut public* charged that the theater was "a gathering-place for criminals *disguised as decent folk.*"[61] Of course an unmasking might prove to have been unnecessary, but it would permit the actor to play his part henceforth without suspicion: after declaring his unswerving support for the Revolution the night of his arrest, Dugazon went on to portray M. Modératin for many weeks to follow.[62]

Dramatic experience during the Terror was hence a curious coexistence of the all-embracing and the exclusionary. Its own impulse to unmask was a condition of its fragile transparency. Just as revolutionary leaders, impelled by the threat of invasion by foreign armies and the paralyzing fear of internal enemies, increasingly relied upon purges and proscriptions to enforce national unity, so too did spectators adhere to a mentality of coercion in the service of unified dramatic experience. A letter published in the *Journal des spectacles* demanded that theater directors be forced to stage revolutionary works: "I say *forced*, because republicanism is often a motive of exclusion."[63] This view of republicanism, combined with the belief that plotters threatened to disrupt common exhilaration by impugning the principles of the Republic, created the mentality that led spectators to denounce "counter-revolutionaries" so zealously. Just as the Revolutionary Tribunal had only two possible verdicts to render to accused traitors, the guillotine or freedom, so were views of drama and opera animated by a ruthless dichotomy. In its glowing review of *L'Heureuse Décade*, the *Feuille du salut public* wrote that "in a time of revolution, everything that is not *strongly for* is *against*; all it takes is some good sense to see the truth of this maxim."[64]

Although the conversion of audiences in the autumn of 1793 to new dramatic perspectives resulted in part from the cumulative development of Jacobin ideas, it must also be viewed as one of the cultural effects of the Terror, which began officially on 5 September. Just as the exclusionary mentality embodied by the Terror surfaced well before the Jacobin dictatorship, so also had sectors of the press and scattered spectators called for the purging of repertoires long before entire audiences cheered allusions to contemporary events. Until the apparatus of the Terror could actually eliminate the opponents of Jacobin principles, however, strong enthusiasm was but one of the possible responses of spectators.

To suggest that fear of the guillotine was an element of the dramatic experience of the Terror—and by now, it should be remembered, the device was so prominent a presence that it earned such darkly endearing nicknames as the "little window" and the "national razor"—in no way diminishes the sincerity of spectators' dramatic vision of transparency. If genuine revolutionary enthusiasm involved a willingness to denounce, the act of denunciation itself implied that no one, not even the accuser, was fully safe from scrutiny. As the director of the Lycée des Arts put it, pleading the innocence of the pantomime *Adèle de Sacy*: "The good republican does not dread denunciations, for they are the touchstone of citizenship; but every denunciation must be examined, tested to its depths; this is the duty of surveillance, and it is only then that public esteem brings justice to the accuser."[65]

For audiences and artists who had gradually come to the ideal of transparency through their discussions of censorship and their experiments in education through theater, the threat of the guillotine was simply the culmination of a natural chain of reasoning that led from suspicion to unmasking to purification. Viewed from the parterre, with spectators all around singing the "Marseillaise" and the "Carmagnole," the guillotine seemed less a tool of coercion than a reminder of agreement. It guaranteed that this glorious, contagious display would keep within itself a salutary dose of distrust, the needed glint of fear. It was undoubtedly with just that fear, an overcompensating, vaguely accusing, and above all aggressively patriotic fear, that the director of the Lycée announced at the Jacobin Club that good republicans had nothing to fear.

Fueled by the spirit of purification that denounced all things not strongly for the Revolution as against it, the dramatic vision of the Terror was never stable, never satisfied with the state of public spirit, never convinced that there was a perfect transparency of interests among the citizens on the stage and in the audience. The moments of true unity seemed too brief, the state of permanent fusion between actor and audience remained just beyond reach. In early 1794, the very time when the number of "aristocrats" executed was highest, a police spy at the Opéra reported that although the audience listened with its "typical" enthusiasm, he feared the theater was still "an aristocratic foyer, . . . a rendezvous of men who want to speak freely."[66] Rumors still circulated in the spring that nobles were hiding in the backstage areas of theaters, and in July the Commission of Public Instruction issued an alarming report that found theaters "still encumbered with the debris of the former regime . . . with interests that no longer concern us and with manners that are not ours."[67]

This late in the Terror, however, the problem sensed in theaters was not one of aristocrats. It was one of representation. For despite the moments of unanimous exultation, when performance seemed to give way to participation, in truth these scenes and reenactments remained representations: the street-clothes, the speeches, the revolutionary songs were all coordinated trappings of a mere illusion of transparency. At times the illusion was strikingly successful, as the arrest of performers made abundantly clear. But as soon as spectators stopped singing or dancing and the action onstage continued, the chasm between actor and audience reopened and the specter of private experience reappeared: ten months into the Terror, the *Moniteur* found cause to worry that "certain frivolous people" in the audience could "escape the national movement by isolating themselves in the audience."[68]

Some believed that more revisions and refinements in censorship could achieve the elusive goal of complete identity between stage and street: *Horace*, *Calas*, and *Britannicus*, once considered models for civic virtue, were among the many works removed from the stage in March 1794; *William Tell*, singled out the previous August for its lessons in morality, underwent a thorough revision in May 1794 to emerge as *Les Sans-culottes suisses*.[69] Given the receding horizon of transparency, however, these changes were likely to be as unsatisfying as earlier purges and purifications of the repertoire had been.

Joseph Payan, secretary to the Commission of Public Instruction, grasped the maddening truth that any stage representation was ultimately inauthentic, even if its subject were unimpeachably revolutionary. No matter how much they resembled the spectators in the hall, performers re-created scenes that had already occurred. They were an elite that represented the experiences of the nation by proxy, a reality that no amount of singing and dancing by spectators could alter. The Rousseauist political analogy rang false as Payan exposed the naïveté in believing that reenactments and lessons in virtue could give birth to an indivisible general will. Writing on behalf of the commission less than a month before the fall of Robespierre, Payan vigorously attacked all stage re-creations of great events: they were gross trivializations, he wrote, "masquerades [that will] become the festivals of preference for 'good society.'"[70] Only actual participation—that is, physical presence as the events unfolded—could solve the problem of representation. The result of this logic would be the elimination of all spectacles, a conclusion that Payan suggested implicitly but left unstated.

Thermidor and the Return of Disbelief

Most of the cliches about Paris after the fall of Robespierre—the sudden hatred for Jacobin "blood-drinkers," the humiliations exacted on former revolutionaries by dandified "muscadins," the silliness and superficiality, the general indifference toward old revolutionary symbols—also apply to audiences after Thermidor. If the theater had been the nation assembled, then its own Thermidorean reaction had all the trappings of the national mood. Women draped in diamonds and Grecian tunics and wearing outlandish wigs reappeared at the Feydeau not to listen but to "make themselves noticed."[71] Youths whose rowdiness belied their elegance interrupted performances by shattering the busts of Marat that still adorned theater stages or by forcing performers with a revolutionary past to sing the "Réveil du peuple." And in an irony possible only in the topsy-turvy universe of post-Thermidor, one of the first performers to be denounced as a former Jacobin by the *jeunesse dorée* and forced to make a public apology was none other than Dugazon.[72]

More revealing for charting the dramatic expectations of audiences, however, was their enthusiastic welcome of old repertoires. Two months after Thermidor, Gluck's *Iphigénie en Tauride* ("of which the public has been deprived for such a long time," commented one newspaper) returned with its kings and priestesses and was deliriously applauded.[73] In November 1794 the Opéra-Comique brought back four works dropped during the Terror.[74] And in the following year, the company of the Comédie-Française, reunited after spending nearly a year in various Parisian prisons, mounted a new production of *Pamela* that audiences received warmly.[75] It was perhaps with reason that the *Vedette* ended a survey of Parisian theater audiences in 1795 with the observation that "such is Paris—revolutions change nothing."[76]

As telling as the return of old productions was the nature of new works after Thermidor. Whereas theaters had earlier injected virtually all their productions with republican maxims, they now produced numerous plays and operas that avoided all possible references to the Revolution. *La Perruque blonde* at the Théâtre de la République poked fun at a simple village girl for buying a wig and wearing perfume, the opera *Sapho* was unrelieved tragedy in which everyone loved without being loved, the comedy

Châteaux en Espagne was a "true success . . . that owes nothing to circum-stances," *Le Jockey* at the Opéra-Comique brought together a pair of lovers only after they had deceived a disapproving uncle with a clever disguise, and in *La Famille américaine* a mysterious benefactor from Bordeaux rescued a poor American girl from poverty.[77]

The works with contemporary references that theaters produced after Thermidor were quite different from those presented during the Terror. Either they portrayed Robespierre as a tyrant and represented dramatically the fortunate events of 8–10 Thermidor or they portrayed the successes of the French armies. Works such as *La Chute du dernier tyran*, *La Nuit du 9 au 10 Thermidor*, and *L'Intérieur des comités révolutionnaires* appeared in theaters fairly soon after Robespierre's death and were for the most part short-lived. Markedly more successful, although still few in number, were the *pièces de circonstance* based on the foreign wars. *Les Epreuves du républicain*, whose plot was loosely constructed around several unnamed battles with the British, was applauded with enthusiasm at the Opéra-Comique. At the same hall, *Encore une victoire*, a comic opera by Rodolphe Kreutzer and Dantilly, portrayed the French victories in Brabant and Liège.

Yet despite the persistence of scattered works with contemporary allu-sions, it is clear that the public's standards of evaluation had reverted to the values held before the Terror. Both in newspaper critiques and letters from spectators, the criterion of purely dramatic interest now returned. Despite the massive public repudiation of Robespierre after his execution, for in-stance, the evident similarities between a tyrannicide in Greece in the opera *Timoléon* and the Convention's arrest of Robespierre were received coolly. "The author . . . has sacrificed dramatic perfection for a pressing obligation to depict the violent death of an ambitious man . . . who aspired to supreme authority," explained one account.[78]

Another spectator, proclaiming that he was tired of seeing contemporary references in dramatic works, was yet more blunt. Writing within weeks of the execution of Robespierre about *La Chute du dernier tyran, ou la Journée du 9 Thermidor*, he attacked the practice of turning actual events into "operas, vaudevilles, dramas, and scenic trifles" and saw in such pièces de circonstance a "true decline of art."[79] Perhaps the most eloquent evidence of a return to the dramatic standards held before the Terror was a letter the *Moniteur* published from a spectator who rhapsodically described how a vaudeville version of the Cinderella story moved him. "Return to nature," he pleaded. "I cried, but my tears were not drawn out painfully; they flowed naturally, I shed them with pleasure."[80] Both in their taste, evidenced in what moved them, and in the manner by which they showed their approval, spectators after Thermidor closely resembled the audiences of the Old Regime.

The disappearance of political pièces de circonstance from the stage does not mean that post-Thermidorean spectators had lost interest in politics. Although audiences never again showed the unanimous exaltation seen during the Terror, after Thermidor they nevertheless seized upon lines or songs to show their political convictions, usually in support of the Convention and strongly against Robespierre and the Terror. The production of Voltaire's *Mort de César* at the Feydeau prompted audiences to shout "a thousand times" the words " 'Vive la République! Vive la Convention!" and a line referring to the "cruelty of men" in the *Prisonnier* at the Favart brought a cascade of sympathetic applause.[81] In the skirmishes involving the "Réveil du peuple" and the "Marseillaise" that resumed in the fall of 1794, it was the latter that most often suffered ridicule and scorn from spectators.[82]

Yet this political agitation, a sign of the greater political pluralism now possible, should not be confused with a dramatic perspective that took stage fiction for reality. The lines that provoked the loudest displays were often in works that had no evident relation to current events. Even the most active anti-Jacobin agitators in audiences implicitly recognized the difference between the person and the persona of the actor. Georges Duval, one of the jeunesse dorée that invaded parks, cafés, and theaters in 1795 to taunt former Jacobins, related that although his cohort successfully prevented any actors or singers with a Jacobin past from performing until they had given a public mea culpa, the performers were thereafter enthusiastically cheered in whatever role they played "to prove that our reconciliation was sincere."[83]

What explains this return of dramatic distance, this willingness among audiences once again to suspend disbelief? The dismantling of the Terror and the collective relief no doubt goes far in explaining the new tone in accounts of the theater. "The arts will reappear," a critic wrote on the release of the actors of the Comédie-Française; another reviewer took the liberty to label the patriotic works "indecent caricatures, . . . disgusting and cold rhapsodies that have sullied our stage."[84] There was a clear sense after Thermidor that the dramatic arts could once again follow their own relatively autonomous path of development, influenced by, but not identical with, politics.

But the return of dramatic distance after Thermidor was more than a simple manifestation of collective relief. It was a sign that audiences no longer viewed themselves as "actors," nor the actors as "citizens," in the spectacle of the Revolution. Thermidor, and the manifest acceptance of its legitimacy by the public in and out of theaters, effectively changed the relationship between the people and government, society and state. By imposing its own authority over that of the revolutionary sections and committees, the Convention successfully substituted the principle of representation for the immanent and indivisible sovereignty of the "nation assembled." To recognize the Convention's authority was thus to recognize the state and society as separate entities and to reject the former politicization of every aspect of private life. Spectators no longer fused their personal fears and ideals with those of the actors on stage because the theater had for them ceased to be the locus of the national will.

The relative calm that slowly returned to audiences by 1796 was a clear sign of this depoliticization. If some regretted the lack of patriotism it seemed to represent, others recognized that it also meant blood was no longer being shed nor performers arrested as a result of political passions. "The general sentiment appeared to us to be overall contentment," reads a description of the audience in a public festival in 1796.

> No enthusiasm but the forgetting of positions and parties, the abandonment to pleasure, simple and frank happiness. Let us repeat this, it is a good thing that all enthusiasm is absent today: in 1790 every person was an actor for the public interest, we were making a constitution, a revolution; we needed enthusiasm. But today, the Revolution and Constitution are accomplished. It is up to the government to tend to our affairs, and the public spirit cannot show it better than by enjoying the pleasures offered it with confidence and security.[85]

"No enthusiasm but the forgetting of positions and parties, abandonment to pleasure, simple and frank happiness." Was the critic for the *Vedette* right in asserting that the Revolution had changed nothing inside theaters? Except for a few scattered voices, no one seemed to miss the moments of solidarity between stage and audience that the Terror had achieved. By most accounts the dress, behavior, repertoires, and dramatic expectations of audiences in 1795 were not much different from what they had been in 1789. But even as Thermidor ushered in a new ostentation as it removed the fear and distrust that had masked earlier dramatic experience, other aspects of theater from the Terror remained. Spectators still saw regular reenactments of battles marking the spread of liberty throughout Europe. As Napoleon knew well, if anything could heal the divisions of the Revolution, it was national unity through national conquest.

The republican dramas and scènes patriotiques that flourished during the Terror had trained spectators to be sensitive to the slightest contemporary allusion, real or imagined, in the plot and had focused their attention on the performers with unprecedented concentration. Even as audiences after Thermidor shunned plots constructed around current events, their occasionally tumultuous responses to lines with perceived references to Jacobins or royalists attest to an immediacy of experience unknown in the Old Regime. That an actor waited until the defeat of the enemy Saracen troops in *Armide* to announce from the Opera stage the French victory at Marengo is a blend of fact and fantasy hardly conceivable before the Revolution.[86]

The decade of experiments in plot and reverses in reception ends with a paradox: capable of a closer identification with actor and plot than ever before, spectators demanded more superficial works than ever before. But was this not the paradox of the Thermidoreans, too, whose task it was to rehabilitate political life by removing politics from the lives of a population still very capable of fighting old battles? For the Thermidorean regime and the Directory after it, the way out of the Terror and back to a semblance of order and national unity was through collective forgetting, "a forgetfulness always aware of the need to forget," as Mona Ozouf has written.[87] This was likely the same peace that audiences sought when they sentimentally cheered for Cinderella, or for lovers disguised as jockeys, or for poor American girls favored by mysterious millionaires.

4

The French Revolution, Anthropological Medicine, and the Creation of Medical Authority

ELIZABETH A. WILLIAMS

For some time historians have agreed that something they call a "medical revolution" took place in France during roughly the same period as the great Revolution itself. Yet the dimensions of this medical revolution and its long-term consequences for medicine and for French society at large have been matters of much dispute. Medical historians of an earlier era celebrated as revolutionary the emergence of the hospital, the techniques of pathological anatomy, clinical training, and other much-admired creations of the era. More recently historical judgment has shifted, thanks to the influence of Michel Foucault and other severe critics of the medical establishment. In this literature, historians have focused on the more menacing features of medical modernity including incarceration, invasive procedures, and new modes of repression and control of the body.[1] One of the central points of contention in the historical debate over the medical revolution has been whether medicine emerged from the Revolution with its "power," "authority," "prestige," or "influence" significantly enhanced.[2] That the medical system was changed in important ways—the structure and character of education and training, the role of the hospital, licensing, governmental roles and functions—seems well established. But whether all these changes entailed a genuine rupture with the past in terms of the power or authority of medicine in society—which under the Old Regime derived chiefly from corporate prerogatives—remains unclear. In this paper I will argue that such a transformation did occur, in conjunction with the larger political and social events of the Revolution itself, and that the most fruitful way to envisage the changes brought by this transformation is to think of them as entailing the creation of a new medical "authority." Moreover, I will argue that medical authority derived not merely from the technical, legal, or bureaucratic advances of medicine but primarily from its success in reconstituting itself as an anthropological endeavor, as an embracive "science of man." It was in the context of the Revolution, with its general restructuring of cultural values, that medicine began to supplant traditional authority in diverse domains of intellectual and social experience.

Some Keywords

To get at the problem of whether medical authority was either created or significantly augmented during the Revolution, we must first consider the words historians have most frequently used to talk about this phenomenon. Raymond Williams argues that it is in the semantics of our debates about society and culture that much of the real argumentation goes on, and he urges that we attempt where we can to bring to consciousness the layers of meaning embedded in "keywords."[3] If we peruse the literature on the medical revolution, we find a number of words used more or less synonymously to describe what many regard as a significant shift in the status of medicine but are as yet unsure how to describe or categorize. The words most often used to discuss this shift are "power" (usually after Foucauldian usage), "authority" (in disparate sociological senses), "prestige" (usually not in a theoretical sense), and the vague, but seemingly indispensable, "influence." These terms all have their advantages and their problems, and it is not my purpose to suggest that the debate should be rigidly connected to one of them and detached from all the others. Rather I want to suggest that the import of these terms needs to be examined more closely, so that the character of the medical revolution may come clearly into focus. As Weber once wrote, it is precisely our inability to capture the protean phenomena of empirical reality that makes it all the more imperative that we seek precision in our categories of analysis.[4]

The most problematic of these usages is "power," a word that has been used more and more generally because of the influence of Foucault. Even those who are profoundly drawn to Foucault complain about his obscurity, but whatever the problems raised by his terminology, it is an inescapable point of reference since it is his work that has done the most to redirect historical research on the coming of medical modernity.[5] Foucauldian power, used in reference to things medical, has at least three valents: the epistemological power of "the gaze," the new disposition of doctors literally to "see inside" their patients by using the techniques of pathological anatomy ("opening a few corpses") or in clinical experience to keep the bodies of patients visible, open to surveillance; the discursive power of statements uttered to capture observations made by means of such techniques; and, at a reduced level of significance, the social or institutional power conferred by doctors' control of the clinical setting, including the power to incarcerate and, seemingly more important, to build up tables, graphs, and grids of intimate information about other human beings.[6] In laying out these "powers" in a linear series, some violence is obviously done to the spirit of Foucault's work, which attempts to convey what Marcel Mauss called the "total social fact."[7] Foucault seeks, I think, a means to conceive the reality of power as experienced by both user and receiver by treating simultaneously the physical setting for the conveying of knowledge, the means by which knowledge is gained, and the statements in which knowledge is rendered.

Foucault's treatment of power has raised critical problems that will in all likelihood take a generation to work through. But since historians cannot— or in any event do not—wait for critical consensus, the Foucauldian concept of power has already clearly marked much historical labor. The net effect of Foucault's influence has been unclear, however, in good part because many of the studies that build on his insights and use his approach also attempt to answer a range of theoretical imperatives laid down in vastly different frameworks provided by sociology and, to a lesser extent, anthropology.

The seemingly endless debate on the professionalization of doctors and its larger social consequences has operated on a plane far removed from Foucault, despite one salutary effort by Jan Goldstein to achieve some harmony between the two approaches.[8] The contrasts between the frameworks provided by Foucault and by the sociological-anthropological literature are too numerous even for summary, but one crucial issue may serve to illustrate the extent of the incompatibility. All recent literature on the professionalization of doctors stresses that French doctors after the Revolution and indeed through the nineteenth and the twentieth centuries did not form a "profession" in the Anglo-American fashion. They had no professional organization, were not responsible for their own program of training, did not establish their own criteria for licensing, and were stratified into two levels of practitioner (physicians and *officiers de santé*) in answer to reasons of state rather than to medical concerns. Instead, this literature tells us, French doctors depended for their "authority" (not "power" in this un-Foucauldian literature) on the state. According to this perspective, even a medical corps as seemingly autonomous as the American depends on "the borrowed authority of the state," and this dependence is clearest of all in the French case.[9] With this view as its point of departure, the sociologically framed literature concentrates on exploring matters such as the Revolution's extension of a state-medical bureaucracy, the creation of a medical monopoly and the various campaigns against illegal practitioners, the role of the medical corps in the military establishment, and the government-controlled training, education, and certification processes.[10] It is hard to imagine how there could be a greater difference—in historical tone if nothing else—between the medical arena portrayed in this literature and the murky, malevolent, corpse-stinking world of Foucault's clinic. This contrast has everything to do, I would suggest, with the differing conceptions of power and authority on which these works ultimately rest. Although Foucault never denied the importance of state power and although he claimed to have given close attention to the concrete apparatuses of power, his work overall conveys the impression that power resides primarily in "knowledge," that is, in autonomous discourse generated by anonymous speakers.[11] In any event his work does not encourage the kind of attention to precise linkages between state power and the concrete legal, bureaucratic, and organizational mechanisms of subordinate agents that is called for by the sociological approach.

The problem of how medicine enhanced its status during the Revolution becomes even more complex when we turn to the two other words that appeared on our initial list of partial synonyms—"prestige" and "influence." The use of these weaker words rather than "power" or "authority" has served two ends in the literature. One is to suggest that medicine as a social enterprise owed its new success to intellectual innovations, an argument that raises problems of emphasis and timing (which innovations were the most important, when they took place, how long it was before they were recognized). Another is simply to de-emphasize the question of whether any genuinely dramatic transformation occurred while still acknowledging medicine's obviously greater influence in the post-revolutionary world. To my mind these words are too modest to capture the truly revolutionary change in the status of medicine that occurred in the context of the larger revolutionary struggle.

Again, it is important to sort out the contexts in which these words are most often encountered. The word "prestige" usually appears in relation to

the putative new scientificity of medicine as it changed and developed in the
revolutionary era. Jean-Pierre Goubert writes, for example, that after the
Revolution "it was no longer a question of the medical corps simply using
established practices and language. Henceforward it was to benefit from the
prestige and the sense of certainty conferred by the great names of the
scientific world, especially those in botany, chemistry, hospital medicine,
and pathological anatomy."[12] Similarly William Albury notes that once
J.-N. Corvisart linked his new conception of the body's constant susceptibility to disease with Georges Cuvier's theory of the "internal conditions of
existence," medicine took on "some of the aura of scientificity and certainty
surrounding biology."[13] Putting aside the question of whether in fact there
was any such thing as "biology" in 1806 (the year Corvisart published his
major treatise) or, if indeed there was, whether biology itself enjoyed an
"aura of scientificity and certainty," we are left wondering what exactly this
"prestige" of science was and, more important, how medicine was able to
appropriate it.

Difficulties inherent in the idea of the prestige of science become glaring if
we compare it to Foucault's power of discourse. Although everything Foucault wrote was based on learned writings (of doctors, jurists, scientists), he
nonetheless suggested in his theory of discourse that discursive power rests
not on any inherent rationality, scientific legitimacy, or personal or institutional standing of those who utter statements, but on the simple fact that
those statements can be made. Although one might be inclined to interpret
this condition of "being able to be said" as indicating the existence of some
external imprimatur (from the state, the church, publishers, newspaper-
owners), Foucault seems in fact to have meant that discourse had power
because, for whatever reason, it existed while other hypothetical discourses
did not.[14] This perspective, which is of course maintained in much of literary
theory too, has encouraged movement away from concentration on canonical
texts and toward recovery and examination of any and all texts.[15] The difficulties such an approach poses for the history of science, which has its canon too,
are legion. If all scientific discourse is powerful merely because it exists, what
quality is it that conveys the apparently greater prestige of some kinds of
science rather than others? This question is crucial to discussions of the
medical revolution since it is so often asserted that medicine's status altered as
it came to incorporate the techniques and approaches of the increasingly
prestigious natural sciences. Seen in this light, the origin and nature of scientific prestige become problematic.

Primarily a sociological concept, "prestige" usually functions in tandem with the related constructs of "status," "position," or "role," except in the limiting case of the independent, self-contained "genius" or, in Weberian terms, of the "charismatic" leader.[16] The limiting case of the genius is an important one in the history of science, where a scientific genius is presumed to have prestige not because (or at least not solely because) he holds an important position but because his science is better in some way (more innovative, well-grounded, fruitful, far-sighted) than that of his contemporaries.[17] Bruno Latour has recently attempted to demonstrate that Louis Pasteur enjoyed prestige not because he was a scientific genius (long everybody's basic assumption) but because he had a genius for self-promotion. The case he makes is not convincing, but it does bring into focus the problem of deciding whence scientific prestige derives if we stop thinking about science in terms of truth, progress, or rationality and start thinking simply about scientific discourse, like any other discourse, simply as what can be said at a given historical moment.[18]

Thus even if we accept that science enjoyed increasing prestige thanks to the French Revolution, there remain the difficult methodological problems of how to demonstrate this access of prestige in general, and harder yet, of how to demonstrate that particular, specialized byways of science enjoyed more of it than others. William Albury, in taking Cuvier as the measure of prestige, rested his case not only on the long tradition of historical adulation of Cuvier but also on the fact that Cuvier worked at the Muséum d'histoire naturelle, which was one of the few learned bodies in Paris not to be closed down by the Convention in 1793.[19] But one may ask whether this fact demonstrates some special prestige of biological science or merely demonstrates that the particular group of Jacobin politicians in power at the moment when the academies were closed saw some special public utility in natural history, a view argued by some historians.[20] In any event, to say that medicine came to enjoy the prestige of natural science leaves in place, as we noted above, the difficult questions of how and under what kinds of circumstances one field, discipline, or discourse can appropriate the prestige of another. In the case of medicine this process has been attributed to many different innovations: the heightened importance of pathological anatomy, the development of tissue theory, the widespread use of statistics, the cleansing of the *materia medica*, and so on.[21] Yet as I will argue below, the medicine that gained new authority in the context of the Revolution was not so much the new medicine of pathological anatomy and the rest, with its prestige borrowed on the basis of technical innovations, but an old medicine, rooted in vitalism, that mapped out a near-universal domain of medical interventionism and, most important, successfully pressed its claims in the political arena.

Finally, there is the word "influence." The literature on the troubles of influence is vast.[22] Yet this literature, though generating discomfort about the word, has not succeeded in banishing it completely. To have no concept of influence seems to fly in the face of one's felt experience of influence, if nothing else. And some scholars have responded to criticism of the concept by developing elaborate frameworks for its use.[23] Influence thus continues to be a much-used concept not only in intellectual history (so-and-so influenced so-and-so to think such-and-such) but in social, political, and institutional studies as well. In respect to the medical revolution, a range of facts has been adduced to prove the new influence of medicine and doctors: the growth of the medical bureaucracy, the increase in the numbers of practitioners in the postrevolutionary period, the path-breaking creation of the medical monopoly, the establishment of new medical periodicals and societies, the enhanced role of the hospitals, the proliferation of medical manuals and guides.[24] Yet contrary evidence has been registered too: doctors were unable to establish an autonomous profession; they failed to set up a medical cameralist system comparable to those established in Central Europe; there were few or no doctors in many areas after the Revolution; doctors had less public importance and lower status and income than lawyers; medical science was rapidly outpaced and overshadowed by those branches of life science that readily embraced experimentalism.[25] For many historians, then, the whole problem of change in the status of medicine would seem to come down to a matter of degree, which of course raises the question of why we think in terms of a medical "revolution" at all.

In my view it is wholly apt to think in terms of a medical revolution precisely because the changes in the status of medicine during the Revolutionary era were not merely incremental improvements in medical prestige or influence but part of a larger structural revolution in social and cultural authority. A sociological analysis of what constituted authority in French society before and after the Revolution is beyond the scope of this paper, but if we recall that one of the Revolution's primary effects was to shift social valorization from birth, inherited status, and privilege toward function, merit, and expertise, then it would seem that the new importance of doctors as social actors eventuated from the more profound alterations in public values caused by the larger social struggle.[26] That public recognition of medicine's authority was prior to enhancement of its social prestige is indicated by the lag social historians have noted between the legal and official gains of medicine and popular images of medicine and doctors. Jacques Léonard in particular has emphasized the slow and gradual shift in perceptions of medicine, a view that fits well with general historical observations that in social change, law, formalities, and officialdom alter well before shifts in perceptions, attitudes, and behavior.[27] I believe this is clearly the case in respect to the status of medicine. To say that medical authority was created by the Revolution does not mean that overnight there were doctors everywhere, respected by everybody. It means that the fundamental bases of authority in society had shifted and that the way was thus opened for myriad minute phenomena of social life to shift too.

Clearly this argument lays heavy stress on the "official acceptance" of medicine, or put differently, the relations between medicine as a social-intellectual enterprise and the state, as it developed and changed in the course of the Revolution. It insists that the fate of medicine was determined by the particular course taken by the larger Revolution, specifically the outcome of the struggle to determine what new bases of authority would emerge from the revolutionary contest. What happened to medicine, in short, depended on who triumphed in the Revolution. Conceived in this fashion the fate of the medical establishment was as fully and intimately linked to the outcome of political struggles as was that of any of the diverse actors in the Revolution's overt drama of politics.

The Chronology of the Medical Revolution

It has become a commonplace to accept the chronological framework of 1770–1830 as the period of the medical revolution.[28] Why this is the case is not clear, though for the point of origin it seems that the fallback to 1770 allows the crucial decade of the 1770s, and thus the work of the royal commission that became the famed Société Royale de Médecine, to come under the revolutionary rubric.[29] By the same logic, however, it would appear necessary to go back considerably beyond 1770, to at least 1731, when the Académie de Chirurgie, a group that was ultimately to alter surgical training, certification, and practice, came into existence.[30] The end-date accepted in the literature, 1830, has an even less clear rationale than 1770, since it seems to imply that trends set in motion during the Revolution continued through the Restoration but then stopped. The 1830 cutoff point does encompass the founding in 1829 of the *Annales d'hygiène publique et de médecine légale,* which many historians take as a critical sign of the gearing-up and new importance of hygiene, whose subsequent role in France's social and intellectual history was so pronounced.[31] Still, one could as easily insist that the date be pulled forward to 1849 to include, for example, the restructuring of the public assistance system. The dates as they stand are, in short, vague and ill-reasoned.

Worse yet, this framework encourages us to slip over the concrete significance of the period 1789–1815. Goubert denies that using the 1770–1830 dates has this effect, arguing that to focus on those years is not to "deny the existence or significance of the French Revolution" but to "perceive its true duration and take its true measure."[32] This point of view has its merits; it would be pointless to try to downplay the importance of the Société Royale de Médecine or to dispute the long-term impact of the diverse critiques of medicine written in these years. All the same, it is my view that a genuine medical revolution could come about, and did come about, only because there took place a political and social revolution of which it was but one constituent part. The central event or development of the medical revolution was thus the creation of a new kind of authority, one that has been called "usufructory" in nature, whose establishment was possible only because of the breakdown of traditional authority generally. In this view the Revolution destroyed the ancient sacral authority of monarch and church and substituted a new species of authority dependent on the pragmatic demonstration of utility and efficacy.[33] This conception of the medical revolution ties it, then, not to a long and gradual process of social, institutional, or attitudinal change but to a decisive moment of political revolution. This is in no way to say that the Revolution was exclusively, or even primarily, political in character but that the political revolution was the necessary condition for the general shift in authority away from sacral representatives to a broad array of instrumental agents—with the state apparatus itself at the core—that substituted the promise to fulfill pragmatic ends for the claim of traditional authority to embody providential design. This constitution of "usufructory" authority became, I would argue, the general aim of revolutionary politics after the radical revolution failed in its attempt to establish a genuine popular consensualism. It was, accordingly, only from the Thermidorian Convention forward that the medical revolution—which was for the most part elitist, bureaucratic, and antipopular in character—really got under way. It was after Thermidor that medical revolutionaries most forcefully articulated a new anthropological vision of medicine—medicine as a general "science of man" that could replace discredited traditional authority with its own authority on subjects that were, as one physician put it, "infinite in their scope."[34]

Medicine as Anthropology

Why medicine should have played a primary part in the new constitution of authority in French society is a complicated matter. Again Foucault—who has a provocative, if finally unacceptable, explanation—helps to clarify matters. Foucault argues in his peroration to *The Birth of the Clinic* that medical discourse wielded its peculiar power at this historical juncture because, given the centrality of pathological anatomy, medicine had become preoccupied with death, and death alone could confer the new individuality that ushered in the "age of man."[35] Whatever the critical utility of this view in examining the death-fixation that is often taken to be characteristic of modernity, it is profoundly paradoxical as a historical formulation. The medicine that first made the conquest of authority during the course of the French Revolution was not the new medicine of the morgue but an old, "philosophical" medicine that was preoccupied not with death but with a unitary, holistic process it had for some time distinguished as life. The leading figures in the creation of medical authority were uniformly schooled in medical vitalism, which as taught principally by the Montpellier doctors of the eighteenth century, posited the presence in living beings of some kind of primordial force, energy, or principle that was not subject to the physico-chemical laws governing brute matter.[36] Some of these doctors regarded the distinction between the living and the dead, the organic and the inorganic, as absolute. Others saw a continuum between inert matter and the most sophisticated organized beings. Vital force itself was variously conceived: to Pierre-Jean-Georges Cabanis (1757–1808), arguably the most important champion of anthropological medicine, it was a "vivifying principle or faculty" that was essentially equivalent to sensitivity. Xavier Bichat (1771–1802) rejected the idea of a unitary vital principle but developed in its place a doctrine of five irreducible vital "properties" that were essential in the performance of functions that staved off death. François Chaussier (1746–1828), who taught a whole generation of new doctors at the Paris Ecole de Santé, referred to one vital force manifested in the three vital properties of sensitivity, motility, and caloricity.[37] Despite this diversity, some concept of vital power was important to all these figures not only because vitalism swept away a plethora of creaking mechanist explanations of body functions but also because to revolutionary medicine it represented a path away from dualisms that consigned mind, soul, morality, and judgment to a metaphysical realm not to be approached by physicians, whose sole legitimate concern was the body. Vitalist medicine, as well as the revolutionary doctors who embraced it, flatly rejected the ancient dictum that medicine treats the body while philosophy treats the soul.[38]

That this medicine was holistic and vitalist had wide implications for medical practice, both in the sense of what doctors ought to do with individual patients and in the broader sense of what medicine as a complex of doctrines, institutions, pedagogical dicta, and sociopolitical agencies should be. Medicine defined as the field of inquiry that encompassed both the physical and moral domains took as its objects ordinary ailments of the body, mental maladies, and disorders of the passions. Medicine as guardian of "health" broadly conceived had for patients both individuals presenting themselves at hospital doors and society itself. Medicine as vitalist doctrine prepared the way to a naturalized "science of man" in which the disjuncture between science and metaphysics was resolved. All of this meant that to revolutionary doctors there were few matters of either individual or public activity that did not to some extent have medical implications. Education, political practice, occupation, weather, family life, diet, and sexuality were all matters that entered, by one route or another, into the sphere of medicine and were the subjects of rapidly proliferating observations, exhortations, and proscriptions.[39]

If we examine some of the individual programmatic statements made by doctors about the new "science of man," we obtain a sense of how extravagant many of these medical claims really were. The series of addresses Cabanis delivered to the Institute between 1796 and 1800 constitute the most grandiose, and certainly the most celebrated, statement of what would be the content of the new medicine. The most important of these addresses concerned the nature of the general vital force of sensitivity and the centrality of sensation in all human experience. For Cabanis, the capacity to feel was the very crux of life; he replaced Descartes's *cogito* with the very different aphorism that "from the moment we feel, we exist."[40] Cabanis regarded it as one of the most important tasks of medicine, moreover, to correct the misapprehensions of eighteenth-century "philosophical" sensationalism. He condemned Condillac's "monstrous, hypothetical statue," which had been stirred to consciousness only by the effect of external sensation, arguing in place of such a view that consciousness was determined not only by the play of the senses with the external world but also by what he called "internal impressions"—the feelings generated by the viscera themselves in varying states of movement and repose, ingestion and excretion, sleep, dreams, sexual excitement, hunger, fatigue, and so on.[41] If the operation of the sense organs and the impressions generated by the internal organs and functions of the body were responsible for thought itself, as Cabanis concluded and as his associates among the Ideologues accepted, then obviously medicine was the only "science" that could explicate matters of consciousness itself. By this route medicine laid claim to the whole of human experience and was rendered fundamentally anthropological in nature. If medicine constituted itself in this fashion, it had no need to borrow its positivity elsewhere; indeed medicine was itself the source of all positivity because it alone could judge the validity and quality of intellectual operations themselves.[42] Cabanis's remaining Institute addresses were devoted to showing, in practice, what the concrete implications of such a conception of medicine were. With physiology at its base, the medical "science of man" was equipped to undertake every kind of study involved in the "analysis of ideas" and in the investigation of morality and ethics. (Thus physiology, the analysis of ideas, and *morale* were the three divisions of the "science of man.") In this light Cabanis approached the investigation of temperament, sex, and the "stages of life"; the influence of climate; the character of instinct, *délires*, and sleep; the nature of sympathy; hygiene and its influence on "moral operations"; the link between disease and mental function; and the character of ideas and passions. He ended with an analysis of the general influence of the "moral on the physical" and a survey of the effects medicine could exercise on morality.[43] An ambitious agenda for anthropological medicine had thus been set.

Another brief for the centrality of medicine was written by Jean-Louis Alibert (1766?–1837), who from 1796 to 1802 was permanent secretary for the Société Médicale d'Emulation, a pivotal medical group that was founded under the Directory by a cluster of doctors who had embraced the larger Revolution and were determined to see it utterly transform medicine.[44] Writing under the rubric "Discours sur les rapports de la médecine avec les sciences physiques et morales," Alibert insisted that the day when medicine subordinated itself to other sciences was past: "A better fate is reserved to medicine in our day; it is no longer the accessory sciences that have conquered medicine—medicine has conquered the accessory sciences. . . . [Medicine] rules their efforts and directs at will the useful application of their discoveries."[45] Medicine, he continued, was a "science infinite in scope," an "art

designed for the surveillance of . . . all human destiny"; a science to which
"no moral question was foreign."[46] Again the source of medicine's claims was
the intimate relation between the physical and moral, the latter a category
that included intellectual operations, passional or instinctual phenomena,
and moral judgment. This link Alibert regarded as wholly established, though
he conceded that the precise "organic means" governing the "intellectual
forces" were not yet understood. The practical services medicine could render
were thus innumerable: as the science of sensitivity, it would be the beacon for
metaphysics as "re-created" by Bacon, Locke, and Condillac. It would lead in
analyzing and treating the mental maladies that were most inimical to human
progress, the "furors, manias, melancholic languors, and thousand other
partial or total eclipses of the human intelligence that sadden the heart and
put human reason to shame."[47] It would ground all future work on "sympathy" and "sociability," which now appeared to be "for animated bodies what
attraction and affinity were for inanimate matter."[48] Medicine alone could
write the "unbounded history of the human heart," curbing and controlling
"the passions that destroyed all felicity."[49] Lastly, "the alliance between medicine and politics" would be forged in the labors of public hygienists and
doctors whose special task was to advise and assist "the judicial art."[50]
Alibert's rhetoric was much admired; the Ideologues' journal, *Décade philosophique*, hailed this text as "remarkable in the breadth of its philosophy and
imagination, in its methodical organization and animated composition, the
merit of its science and . . . its style."[51] But a number of similar prospectuses,
not so dramatic stylistically but equally ambitious thematically, are to be
found in the writings of Philippe Pinel (1745–1826), Jacques-Louis Moreau
de la Sarthe (1771–1826), Jean-Noël Hallé (1754–1822), and other doctors
who were associated with the Société Médicale d'Emulation and bent on the
anthropologizing of medicine.[52]

Not everyone, certainly, looked kindly on the broad claims of doctors. In
the early years of the Revolution, the Constituent Assembly had left languish-
ing Joseph-Ignace Guillotin's detailed program for the development of a national system of medical care to be accomplished by a medical profession with
greatly enhanced authority. Among Jacobin leaders there were many who
believed with Rousseau that social health would restore the salubrity of
"natural man" and eliminate the need for medicine; others were interested in
medicine only insofar as it could show immediate practical results on the
battlefield or in the care of orphans and the indigent. And although the image
of the Jacobins as the standard-bearers of a "fanatical" anti-intellectualism
has no doubt been overdrawn, it remains true that the Jacobins upheld as a

replacement for clerical authority not some new brand of elitist scientism but their own version of public morality as taught by universal reason.[53]

These observations raise for speculation the fascinating question of what might have happened to medicine in a world formed by Jacobin vision, a question that the Foucauldian perspective on autonomous discourse would render utterly meaningless but which any historical view that insists on the importance of specific moments of political decision validly raises. My own view is that medicine took on its peculiar importance in French society, and achieved its new authority, within the decisive context of the defeat of Jacobinism, the momentary victory of the "moderates" who controlled the Directory, and the ultimate triumph of Bonapartism. It was in the decade after 1794 that medicine made most of the concrete legal, institutional, and social gains to which historians have attached so much importance. And it was these gains that made possible the continued exercise of medical author-ity long after the specific historical juncture in which they were made had passed. The Jacobins rejected as spurious the claims of the doctors, but for those who continued the revolution, the truth of medical claims was clear. Medicine, wrote one commentator in the year VI, was an art that required men of "rare qualities," and he suggested that the government must move to safeguard this science that was so vital "to public morality and internal politics."[54]

The crucial determinant in the medical revolution was, then, the underly-ing attitude of the revolutionaries at large to the whole problem of authority itself: was it necessary to establish above and beyond the general population some authority to replace that which had been undermined? The answer of every political configuration constituted from 1794 forward was clearly affirmative. A statement issued by the Directory in the year VI is telling: "The public is the victim of a crowd of poorly educated individuals, who on their own authority have called themselves masters of the art, distributed remedies at random and compromised the existence of many thousands of citizens. . . . A positive law should compel anyone who pretends to profess the art of healing to go through a long period of study and to be examined by a severe jury."[55] The specific form this new authority might take altered of course with each change of government. The Directory and early Consul-ate, the revolutionary regimes in which the Ideologues played their greatest political role, were sympathetic to the broad theoretical and scientistic claims of medicine, and it was thus under their direction that the reconstitu-tion of medical education and training in a new scientific framework was undertaken. These years saw the establishment of the three "schools of health" to replace the old faculties of Paris, Montpellier, and Strasbourg, the organization of the new medical curriculum, and the creation of clinical teaching in the hospitals. The nomination of faculty and administrators to the Paris Ecole de Santé, which opened its doors in January 1795, indicated the inroads made by the new anthropological medicine. Pinel, who had been excluded from the teaching establishment under the ancien régime, was accorded a chair in internal medicine. Chaussier was charged with the teaching of anatomy and physiology. Cabanis was made professor of internal clinical medicine in 1796.[56] The dean of the school was Michel-Augustin Thouret, who in the early years of the Revolution had worked closely with Cabanis on a plan for hospital reform that envisaged the closing of the giant establishments of the ancien régime and their replacement by small hospices in which there would be intimate contact between doctor and patient.[57] Curricular changes also reflected the new scope of medicine: a course in Hippocratic medicine was reserved to Thouret personally, the first official chair of hygiene was created, the study of medical history (from which Cabanis had drawn the principal insights of a famous treatise on medical "certainty") was inaugurated.[58] Three of the twelve chairs of the new Ecole de Santé were linked to clinical teaching at the Hospice de l'Unité (the old Charité), the Hospice de l'Humanité (formerly the Hôtel-Dieu), and the Hospice de l'Ecole (the hospital of the defunct Académie de Chirurgie in whose facilities the Ecole de Santé was lodged).[59] Such a pedagogical setting was precisely what was required, Cabanis had consistently argued, if doctors were to be trained to gather and analyze the minute particulars about patients (age, sex, temperament, occupation) essential to the diagnosis and treatment of individual maladies.[60]

Once medical training was reorganized, the Directory took the first tentative steps since the dissolution of the guilds and the closing of the academies toward the reestablishment of official licensure. In 1796 it established a *mode de réception* for all officiers de santé, a category that included all practitioners until the two-tier system of doctors and officiers was created in 1803. Two years later a certification program was instituted to reward those who had passed three examinations at the medical schools. Although this certificate conferred no special legal authority, it did move in the direction of privileging official medical science in the face of all competitors.[61] In a similar spirit the Directory sanctioned, and in some cases actively encouraged, the founding of a score of medical societies, at least six of which published their own journals. Of these the publications of the Société Médicale d'Emulation reflected most clearly the preoccupations of anthropological medicine, with contributions on "moral medicine," the medical importance of odors, "periodic and inter-mittent manias," hermaphroditism, the use of the guillotine, fogs, certitude in metaphysics, "nymphomania," statistical measures of workers' health, the relations between hysteria and depression, climatic patterns in the Antilles, and the like.[62]

With the ascendancy of Bonaparte, the character of the *Mémoires de la Société Médicale d'Emulation* abruptly changed: articles suggesting an inti-mate physical-moral relation were no longer included. This was but one sign of a transformation in the general disposition of the regime toward medical ambitions. The changes in medicine instituted under Bonaparte were le-galistic, formally bureaucratic, and aimed at solving immediate, practical problems. In 1803 the legal monopoly was established, a move that one historian has suggested was intended as much to control the activities of itinerant empirics, midwives, and popular healers as it was to validate the medical practice of doctors.[63] In 1802 the regime established the *Conseil de Salubrité de Paris et du Département de la Seine*, a council of advisors that elaborated the new medical framework that came to be known as "public health."[64] Centralized control of Paris hospitals was sought with the found-ing of the *Conseil général d'administration des hôpitaux et hospices de Paris*. This move prepared the way to establishment in the hospitals of the intern-extern program, which made available a pool of student labor for myriad minor tasks in the hospitals and helped to shift the emphasis, in education of the elite interns and externs, away from theoretical subjects toward practical training in surgical techniques, the care of wounds, and dissections.[65] This de-emphasis of the theoretical was characteristic of the whole Bonapartist approach to medicine and its functions.

Although Bonaparte showered favors on some individual physicians, he was generally hostile to doctors and to medicine, especially to medicine's anthropological self-construction in the fashion of Cabanis and Alibert. His closing of the Second Class of the Institute (the division to which Cabanis had delivered his addresses on the future of medicine) was directed as much at the pretensions of such doctors as it was at the political base of his enemies among the Ideologues.[66] The same disposition is evident in the regime's approach to medical education, which had several dimensions. In 1808 the medical schools were transformed into faculties of the new Impe-rial University and their administration brought, like the rest of the univer-sity, under the control of the "Master," a post held first by the intensely conservative Louis de Fontanes. From 1806 forward the regime moved to create a number of regional medical schools (*écoles préparatoires de méde-*

cine) whose purpose was to train not full-fledged physicians but second-tier officiers de santé.[67] This program served not only to attenuate the professional exclusiveness of physicians but also to divert resources away from Paris, Montpellier, and Strasbourg, whose overweening position in the teaching of medicine constituted a potential ideological threat. With the closing of the Second Class of the Institute, the transformation of such independent forums as the journal of the Société Médicale d'Emulation, and the restructuring of the teaching establishment, the era of grandiose medical rhetoric came to a close. Still, far from bringing the medical revolution to an end, the Bonapartist phase of the Revolution assured to medicine its most important concrete legal and bureaucratic gains of the whole period and in the elaboration of a framework for public health and hygiene realized at least some of the major ambitions of anthropological medicine. In the context of Bonapartism, the theoretical claims of the doctors had to be minimized since they clashed with the bid for prerogatives made by the new "Gallican" church, an institution that in Bonaparte's view held greater promise for service as an instrumental agent of the state than did medicine. By augmenting practical medical authority while simultaneously restructuring and privileging clerical authority, Bonaparte created the conditions for a continuing struggle between doctor and cleric, medicine and church, that became a distinctive feature of French political, social, and intellectual life in ensuing decades. The intensity of that struggle is itself proof of the irrevocable arrival of medical authority in France.[68]

After the Revolution

The extent to which these changes of the revolutionary era in fact entailed the creation of a new medical authority became fully clear only in the aftermath of the Revolution. During the Restoration an intense campaign against the pretensions of medicine was waged by conservative intellectuals, and when the new government came into power, there was prolonged discussion of revamping the whole system of medical education.[69] These plans came to nothing, however, and indeed during the years of the Restoration only one major attack on the new medical establishment, the temporary closing of the medical faculty and the firing of the liberal professors in 1822, was undertaken. Even this move led to an improvement for the teaching establishment: when the faculty was reopened in 1823, it was allowed twenty-three chairs in place of the original twelve founded in 1794.[70] In all other major respects, the doctors were left to their own devices, and in important ways the Restoration government moved to reinforce and validate their new authority. The founding of the Académie Royale de Médecine in 1820, for example, accomplished the two ends of granting official recognition to the labors of medical scientists and of channeling medical endeavors in directions the government favored and approved.[71]

None of this would seem to fit very well with what we know of other measures taken by the Restoration regime to restore clerical authority and to undo the work of the Revolution.[72] But in fact there is no real contradiction. Except for the years when the regime was dominated by ultras, the Restoration government proved itself content to accept, use, and indeed augment the authority of medicine so long as certain basic conditions were met. It was made clear early on that the regime would not tolerate the public expression in medical quarters of what its polemicists called "materialist" or "physiological" doctrines of mind, soul, and morality but was prepared to see and even to encourage the extension of medical authority throughout society.[73] The doctors themselves eased this rapprochement along by abandoning almost universally the more extreme claims of anthropological medicine (its claims, for example, to provide the only access to an understanding of consciousness, to be the natural arbiter of moral and ethical disputes, to be the "beacon of metaphysics," and the like) and by developing instead those elements of the medical "science of man" that entailed no controversy and, better yet, could be shown to have immediate public utility.

The clearest case of this direction taken by anthropological medicine is that of hygiene. When the *Annales d'hygiène publique et médecine légale* was founded, the author of its opening *discours* engaged in rhetorical flourishes reminiscent in some respects of those of Alibert: "Medicine has for its object not only to study and heal the sick, it has intimate relations with social organization. Sometimes it lends aid to the legislator in the formulation of laws, often it enlightens the magistrate in the application [of those laws] and always it attends, with the administration, to the maintenance of public health."[74] Yet the stress laid on cooperation with magistrates and the administration correctly indicated the readiness and indeed clear intention of these doctors to enhance their own authority by furthering the projects and interests of the state.[75] Equally important, if not quite so striking, are the cases of what came to be known as "mental medicine" and "legal medicine." Both of these medical specialties, which began hesitantly to develop under the Restoration and then took off under the Orleanist monarchy, traced their origins to the medical "science of man" of the revolutionary era. But those who fostered their further growth from the 1820s to the 1840s were, like the hygienists, deliberately careful to avoid polemics, institutional struggles, and policy battles that would entail direct confrontation with the defenders of clerical prerogatives. They were not always successful, as may be seen in the protracted struggle in the late 1820s between conservatives and alienists over whether "monomania" was a valid medical category and legal defense.[76] But their efforts were for the most part rewarded. From the 1820s to the 1840s, the Académie de Médecine, which came to be the standard-bearer of official medicine, excluded from its discussions any topic that even hinted at consideration of the material foundation of the intellectual faculties. Yet at the same time it showed great receptivity to the limited, "safe" questions of mental medicine involving the diagnosis and treatment of nervous ailments. Scarcely a year passed that some paper similar to one offered in 1836 by the conservative Frédéric Dubois d'Amiens on the "philosophical investigation of idiocy and dementia" failed to appear in the Academy's *Mémoires*.[77] Mental medicine, if gauged by official reception at the Académie de Médecine, had arrived. These diverse currents, which stemmed from the original anthropological construction of medicine of the revolutionary years, culminated later in the century in the broad-gauge medicalization of moral and social concerns that historians have charted for the Third Republic.[78]

These glimpses into the postrevolutionary medical world confirm that the fundamental achievement of the medical revolution was the establishment of a new medical authority whose creation was dependent on a fundamental alteration of perceptions about the bases of authority generally, about what constituted a medical matter, and about who was empowered to speak. To argue that in the course of the Revolution medical authority emerged and began usurping traditional authority is not, of course, to hold that kingly "thaumaturgic power" was abruptly banished from popular mentalities nor is it to say that the church as an institution, or religious people as individual social actors, altogether lost their grip. The Weberian schema of modernization that envisaged the progressive "disenchantment" of the world and the inevitable wholesale displacement of religiosity by rational/legal authority has been undercut in our own age by a host of powerful social facts. To say that medical authority was created by the Revolution is rather to argue that a new kind of authority emerged that was not there before, that it could have emerged only in revolutionary circumstances, and that it invaded domains of intellectual and social experience that traditional authority was never again to have exclusively as its own.

5

The Culture of Statistics and the Crisis of Cholera in Paris, 1830–1850

CATHERINE J. KUDLICK

Within a week after the terrifying and mysterious disease cholera-morbus began ravaging Paris for the first time in the spring of 1832, the mainstream press expressed both fear and relief. Clearly the disease that would turn more than eighteen thousand Parisians into black and purplish corpses after several hours of vomiting and diarrhea seemed to show what journalists, government officials, and even doctors called a "preference" for the poor. More than through passionate stories, these middle-class feelings about cholera and poverty emerged through what appeared to be unemotional columns of numbers. Known as the *bulletins du choléra*, the daily mortality figures were reprinted by the government organ, the *Moniteur universel*, and by most popular newspapers as the latest "objective" medical facts about the epidemic and its progress.

In addition to providing valuable information about the immediate crisis of cholera, however, the bulletins marked a pivotal moment in the development of a "culture of statistics" at the level of government policy, popular attitudes, and urban social relations. Formats, categories of information, and the place of the daily mortality figures in the press varied dramatically over the course of the epidemic. These changes—and particularly the responses to them—reveal a great deal about how city officials came to understand a new kind of power and experimented with how best to use it. Meanwhile, for the upper- and middle-class readership of the mainstream press, the bulletins and the "reality" of cholera they depicted helped bring the lives of the poor more squarely within the bourgeois social imagination, as government officials, doctors, and social investigators took a greater interest in the habits and habitats of those who somehow seemed predestined to die.

Seventeen years later in 1849 when cholera returned for the second time and claimed over twenty thousand victims, the role and significance of statistical information had changed considerably. Preferring not to cause panic in the still-jittery aftermath of the bloody revolution of 1848, the government opted to downplay the epidemic by initially printing no bulletins du choléra at all. The official "silence," however, produced the opposite reaction of what the administration had hoped, for the lack of information prompted an outcry from medical journals as well as from the popular press. The bulletins, it seemed, had not lost their power to shape the public imagination; they had become powerful for different reasons.

Using the differing roles of the bulletins du choléra in 1832 and 1849 as a point of departure, this essay examines the rapidly changing culture of statistics in early nineteenth-century Paris. Originally appealing and powerful because of their apparent scientific objectivity and political neutrality, the bulletins quickly came to represent a highly charged rhetoric for both describing and shaping impressions of the Paris environment. Rather than focus on the subjectivity of numbers, I want to explore the complex means by which they derived cultural authority. In the interplay between scientific knowledge and government power on the one hand and popular perceptions of disease and urban social relations on the other, one can see the creation of a political meaning for statistics represented by the bulletins du choléra. Moreover, as we shall see, this culture of statistics developed within a larger historical context where the growth of liberalism, fears of revolution, and the birth of the modern press influenced how all Parisians—from the trained official to the average citizen—would make this culture a fundamental part of their daily lives and their understanding of the world in which they lived.

Counting and Seeing before Cholera

The bulletins du choléra represented but part of a larger enthusiasm for figures that had emerged in the 1820s and 1830s, an enthusiasm reflected in a set of ideas and practices that differed significantly from the political arithmetic of the prerevolutionary period.[1] Since the seventeenth century,

monarchies throughout Europe had sought to compile crude data on population size as a measure of prosperity. A large, rapidly proliferating population
constituted a tremendous military and economic asset at a time when human
bodies were considered a state's principal resource. Not surprisingly, states
kept this statistical information—piecemeal as it was—highly secret. "Political arithmetic," as it became known, then, required the state's clear involvement in the lives of its subjects, while inaccuracy, irregularity, and secrecy
characterized this intervention.

By the nineteenth century, however, statistical information became a
highly public means for "seeing" and describing ongoing social problems
such as disease, poverty, and urban decay. In France the investigations took
on a largely medical character, with the hygienists—a select group of trained
physicians and enlightened city administrators—playing a major part in the
collection, interpretation, and dissemination of data. Concerned that the
former capital of enlightened civility and sophistication had degenerated
into a body being consumed from within by such apparently intrinsic "diseases" as poverty, revolution, filth, crime, and eventually cholera, the hygienists sought to collect empirical data that would lead to some "cure."

Nowhere did the character of the new statistical zeal emerge more clearly
than in the ambitious project to launch a Paris census in 1816–1817, the first
major attempt since the time of Louis XIV.[2] In the shadow of revolutionary
turmoil, the explosive growth of Paris, and—to some extent—Malthusian
pessimism, nineteenth-century officials came to see rapid population growth
as a potential liability linked to other social problems. Disturbed by the
greater visibility of the lower-class population, increasing poverty, and the
changing economic face of the capital, the prefect of the Seine sought to
obtain factual information about the city that culminated in the first edition
of the *Recherches statistiques sur la ville de Paris*, published in 1821. This
massive study included vital statistics on births, deaths, and marriages, along
with data about climate and consumption of foodstuffs.[3] Here, the quest for
accuracy and objectivity played the dominant part in shaping how information was collected and presented; the document relied heavily on the use of
numbers gathered from a variety of sources. Printed as tables, the data created
a composite numerical picture of the capital. For those who had access to it, if
not the public at large, the census helped establish the popularity and legitimacy of using numbers as a primary means of conveying descriptive information, and the categories established for each set of numbers became their
narrative framework.[4] Such data, as well as subsequent censuses in 1826,
1831, and 1846, would serve as the empirical basis for the work of many

urban investigators, while also no doubt influencing the descriptions of writers such as Balzac, Hugo, and Sue.[5]

The Enlightenment, along with both the French and the Industrial Revolutions, had helped define this new concept of statistical description and its objects of investigation, while paving the way for its ultimate acceptance. Ideas such as confidence in science, knowledge through observation and investigation, and optimism formed the intellectual and methodological foundation for the early hygienists. Meanwhile, by broadening the economic, social, and political power bases of the bourgeoisie—the class to which most hygienists belonged—the Great Revolution of 1789 propelled the medical profession to a role of greater national significance, a role to match the international prestige and confidence it had already gained through earlier discoveries in clinical medicine and related sciences.[6] As the middle classes came to be the dominant ruling voice in the first half of the nineteenth century, hygienists found it increasingly both desirable and possible to become involved in government. Because many of them were doctors who had trained on the battlefields as surgeons during the Napoleonic wars, the hygienists saw their engagement in politics as something that transcended their class interests; they believed that their practical experience would enable them to serve as theorists of a new, greatly improved urban order grounded in sanitation and public health.[7]

Enlightenment ideas, the French Revolution, and the accompanying rise of liberalism also created a new meaning for the population as an object of study and as a volatile political actor. By the early nineteenth century, the *health* of the population—not just its size—became an object of *ongoing* concern. In this context, quantified details about living environment assumed greater importance, a fact that called for greater, more regular intervention into the lives of individual citizens. Meanwhile, the promise of liberty and equality, along with the fear of revolt, suggested that the population might in fact play a more active role in shaping society than had previously been the case. The population, it now seemed to many writers and thinkers (including the hygienists), could be studied not simply as an object, but as a subject that could potentially change the urban environment.[8]

The Industrial Revolution and its accompanying urbanization shaped the concept of statistical investigation and created an environment that made it an attractive option for government. The threat of cholera, along with the growing fear that Paris had become a "sick city," inspired a series of both formal and informal investigations similar to the census. Hygienists looked at everything from public squares and open-air markets to cesspools and

private dwellings in order to identify unclean areas where the putrid mias-
mas of disease might arise. Keeping detailed accounts of exactly what they
saw, reporters wrote up descriptions (sometimes several pages long) of individual residences, number of inhabitants, rooms, doors, windows, pieces of
furniture, latrines, available water facilities, and general impressions of the
environment.[9] Recorded both as description and as numbers, the disparate
pieces of information created a composite, almost three-dimensional portrait of the capital. During the Restoration and the July Monarchy, hygienists conducted hundreds of such investigations. The formats ranged from
elegantly published official reports and highly specialized articles in professional journals to hastily scrawled notes written by semiliterate doctors
appended to the minutes of neighborhood sanitation commission meetings.
As we shall see, they contributed much to popularizing statistics as an
option for government policy and created a whole new way of seeing and
describing the Paris environment.[10]

Certain generalizations can be made about these reports that shed light
on the prevailing culture of statistics represented in the daily mortality
figures for cholera. As studies by hygienists, the inquiries shared the underly-
ing assumptions and methodology implicit in their work. Most important,
they articulated a *medicalized* view of the population and urban space. With
their medical training and background, hygienists such as L. R. Villermé and
J. B. Parent-Duchâtelet inquired into the links between material and economic conditions on the one hand and health and "civilization" on the
other. Seeing the physical environment as the source of "disease"—broadly
conceived to encompass filth, poverty, and prostitution, along with a multitude of illnesses including cholera—they geared their investigations toward
a deeper understanding of the capital's poorer neighborhoods. In other
words, they measured humanity's progress from a perspective that focused
on the population and its environment in terms of characteristics relating to
health: births, deaths, diseases, and basic sanitary conditions.[11]

Methodologically speaking, the investigations relied heavily upon observation, categorization, and counting. By using quantitative knowledge to
understand qualitative social and economic problems, the hygienists hoped
to introduce a new, predictable, reliable—scientific—means for curing "disease" broadly conceived. Looking back on his service during the first cholera epidemic, François Marc Moreau, a prominent physician in the northern
part of Paris, gave a revealing description of sources and methodology in his
1833 work, *Histoire statistique sur le choléra-morbus dans le quartier du
Faubourg St.-Denis*. His material came from a careful scrutiny of registers

from emergency first-aid stations, hospitals, reports of house calls, and death certificates, as well as from police documents. Calling for "facts collected without preconceptions," Moreau articulated a much-repeated view. "To trace the general history of the epidemic that has ravaged the city of Paris," he explained, "the knowledge of detailed facts is of an absolute necessity: it is necessary, in a manner of speaking, to follow this epidemic not only in each neighborhood, but even in each street, in each house, to penetrate, if it is possible, into each dwelling, and to have for each and every one of these places exact and thorough documentation."[12]

Here, as in all investigations of the 1820s and 1830s, detail was of the greatest importance as doctors like Moreau sought to understand society by breaking it down into its smallest components. These could then be counted and classified so that some preliminary conclusions could be drawn from the results. By reaching so deeply into previously hidden urban space, the investigations essentially mimicked the capricious disease itself, while creating a fresh way of seeing the Paris environment.

Such statistical investigations established the methodological and intellectual grounding for the bulletins du choléra. Not only did they suggest that urban space could and should be viewed medically, but they also provided a model for exploring that space by penetrating deeply into areas that had previously remained hidden from public view. Hygienists believed that the urban body could best be explored using a technique similar to that of a surgeon probing the human body. Officials could understand such complications as filth, poverty, and cholera through a kind of urban anatomy by seeing the city as the sum total of each of its component parts. Moreover, as hygienists collected ever-greater numbers of details about the Paris environment, quantifying them in specific categories became a way both of organizing the increasingly vast amounts of information and of creating a portrait of the capital grounded in statistics, that is, "facts." Facts in the form of *detail* thus took on both a new prominence and a changing definition because their power now came from numerical as opposed to narrative description.

Although not invented by the hygienists, the investigations of urban detail contributed much to legitimizing and popularizing a culture of statistics that had grown out of Enlightenment thought but had remained largely in the background until after the French Revolution. As industrialization and urbanization of the early nineteenth century compounded problems of rapid population growth, overcrowding, and urban social unrest, the issues of poverty, disease, and misery became realities that could no longer be ignored. The novelty and promise of statistical investigation thus became an attractive option for government. The epitome of this growing crisis, the arrival of cholera in the spring of 1832, invested the culture of statistics with increased power and social meaning. Nowhere did the scientific and popular appeal of figures become more apparent than in the presentation of the bulletins du choléra in the popular press in March and April 1832.

Numbers, Narratives, and the Early *Bulletins du Choléra*

"In the mornings people opened the newspaper with trembling hands," one Parisian recalled in his memoirs about the great 1832 cholera epidemic. "They weren't looking through them for political news anymore. . . . What they really wanted was the casualty figures."[13] Appearing prominently in most major newspapers, the bulletins du choléra had a significance all their own, one unmatched by any other official representation of the outbreak. Printed as tables, the figures stood in stark contrast to the rest of a densely printed newspaper page. In a very real sense, they represented the early nineteenth-century equivalent of a photograph for a population quite literally learning to see information in new ways.[14]

The bulletins du choléra served as a key link between the official investigations of Paris on the one hand and the largely upper- and middle-class readership of the popular press on the other. Not only did the daily mortality figures provide the public with a running account of the epidemic's progress, they also constituted some of the few concrete pieces of information available at a time when cholera remained an unsolved medical mystery. As miniature, daily versions of the earlier, more comprehensive statistical inquiries, the bulletins helped make the hygienists' ideas—faith in quantification, the desire for objectivity, and the need to present information publicly—a part of the popular imagination at a time when Parisians thirsted for any cholera news they could find at all.

In 1832 conditions seemed especially ripe for placing the daily bulletins at the center of government policy and public consciousness. The ideas of the hygienists helped propel statistical description to the forefront of scientific knowledge, while this enthusiasm for figures had greatly improved techniques for their collection and dissemination. As the first "modern plague," the 1832 cholera epidemic arrived at a time when the importance of the expanding press in shaping popular perceptions was becoming more evident.[15] Having come to power in 1830 by overthrowing the repressive Restoration government of Charles X, the new July Monarchy of King Louis Philippe presented itself as the essence of European liberalism, replete with freedom of the press and limited male suffrage. As literacy, circulation, and newspaper availability increased, and as the Parisian middle classes were brought more directly into the political process, the press became an increasingly valuable tool for promoting the image of an administration fully in control of the crisis. Thus the power of statistical description and particularly the bulletins du choléra resulted from the convergence of two previously distinct developments that had been forced together for the first time during the cholera outbreak. On the one hand, the hygienists had helped make medical knowledge a legitimate concern of government. On the other hand, the growing need to engage more Parisians—coupled with a redefinition of this public to encompass a greater segment of the population—had forged a new role for the press and its representation of the epidemic.

In order to understand the cultural significance of the bulletins, then, it is necessary to realize the hold the press was beginning to have upon the popular imagination, particularly during the cholera epidemic of 1832. After the initial excitement at the beginning of the 1832 epidemic, an entertainment daily printed a modern parable that demonstrated the central yet problematic place the press occupied for the public.[16] Entitled "A Correspondence," the article consisted of a fictitious exchange of letters between a writer and Cholera-morbus, "a man all in black and having an evil look." Cholera opened the exchange by informing the writer that he should be ready at high noon when the disease's servant would come for him. The intended victim casually wrote back that he would gladly oblige but that noon was too early because he had an important article to finish that day. Upon learning that the writer was in fact a journalist, Cholera gave him a reprieve, saying that had he known the writer's occupation, he would never have bothered "a person whom I cherish as much as he respects me." Cholera politely thanked the journalist for his help in claiming more victims and promised the writer somewhat perversely: "I'll never forget you as long as I live." After receiving such a warm letter, the journalist asked Cholera's permission to publish it, which the disease gladly granted, saying that he would "refuse nothing from kindly journalists." The article ends with the writer's suggestion that given the affection Cholera had for journalists, their occupation offered the best immunity against catching the disease.

Humorous and sarcastic, the epistolary exchange revealed an ambivalent attitude toward the press and its prominent role in conveying information through the printed word. In fact, publishing the story at all suggested the popular paper's own fundamental confusion about what role it should play in educating the public about the dangers of the press. On the one hand, the cooperative, almost conspiratorial, relationship between Cholera and the journalist made clear a certain animosity and resentment in this attack against the glib mainstream press. The fear inspired by sensationalist newspaper articles, the piece suggested, constituted a danger as formidable as the epidemic itself. Because current medical wisdom held that fear predisposed one to catching the disease, it lent a certain legitimacy to the modern parable's implicit argument that the press spread cholera by spreading news of it. On the other hand, the content of the correspondence as well as its inclusion in the paper clearly demonstrated the power of the press, a power that might just as easily be used to confront the epidemic. If journalists took their responsibilities seriously, they wielded influence that could help fight the fear that had given the disease free rein.

The ambivalence about the power of newspapers emerged even more clearly as various papers debated whether to print mortality figures at all. Papers appeared uncertain of what the bulletins meant for presenting the epidemic's "reality." *Le Corsaire*, an entertainment daily that often poked fun at the government, observed that the "sad lists of mortality don't diminish the scourge, they only serve to heighten fears," and consequently never published them [17] The Saint-Simonian newspaper, *Le Globe*, hesitated to present the bulletins, explaining, "Not everyone is strong enough to endure this daily enumeration of pain and suffering that strikes their neighbors."[18] One haughty theater tabloid ridiculed the obsession with statistics in general, condemning publications that competed for readers by offering "the prettiest, the longest, the most complete lists of the dead and dying."[19] This paper, like others that refused to print the figures, was apparently convinced that the information would only serve to frighten the public.

More often, however, papers took up the cry for "rigorous exactitude," accusing the government of willfully misleading Parisians with grossly reduced figures. *Le National*, a left-wing daily fervently opposed to government policy, automatically assumed that published mortality figures were only half the real number.[20] Another popular newspaper went so far as to express concern that Paris did not have "a central place where papers could obtain information [that was] rigorously exact."[21] *Le Bonhomme Richard* waited a couple of weeks into the epidemic before passing judgment, announcing that the civil register contained a much larger number of cholera deaths than did the *Moniteur*, a commonly held assumption.[22]

The avid quest for "Truth" must be viewed in terms of how difficult it was to secure and report information about deaths. Although post-Napoleonic France was renowned for its highly centralized bureaucratic apparatus, the cumbersome system was by no means prepared to collect and record the avalanche of information that would inevitably accompany a cholera epidemic. Even in normal times the act of reporting a death constituted a major bureaucratic chore. To record a death in the city of Paris and thus ensure that it would be counted with the mortality figures, one needed a doctor's confirmation, a witness to certify it, a member of the mayor's office to collect the announcement, and a notary to register it.[23] On the average it took approximately three days after a death for the information to make its way into the pages of daily newspapers. The daily bulletins required an efficient, uniform, and coordinated strategy among neighborhood hospitals, first-aid stations, and reports of house calls. The quality and quantity of information varied considerably among arrondissements and among individual medical posts, especially during the busiest periods of the epidemic.[24]

Although the complexity of reporting a death made it seem a nearly impossible task, the press campaigned aggressively to present "the truth" to readers. Accuracy or "exactitude" was of the utmost importance, for medical and administrative purposes and for presenting the epidemic to the public at large. "Our readers are grateful to us for telling them the entire truth, regardless of how sad this truth [is]," the *Journal des débats* boasted during its earliest coverage of the epidemic. "Better to know [the truth] such as it is than to allow the public to be misled by the thousands of exaggerated stories that circulate about this fatal event."[25] In writing of the early mortality figures, one popular newspaper warned its readers: "This information is exact; but we are far from presenting it as the complete portrait [*tableau complet*] of cholera cases observed during the day." Citing the fact that "no regular service [for collecting data] has yet been established," the editors pointed out that "many observations have gone ignored, just as many that have been given lack authenticity." For the following day the paper promised a table that would provide the most up-to-date information on the epidemic.[26] Even the *Moniteur* apologized to its readers for failing to include figures it had yet to receive from the suburbs.[27]

At some fundamental level the papers believed—and wanted their readers to believe—that "rigorous exactitude" would reveal the "truth." In 1832 the epidemic "truth" constituted a reality that was within humans' capacity to record, if not to understand. Accordingly, it had to be discovered and could be presented to the public in the concrete manifestation of the bulletins du choléra, at a time when no one really understood the disease. By picking up a daily paper such as the *Moniteur* or the *Journal des débats*, one could potentially come close to touching "truth" both figuratively and literally, because ideally the paper contained the known facts that would illuminate this truth.

Because "truth" conveyed through daily statistics had rarely been an ongoing part of public discourse, officials did not initially grasp how to appropriate the bulletins' social and political power in 1832. Relying largely on trial and error, authorities unknowingly experimented with how best to present and use the bulletins. On 31 March, for example, the official government organ, the *Moniteur universel*, published the first bulletin du choléra, which listed reported cases as well as actual deaths. In keeping with the government's naive desire to present everything known about the epidemic, the bulletin also contained the names, occupations, and addresses of the victims. [See illustration 5.1.]

Although the *Moniteur* printed the data as the most current information about the epidemic, the public did not always read it that way. The early exposés immediately caused a public outcry; because cholera struck the poor

928

PARTIE NON OFFICIELLE.

INTÉRIEUR.

Paris, le 30 mars.

IIe BULLETIN SANITAIRE DE LA VILLE DE PARIS.
État des personnes atteintes du Choléra depuis le 22 mars jusqu'au 30 à minuit.

5.1 The initial *bulletins du choléra* consisted of the names, occupations, and addresses of cholera victims. *Moniteur universel*, 31 March 1832.

neighborhoods of the capital with the greatest intensity at the beginning, names from the lower classes dominated the lists. Using recognizable imagery in the form of street names, arrondissement numbers, lists of occupations, and even family names, the initial cholera statistics seemed to present the disease and its victims as problems that could be kept at a comfortable psychological distance from the bourgeoisie by linking them to the alien world of the poor. The opposition press implicitly questioned the administration's objectivity when it lambasted the government's insensitivity and prejudice against the poor.[28] Writing some years later, the socialist Louis Blanc claimed that printing the names had been a deliberate policy of class hegemony "either to dissipate the fears of the fortunate or to flatter their pride."[29]

It is doubtful that such rosters reassured the upper classes the way members of the opposition suggested. Readers of the *Moniteur*, who were in general among the wealthier Parisians, immediately voiced their strong disapproval. After only three days, complaints to authorities and editors forced the paper to replace the names and occupations of victims with simple summary statistics. "The identity of a few names gave rise to terrible misunderstandings, causing considerable discomfort for families living in the suburbs," the *Moniteur* explained to readers on the day the paper shifted to using figures alone.[30] The public outcry against the lists demonstrates the extent to which both the disease and the information were already invested with a vast social and cultural meaning. In effect, the black ink of the modern press had replaced the ancient tradition of marking the houses of plague victims with a large white "X."

At the same time that the daily figures promised a kind of anonymity and objectivity, they in fact helped readers and government officials to discover the subjectivity of numbers, as revealed by the changing formats of the bulletins. Although the administration stopped disclosing details about individual victims, the prefect of the Seine still provided daily mortality figures that appeared in most newspapers until late August. Interestingly, it took the press several attempts to settle upon a more palatable form for presenting the data to readers. On 2 April, for example, the *Moniteur* opted for detail. It printed two tables, one for deaths and one for new cases, each table broken down by arrondissement, sex, members of the military, and cases in the suburbs. The day's totals and the cumulative total for the epidemic punctuated each daily report. Soon after, a new category appeared, separating out "homeless persons," a distinction that could be either reassuring for the comfortably-housed readership of the popular press (because it linked cholera safely with "the other") or frightening to these readers (because it made the threat of wanderers more visible). [See illustration 5.2.]

When the hysteria surrounding the cholera outbreak reached a climax around 5 April, the mortality figures occupied an even more important yet complex place in telling the epidemic story. The bulletins reported a dramatic rise in deaths, with nearly eight hundred victims a day in the first week of April.[31] It is particularly interesting that papers had to present the figures against the backdrop of frightening urban social unrest prompted by rumors that cholera was really a government assassination plot designed to rid the city of its unwanted poor. In this context of chaos, the *Moniteur* experimented with highly stylized tables that used figures divided by thick ink lines, a format more commonly found in the hygienists' published investigations than in a daily newspaper. [See illustration 5.3.] Linked to the credibility of the hygienists, the stylized tables suggested legitimacy and accuracy that might give added veracity to the numbers contained in them. As the epidemic began to stabilize, the bulletins became simpler and more stylized, stressing new kinds of information. After the initial flush of enthusiasm for figures in the wake of deaths that climbed into the hundreds per day, the information now conveyed only the most basic points while no longer attempting to impress the public with sheer detail. A regular, repeated, familiar format appeared to comply with expectations officials had created when making the information available in the first place. Every couple of weeks the paper printed elaborate summaries of the data it had acquired about cumulative mortality figures. [See illustration 5.4.][32] The epidemic and the bulletins' narration of it had become almost routine, yet not routine enough for the daily figures to be eliminated completely.

Once the bulletins had become a part of daily life, spoofs of the information appeared in the popular press, a further indication of the hold that the culture of statistics had on the public imagination. *Le Corsaire* printed parodies of the bulletins du choléra on several occasions. In the first instance the paper compared cholera mortality with figures from the Revolution of 1830 as well as with numbers of what it called "unexpected mortality" from the insurrection of 5 and 6 June 1832.[33] Six days later the parody was more explicit, this time offering information on criminal cases. [See illustration

5.2 Typical bulletin from the first week of the first epidemic. *Moniteur universel,* 3 April 1832.

Bulletin officiel du 1er avril quatre heures du soir,
au 2 avril quatre heures du soir.

NOMBRE DES PERSONNES ATTEINTES.

1er arrondt.	4 hommes	3 femmes.
2e. ——	2	1
3e. ——	1	1
4e. ——	5	7
5e. ——	3	4
6e. ——	12	8
7e. ——	18	14
8e. ——	13	9
9e. ——	13	11
10e. ——	22	9
11e. ——	19	5
12 . ——	21	12
Militaires..........	6	»
Personnes sans asile.	19	10

Total de la journée.. 158   94   252
Total des jours précédens..................... 483

Total général............... 735

DÉCÈS.

1er arrondt.	4 hommes	» femmes.
2e. ——	2	»
3e. ——	1	»
4e. ——	3	2
5e. ——	2	1
6e. ——	8	3
7e. ——	8	6
8e. ——	4	2
9e. ——	8	5
10e. ——	12	4
11e. ——	3	2
12e. ——	3	4
Militaires	2	»
Personnes sans asile.	9	2
Banlieue.........	»	» 4
Militaires	»	» 2

Total de la journée.. 69   31   100
Total des jours précédens 167

Total général............... 267

Etat numérique des personnes atteintes et de celles mortes du choléra depuis le 5 à midi jusqu'au 6 à la même heure.

Nouveaux cas à Paris et dans la banlieue.		Décès à Paris et dans la banlieue.	
Hommes.	Femmes.	Hommes.	Femmes.
335	174	165	77

Total.	509	Total.	242
Tot. des jours précédens.	1851	Tot. des j. précéd.	670
Tot. général.	2360	Tot. génér.	912

(Nº 2.)

PRÉFECTURE DU DÉPARTEMENT DE LA SEINE.

Etat des sommes versées à la Caisse municipale le 6 avril 1832, pour venir au secours des individus atteints ou en danger d'être atteints par le choléra-morbus.

MM.	fr.	c.
Flayol, avocat, au nom et comme trésorier de la conférence du droit public du Prado	200	
Raymond	100	
Mᵉ Vaulchier	60	
Cadet Dubreuil	50	
L'ambassadeur d'Espagne	1,000	
De Montcarville, directeur-caissier du *Journal des Débats*	10,000	
Marbeau, caissier des Invalides de la marine	200	
Richard, trésorier, au nom des officiers, sous-officiers et gardes de la garde municipale	1,063	40
Paixhans, colonel d'artillerie	60	
Le comte de Carvoisin	500	
Le trésorier de la préfecture de police	6,600	
Le lieutenant-colonel Boyer, aide-de-camp du Roi	50	
Le comte France d'Houdelot, colonel *idem*.	50	
Les agréés du tribunal de commerce	300	
Gramaire	50	
Chaumette Desfossés	100	
La Banque de France	12,000	
La 7ᵉ mairie	3,013	25
Le général-commandant, les officiers et sous-officiers, les professeurs et employés de l'Ecole d'état-major	374	50
La 3ᵉ mairie	10,489	35
Lorin, au nom et comme trésorier de la Cᵉ des commissaires-priseurs	1,000	
La 2ᵉ mairie	1,745	
J. A. G. Eynard de Genève	500	
Brière Valigny, président de chambre à la cour royale	100	
La 5ᵉ mairie	2,700	
L'ambassadeur de Bavière	500	
L'ambassadeur de Suède et de Norwège	500	
Dubois d'Angers, député	100	
Total	53,405	50
Souscriptions des jours précédens	243,657	85
Total général	297,063	35

5.5.] "It is assured that the newspapers on sale are about to have daily bulletins of trial judgments," the paper joked. "These will be calculated like those for cholera." A model followed, which included categories such as numbers of judgments, lengths of sentences, and condemnations. Like the bulletins, the parody provided figures for that day and the one before, as well as numbers from the previous year. Just in case the comparison proved too subtle, the mock bulletin closed with an observation that condemned government intervention, likening prison terms to the cholera measures that brought the government into every aspect of daily life. "One will be considered on the road to recovery [only] when one is under police surveillance," the paper proclaimed.[34] Such mockery demonstrates the extent to which disease and social unrest were fused in the minds of contemporaries, while showing how deeply the mortality figures had permeated popular consciousness. The spoofs could work only if the majority of readers had internalized the cultural import of the bulletins du choléra, for no cultural code can be consciously manipulated or broken without a widespread understanding of the rules that shape it.

The enthusiasm for figures permeated other aspects of the ongoing epidemic "story" in the press as well. Charity donations on behalf of cholera patients quickly assumed center stage, relying on a format strikingly similar to that of the earliest daily mortality tables. [See illustration 5.3.] The *Moniteur* published the names of donors with the figures for their financial contributions and sometimes included their addresses and occupations. The paper also printed daily and cumulative totals of donations just as it had initially given such totals for cholera cases. It was almost as if the administration had set up the charitable lists to represent a rival "epidemic" that could somehow battle the pessimism inspired by the rising mortality figures for cholera.

Sensing the potential of the information presented in the bulletins du choléra, authorities sought other ways of achieving a measured balance between enlightening and alarming the public. Frequently the *Moniteur* tried to dilute unpleasant statistical realities with what one contemporary described as "reassuring formulas, altered with remarkable talent, genuine language of

5.3 As the bulletins became more a part of daily life in 1832, they settled into a regular, predictable format using the solid lines of established statistical reports. Note here that the figures are directly juxtaposed with those for charitable contributions. *Moniteur universel,* 7 April 1832.

BULLETIN OFFICEL SANITAIRE DE PARIS.

Décès dans les hopitaux, hospices, etc.... 29
A domicile........................... 18

Total........ 47
Augmentation sur le chiffre d'hier...... 10
Il est à remarquer que sur cette augmentation de dix décès, huit proviennent de l'hospice de la Vieillesse (hommes), à Bicêtre.
Décès par suite de maladies autres que le choléra................................. 37
Malades admis dans les hopitaux, hospices, etc............................. 59
Sortis guéris dans la journée.......... 74
Augmentation sur le chiffre de la veille... 21
Lits vacans........................... 2,372

Souscription en faveur des orphelins. 25 f. 00c.
Versemens antérieurs........... 20,612 05

Total general.... 20,637 05

Résumé du mouvement des hopitaux et hospices civils de Paris dans la journée du 10 mai.
CHOLÉRIQUES.

NOMS des HOPITAUX ET HOSPICES.	INDIVIDUS EXISTANS le matin.	MALADES ADMIS pendant le jour.	SORTIS après guérison.	DÉCÉDÉS.	LITS DISPONIBLES.
HOPITAUX.					
Hôtel-Dieu	181	15	16	4	330
Notre-Dame-de-Pitié	97	3	1	»	101
Beaujou	64	2	1	1	48
Charité	94	1	7	1	100
Saint-Antoine	83	6	9	2	58
Necker	38	2	2	1	1
Cochin	11	»	1	»	102
Saint-Louis	201	8	12	7	509
Vénériens	5	»	1	»	156
Enfans-Malades	11	»	1	1	132
Accouchement	»	»	»	»	»
Maison royale de santé	13	8	2	»	»
Enfans Trouvés	»	»	»	»	»
Bons-Hommes	12	»	3	»	296
Réserve	120	2	9	1	674
Lazaristes	24	»	2	»	27
Clichy	53	4	»	»	3
Saint Sulpice	48	»	1	»	35
HOSPICES.					
Vieillesse (hommes)	64	4	1	8	»
Vieillesse (femmes)	60	2	1	3	»
Incurables (hommes)	5	»	»	»	»
Incurables (femmes)	11	2	3	»	»
Ménages	3	»	1	»	»
Totaux	1198	59	74	29	2372

BULLETIN SANITAIRE DES DÉPARTEMENS.

AISNE. — *Laon*, 10 mai.

Arrondissement.	Communes.	Malades.	Décès.
Saint-Quentin	9	42	15
Vervins	4	84	43
Laon	20	339	118
Soissons	18	249	124
Château-Thierry	12	102	57
Total depuis l'invasion.	63	816	357
Augmentation sur le chiffre d'hier	3	70	22

AUBE. *Troyes*, 10 mai.
Arrondissement de Troyes. — 64 nouveaux cas se sont manifestés dans la ville de Troyes : 24 personnes ont succombé.
Arrondissement de Nogent. — Quatre nouveaux cas et un décès ont été constatés.

CORRÈZE. — *Ussel*, 7 mai.
Un cas de choléra vient de se manifester dans la commune de Combronal, canton de Meynac. L'individu a succombé dans quelques heures.

EURE. — *Evreux*, 10 mai.
Arrondissement de Louviers.—Nouveaux cas.... 7 / Nouveaux décès.. 3

INDRE-ET-LOIRE. *Tours*, le 10 mai.
Une dépêche télégraphique annonce que ce jour il y a eu 4 nouveaux cas de choléra.
Total depuis l'apparition de la maladie, 37 malades, 22 décès, 8 guérisons.

LOIRET. *Orléans*, 10 mai.
Arrondissement d'Orléans. — Orléans : 25 cas nouveaux, 8 décès. Quatre communes dont déjà été atteintes dans cet arrondissement, qui compte, depuis l'invasion de la maladie, 228 cholériques, 96 décès.
Arrondissement de Montargis. — 3 nouveaux cas et 2 décès sont signalés dans la ville de Montargis. Dans l'arrondissement, on compte, depuis l'invasion de l'épidémie, trois communes atteintes ; 48 cholériques, 30 décès.

MARNE. *Reims*, 10 mai.
Sept nouveaux cas et cinq décès sont annoncés dans la ville de Reims. Ainsi, depuis l'invasion, 82 personnes ont été atteintes, 30 ont succombé.
Un cas du choléra s'est manifesté dans la commune de Cormontreil.

HAUTE MARNE. *Chaumont*, 9 mai.
Deux cas viennent de se manifester à Saint-Dizier.

MEUSE. *Bar-le-Duc*, 9 mai.

Arrondissemens.	Malades.	Morts.
Bar-le-Duc	422	146
Commercy	97	36
Verdun	47	22
Montmédy	»	1
Total depuis l'invasion..	566	205

Augmentation sur le bulletin d'hier, 52 malades, 20 décès.

5.4 Summary bulletin of the type that appeared in the *Moniteur* approximately every two weeks. As the epidemic moved from the capital to the provinces, the paper presented more detailed information from other departments. *Moniteur universel*, 12 May 1832.

— On assure que les journaux vendus vont nous donner
un bulletin journalier des condamnations des tribunaux exceptionnels. Ce bulletin sera calqué sur celui du choléra.

MODÈLE.

Les condamnations par tribunaux exceptionnels se sont
élevés à. 00
Idem par les tribunaux ordinaires. 00

Total. 00
Augmentation ou diminution sur le chiffre de la
veille. 00
—Prévenus admis dans les prisons. 00
Sortis des prisons pour être jugés. 00
Arrêtés pour d'autres crimes que ceux dévolus au
tribunal militaire. 00
Chiffre correspondant de l'année dernière. . . 00
Par la même raison on distinguera les condamnations en
deux classes : la fusillade et l'échafaud seront réputés jugemens *spasmodiques*, et l'exil et la prison à temps, jugemens
sporadiques. On sera déclaré en convalescence quand on sera
sous la surveillance de la police.

5.5 Spoofs of the bulletins appeared later in the 1832 epidemic, an indication that
the daily figures had become an important part of the popular imagination. *Le
Corsaire*, 22 June 1832.

nourishment for lulling the screaming baby to sleep." If mortality increased,
he explained, "it was a good sign, the epidemic would not last. If the number
decreased, it meant that the troubles were coming to an end. If [the number of
deaths] picked up again, it was a last effort before the calm."[35] This double
narrative sometimes resulted in an absurd discrepancy between rising mortality figures and the soothing mood of optimism that the paper sought to
promote in the prose. On 10 April, for example, the *Moniteur*'s front-page
sanitary bulletin joyfully proclaimed that doctors were "almost unanimous
[in supporting] the fact of the very noticeable decrease in the power of the
disease." The accompanying mortality figures offered a blatant contradiction, however, since they faithfully recorded the previous day's total deaths at
861—the highest number for the entire epidemic.[36]

Such an awkward compromise between numbers and narrative makes it clear that in 1832 contemporaries had not yet fully comprehended the meaning implicit in the daily information. On the one hand, officials seemed almost naively committed to furthering hygienist ideals by objectively presenting an epidemic "truth" based on observation and quantifiable knowledge. As the culture of statistics would have it, describing the disease in numerical terms made it seem less baffling, because once quantified it could somehow be conquered. Part of the bulletins' great appeal lay in their apparent innocence, their closeness to a possible truth so lauded by the hygienists, the respected thinkers of the day. Thus, by printing everything it knew about the epidemic, the government hoped to heighten its credibility.

On the other hand, the addition of a paragraph to offer a subjective interpretation of this "truth" suggested that both the administration and the press were arriving at a new understanding of their own positions in the nexus between power and knowledge. As officials and journalists experimented with how to use the bulletins du choléra in 1832, the figures seem to have lost their original allure of offering a neutral, objective language. The experiments also introduced a new balance between a traditional narrative description that used words as facts and a seemingly neutral rhetoric of statistics that used numbers. The apparent impartiality and objectivity of numbers helped redefine the meaning of both "detail" and "fact." By controlling the collection and presentation of mortality figures while redefining the use and meaning of this information, officials could create the image of both the epidemic and their prefectures' attempts to fight it. In other words, not only did officials try to use their information about the outbreak to maintain control over it and the anxious population, but they also redefined what that information was. Knowledge—and particularly its dissemination—became power.

The bulletins du choléra in 1832 reflected much more than a daily rise and fall of mortality; they symbolized a new kind of scientific knowledge that would ultimately contribute to a new strategy of government. The quest for detailed information required that officials penetrate more deeply into urban space than had ever been the case before. In 1832, however, officials had not worked out the methods for gathering and distributing data, nor had they fully comprehended the potential power of the information itself. The popular press shared much of this ambivalence, hence the mixed, often contradictory responses to the bulletins. Clearly, responses to the new statistical description indicated that a fundamental change was taking place in how officials presented statistics and what the public expected from them.

Medicine—through the imprint of the hygienists and their interpretation of the cholera crisis—was becoming a key element in defining how the state understood and used power. These ideas would seep so deeply into the bedrock of society and culture that they would shape public expectations of government when a second cholera epidemic arrived seventeen years later.

From "Rigorous Exactitude" to the "Production of Truth"

E. A. Duchesne, a doctor in the eleventh arrondissement, began his statistical history of the 1849 epidemic with a disclaimer. "I hesitated," he confessed, "I even slowed down my work in the face of the countless difficulties that I came across in my research and in my attempts at verification." He could only bring himself to go on "with renewed ardor," he explained, "by keeping in mind that someone could profit from the comparisons [with 1832]."[37] Duchesne's frank admissions did not represent either false modesty or self-deprecation, for by 1849 traces of humility could be found in other works of statistical description as well. Introducing his report about the second epidemic in the fifth arrondissement, Dr. François Marc Moreau explained that his study was "nothing but simple statistical research, no doubt quite incomplete . . . that I give over to [other] doctors and administrators."[38] Compelled by their desire to solve the mystery of cholera, both doctors also understood their humbled relationship to numbers as "facts" in a way that no writer seventeen years earlier ever had.

Like the admissions of Duchesne and Moreau about their investigations, discussions and presentations of the bulletins du choléra in 1849 suggested a more sober awareness regarding the power of numbers. Along with advertisements promising a wide variety of cholera cures, sporadic mortality figures were often the only real sign that an epidemic had in fact reached the capital in 1849. Newspapers that had once printed lengthy editorials, lists of health instructions, and lofty claims about the accuracy of their figures now published the bulletins infrequently and usually without comment. Often, especially in the early weeks of the epidemic, papers used a narrative format—rather than tables—to represent statistical information.[39]

By 1849, then, officials seemed less inclined to promote the bulletins as symbols of science, progress, and public order. Fearing that the opposite could be true, that news of cholera might reignite the smoldering embers of the June Days of 1848, authorities of the young, increasingly defensive Second Republic decided early in the epidemic to downplay its severity by limiting coverage in the press. Such an approach was only one instance of the government's hostility to the press in the context of a climate hostile to the press generally; since Louis Napoleon Bonaparte's overwhelming electoral victory late in 1848, the republican government had banned various opposition newspapers.[40] This restrictive environment meant that the new daily figures now contained an even more profound social and cultural meaning than their predecessors, especially since health officials' highly publicized quest for "rigorous exactitude" had already created a certain expectation that the government would provide the public with regular statistical information in 1832. Thus while statistical information continued to play an important role in determining how medical officials fought cholera, in 1849 the data occupied a more problematic place in the cultural imagination.

The relative silence of the Parisian press was perhaps the most striking feature of the 1849 outbreak. Three days after the declaration of an epidemic in mid-March, the *Moniteur* first mentioned cholera in a small news item buried in the back pages. Beginning with a brief statement describing a few victims who had died in civil hospitals, the article was accompanied by a small table of mortality figures that lacked the detail of the information published in 1832.[41] Although cholera continued to claim victims in the capital throughout April and May, the *Moniteur* limited its reports on the subject to a short column entitled "Cholera News." Appearing approximately every three or four days, the feature often contained mortality figures without explanation or comment. On the rare occasions when tables replaced the numbers printed in the text, they had a simpler format than their counterparts in 1832, with fewer comparisons and statistical breakdowns by location, sex, or age. This was also true of nongovernment organs. *Le Courrier français*, a popular paper that had filled its pages with news of cholera in 1832, relegated much of its coverage of the epidemic to the "faits divers" section in the back pages. Nestled among accounts of bizarre murders, sensational robberies, and stories of people who set fire to themselves or others, the information about cholera had clearly lost its privileged place.[42] Other papers such as *Le National*, the *Journal des débats*, and *Le Constitutionnel* followed a similar policy of only occasionally reprinting figures verbatim from medical journals. Only when the number of deaths began to rise noticeably in early June did the figures enjoy any prominent attention in the papers. [See illustration 5.6.] But even so, it seemed clear

MINISTÈRE DE L'AGRICULTURE ET DU COMMERCE.

BULLETIN DU CHOLÉRA.

Paris. — Journée du 10 juin 1849.

Décès à domicile..........................	477
Décès dans les hôpitaux et hospices civils........	163
Décès dans les hôpitaux militaires.............	32
Total....	**672**

Mouvement des hôpitaux et hospices civils.

Existant le matin.........................	1,705
Admis pendant la journée...................	335
Total...................	**2,040**
Sortis................................ 47 ⎱	210
Décédés........................... 163 ⎰	
Restant le soir............................	1,830

Mouvement des hôpitaux militaires.

Existant le matin.........................	485
Admis pendant la journee...................	88
Total.................	**573**
Sortis. .... 36 ⎱	68
Décédés.......................... 32 ⎰	
Restant le soir...........................	505

Le chiffre des décès à domicile signales pour la journée du 11 juin s'élève à 211, mais toutes les déclarations n'étaient pas encore connues.

Dans les hôpitaux le chiffre des décès est de 181.

5.6 Only at the height of the second cholera epidemic did the bulletins even begin to approach the detail and prominence of the first outbreak. This table appeared on 13 June 1849, the date that recorded the highest number of deaths for the epidemic.

that the administration no longer relied on statistics to perpetuate its image of being in control.

Significantly, it was the medical press that protested this silence most vociferously. Medical journals had largely been spared the wrath of government censorship policies, while finding themselves forced to defend their position vis-à-vis the administration. On 13 March, when it became obvious that cholera had claimed several victims in the northern suburb of St.-Denis and would soon reach the capital, the most prominent medical journal at the time, the *Union médicale*, noted, "For more than eight days this sad fact has been known, and no official communication has yet been addressed to the Academies [of Science and Medicine] nor [has any information appeared in] professional journals. We can do nothing but criticize this silence."[43] By mid-May, after more than three thousand Parisians with cholera symptoms had entered hospitals, the editors attacked the Academy of Medicine for remaining silent, demanding, "What has it got to hide?"[44] At about the same time, the *Gazette médicale de Paris* lamented the fact that its "colleagues of the press" had failed to register a united complaint about the silence from the administration and the Academy of Medicine.[45] Shortly after the epidemic had peaked toward the end of June, the *Gazette des hôpitaux* joined other medical journals in issuing a plea urging the government to keep statistics as accurately as possible.[46]

Individual doctors argued for publishing statistics on both pragmatic and moral grounds. Many of them, such as the editors of the *Union médicale*, believed that regular information would quell what they considered to be the exaggerated fears of Parisians. Condemning the administration, the respected medical journal announced that "this hesitancy [to provide information] is vexing, it produces precisely the misfortune that it wants to avoid."[47] Editors of the *Gazette des hôpitaux* saw the problem in terms of the government's need to maintain a certain public image. "What kind of confidence can the people have in the administration that is charged with giving them assistance," the editors wondered, "when they see this administration hiding the truth to achieve a goal that they cannot always understand?"[48] Perhaps Paul Caffe, director of a clinic at the Hôtel Dieu and a veteran of the first epidemic, understood the government's role in the culture of statistics most clearly of all. Arguing that continuous and clearly presented mortality figures had spared London considerable panic in 1832 (and conveniently forgetting the social unrest in Paris at that time), he noted that "officially produced truth is the only way of responding to exaggerations in every sense: far from causing panic, truth always calms, [it] reassures the frightened and destroys calculations that are sometimes knowingly false."[49]

Caffe's observation was both to the point and uncannily modern. Like his contemporaries, he feared the consequences of withholding information. But he also clearly saw "truth" where others saw Truth, while understanding the government's active role in *producing* it through statistical description. This idea of "producing truth" marked an important contrast with the quest for objectivity and rigorous exactitude that had preoccupied officials during the first epidemic. In 1849 the administration seemed much more self-aware; not only did officials realize the power implicit in the bulletins, but they were also more savvy about just how this information could be both created and presented. The administration's comprehension of statistics had subtly shifted from merely rendering truth to producing it.

To be sure, since 1832 the meaning of the figures had changed in such a way that many contemporaries now considered it the administration's *duty* to publish them and the public's *right* to read them. "Publicizing statistics is an obligation that the municipal administration must religiously perform at very frequent intervals," wrote Caffe in a remarkably articulate and candid appraisal of the problem. "Everyone has the right to be informed of what is taking place in the city, above all at the moment when each one plays his part in the public interest [la chose publique]."[50] Officials, it seemed, had violated a contract that they had unknowingly agreed to when they had first promised the most detailed and up-to-date figures about cholera in 1832.

The medical press attempted to make up for the official silence with its own statistics to rival the rigor of those presented during the first outbreak, sometimes using the identical vocabulary of the political papers in 1832. On 17 March, the day before officials declared the second epidemic, for example, the *Gazette médicale de Paris* promised its readers "a recapitulation as detailed as possible." The editors' main goal was to "furnish facts sufficient in number and detail for science and medicine, enabling a rigorous comparison between the current epidemic and that of 1832." Accordingly, the paper listed detailed points that it hoped to publish concerning as many patients as possible.[51] The *Gazette médicale* kept its promise and carried numerous case studies, but in general the political press did not reprint this information as it had in 1832.

By 1849, standards of rigorous exactitude no longer dominated the presentation of statistical description. Not only was less information available for the public, but papers also did not always print the most detailed or accurate figures. Having no common source, the political papers' casualty reports varied widely between understatement and gross exaggeration. The *Union médicale*, for example, accused the *Moniteur* of publishing a figure that was "far below" its own.[52] The popular *Journal du peuple*, meanwhile, offered figures that differed markedly from other papers, perhaps due in part to frequent mistakes in addition.[53]

The distortions of the opposition press, which was more prone to gross exaggeration, finally prompted government officials to address the problem of statistics directly. On 8 June, with the number of cases rising steadily, all major newspapers carried a statement from the administration:

> In the interest of public calm, we will not hesitate to publish figures that are probably considerable but that are far from being as terrifying as those spread everywhere by fear and exaggeration. People have gone as far as to say that 1200 persons have died in the city the day of June 5. We can affirm that nothing is more false: they have more than doubled the true number.[54]

The official statement represented much more than a simple desire to maintain "public calm," for ultimately it symbolized a fundamental change in the meaning of statistics for both the government and the population of the capital. Whereas in 1832 the administration had to convince the public of both the validity and the importance of the bulletins du choléra, by 1849 the government's role in collecting and presenting the data had gained acceptance to the point that it had become a *duty* to provide them. Failing to offer information might result in dire consequences, ranging from an uncontrolled epidemic to social unrest. In other words, the lack of statistical information during the second epidemic did not reflect a decline in such data's social or political potency; rather the absence of bulletins and the responses to this absence indicated that the figures were now potent for different reasons. By successfully promoting mortality figures as symbols of science and knowledge in 1832, officials had created a new set of expectations and, ultimately, a new social meaning for the mortality figures. No longer the discourse of distant experts, the numbers became central to telling the daily story to the average citizens of Paris.

The significance of mortality figures had also changed for the administration by the time of the second outbreak. Whereas in 1832 the bulletins had suggested a world of enlightened progress through quantitative reasoning, by 1849 they had come to represent negative omens of civil disorder. Just a year before the outbreak of cholera, revolution had rocked the capital, leaving behind a new regime and a bloody reminder of lower-class discontent. An ongoing revolutionary tradition suggested that the arrival of cholera could be enough to provoke more unrest. Still not fully cognizant of the bulletins' power, however, officials continued to grapple with how best to use them in 1849. Fearful of unrest and perhaps less convinced that numbers for numbers' sake held the golden key to explaining the epidemic "truth," they experimented by downplaying mortality in the press, a move that brought strong condemnation from the medical community and public. Perhaps by the time the next epidemic hit the capital in 1854–1855, an important lesson about the culture of statistics had been learned, for officials imposed complete censorship, and no figures appeared at all.

Knowledge, Power, Culture, and the French Revolutionary Tradition

Behind the daily rise and fall of mortality depicted in the bulletins du choléra lies a much bigger story, one involving a complex interplay among knowledge, power, and culture. As a formidable attempt to impose order on chaos, the daily bulletins represented medical knowledge that would ultimately contribute to a new strategy of government. Even if hampered by logistical difficulties and inconsistencies, the information provided a daily look at the capital and its inhabitants and also established a methodology for acquiring this new knowledge. When officials both knowingly and unknowingly experimented with how to present and use the bulletins, then, they were in fact discovering a new kind of power. But the constant experimentation with the daily figures and the mixed public reactions to them indicates that no one fully understood the potential power of statistical information. No single actor exercised power consciously and unrelentingly. Rather, as the debates surrounding the bulletins reveal, knowledge and power were molded and used within a unique cultural milieu that rested on a complex and often subtle interplay among government, medicine, the popular press, and urban social relations in 1832 and 1849. In their quest for detail and "rigorous exactitude," the hygienists had redefined the meaning and use of *fact* itself. In the bulletins, emphasis shifted from a narrative depiction of "truth" to a numerical one.

The differing official and popular responses to the bulletins du choléra in

1832 and 1849 demonstrates, moreover, a growing awareness of the power of numbers in shaping impressions of cholera, Paris, and its inhabitants. The hygienists' use of statistical description served as the key link between medicine and the state in the 1830s and 1840s. By introducing quantification as a compelling new means for exploring the capital's social and economic problems epitomized by the first cholera epidemic, the hygienists opened the way for making medicine a legitimate and necessary concern of government. Representing a new form of knowledge that connected medical investigations of the urban environment with government policy, the bulletins offered a new means of observing and controlling the potentially revolutionary population of Paris. The need for detail, penetration into urban space, and careful reporting of everything investigators saw provided a vast new base for social inquiry in which it seemed that objectivity itself could be harnessed for political ends.

Because the French revolutionary tradition played such an important part in these struggles for cultural authority, I end this essay with some brief thoughts on its central, if admittedly contradictory, influences. On the one hand, events in 1789, 1830, and 1848 established a precedent for broader public participation that gave a larger segment of the Paris population a role in shaping political culture. Here the press assumed considerable importance as the primary mode of communication between the government and the citizens. Within this context, data such as the bulletins du choléra became a valuable forum for presenting a certain image of official competence, at the same time that the presentation of the daily figures furthered expectations that the government had an obligation to keep the public informed. On the other hand, the revolutionary tradition and the seemingly predictable regularity with which Parisians took to the streets to topple regimes revealed the need to manage the kind of information to be placed at the disposal of the general public. Numbers for numbers' sake was no longer enough; statistical data had to be presented in such a way that it would not lead to the unpleasant consequence of further revolt. Combined with factors such as the rapid population growth of Paris in the early nineteenth century and Enlightenment ideas about human potential, objectivity, and rationality, the revolutionary tradition helped forge a new role for government and a changing conception of the population that the government saw itself as serving. Together, these forces helped define and popularize a culture of statistics that would extend far beyond the cholera epidemics of 1832 and 1849.

CHAPTER

 6

Applied Natural History and Utilitarian Ideals: "Jacobin Science" at the Muséum d'Histoire Naturelle, 1789–1870

MICHAEL A. OSBORNE

The last twenty years have witnessed substantial revision in our understanding of the natural history tradition. It is no longer fashionable to characterize natural history, as many biologists and historians of biology once did, as a collection of arcane descriptive and speculative endeavors informed by Baconian methodology. Paul L. Farber has identified four major research traditions under the rubric of natural history during the Enlightenment: taxonomy, the construction of individual natural histories to infer general laws about the natural world and its inhabitants, comparative morphology, and the study of vital functions.[1] In addition to these activities, however, there existed another tradition—that of applied natural history—which gained clearer definition and institutional momentum in the emerging revolutionary political culture of the 1790s. This article examines the building of scientific and cultural institutions with dual appropriative functions. On the one hand, the arenas of applied natural history—mainly zoos, museums, and postrevolutionary scientific societies—were intended to instruct the public in the practical applications of the elite activity of science. Thus they appropriated to science a new and growing audience of "agriculturalists and amateur naturalists." On the other hand, these institutions engaged in an appropriation that was global in scale. They exhibited the biotic resources of foreign lands and portrayed them as actual or potential conquests of French culture, and especially as rejuvenators of agriculture and industry.

Applied natural history was a scientific manifestation of a larger cultural imperative to appropriate and exploit "the other," the exotic, the unknown. As a research tradition, its function was antielitist and nominally egalitarian. It sought to build national wealth and prosperity through the discovery of utilitarian applications for what had been exotic plants and animals, accouterments of Old Regime wealth, appearing in the private menagerie, the hunt, the landscaped garden, and the feasts of royalty. The ideological essence of applied natural history promised beneficiaries of the new political order material rewards from the scientific exploitation of these symbols of royal privilege.

Those who promoted applied natural history found inspiration in works such as Diderot and d'Alembert's *Encyclopédie* of 1751, which had sanctified the practical and utilitarian vocations of the crafts and trades. Inculcated with an attitude of science as hands-on activity, the literate public sifted the many volumes of the *Histoire naturelle* of Georges-Louis Leclerc, Comte de Buffon (1701–1788), with an eye toward the economic viability of domesticating exotic organisms and experimenting with new technical applications of zoological science.

Although this activity, which was part of a larger campaign to create a scientific agriculture, bloomed most fully during the Second Empire, it had already appeared with great urgency at the time of both the Revolution of 1789–1799 and the Revolution of 1848.[2] First among the advocates of this applied natural history of exotic animals were members of the Geoffroy Saint-Hilaire clan, including Etienne (1722–1844) and his son, Isidore (1805–1861), both of whom took great delight in placing the family motto "to be useful" on their books. As professors of zoology and directors of the menagerie at the Muséum national d'histoire naturelle, they were strategically poised to put the motto into practice through the examination and study of exotic animal resources.[3] Crucial to the well-being of applied natural history was the generally favorable attitude of the National Assembly and the Convention toward natural history, an attitude that would continue during the Directory and the Empire.[4] Specifically favored by the revolutionary bodies were scientific fields with potential utility to the public, fields such as zoology and botany that might, if properly conducted, ameliorate social conditions by bolstering agricultural production.

Applied Natural History in the Old Regime

The intellectual roots of applied natural history can largely be traced to zoologists associated with the Jardin du Roi in Paris and its successor institution, the Muséum national d'histoire naturelle.[5] This group included Buffon, as well as the man of letters and administrator of science Jacques-Henri Bernardin de Saint-Pierre (1737–1814), and above all Buffon's collaborator, Louis-Georges-Marie Daubenton (1716–1800). Prior to the Revolution, the king's menagerie at Versailles had been France's largest exotic animal collection in both variety and absolute numbers of animals. But Versailles was largely an institution dedicated to the amusement of the king and his entourage. Nonetheless, the idea that exotic zoo animals ought to be examined as a potential source of agricultural wealth predated the Revolution. In England, the sort of scientific agriculture promoted by George III and Jethro Tull found strong support among the upper and middle classes. Eighteenth-century developments in France seem to have paralleled those in England, where the humane treatment of animals increased in tandem with their economic value.[6]

Proposals for a different kind of menagerie began to appear in France during the middle decades of the eighteenth century. Reflecting the spirit of Enlightenment rationalism, these projects called for menageries more closely wedded to scientific progress and agricultural improvement. Certain members of the French government, most notably the intendant of finances Jean-Charles-Philibert Trudaine de Montigny and the controller-general of finances Henri-Léonard-Jean-Baptiste Bertin, promoted scientific agriculture by establishing schools of veterinary medicine at Lyon (1762) and Alfort (1765), founding learned societies such as the Société royale d'agriculture, and funding experiments on exotic animals with the hope of agricultural benefits.[7]

Buffon, intendant of the Jardin du Roi from 1739 to 1788, coveted the king's menagerie at Versailles. He wanted to move it to the Jardin du Roi, believing that research on the animals, prepared specimens, and library materials could be scrutinized simultaneously. But only a change in the political order would accomplish his dream, and Buffon found it necessary to use the Versailles animals and those at his personal menagerie at Montbard in Burgundy to prepare the animal descriptions of the *Histoire naturelle*. Although the Jardin du Roi lacked an official menagerie during Buffon's era, a plan developed in 1776 by the architect Viel included space for a menagerie, and the institution housed modest, unofficial collections of a variety of animals, including swans, ducks, peacocks, salamanders, toads, monkeys, and pigs.[8] A more substantial commitment to the applied natural history of exotic animals dates from the 1780s when Daubenton began keeping foreign strains of sheep at the Jardin du Roi.

Although both Buffon and the botanist André Thouin (1747–1824) occasionally commented on the potential economic benefits of menagerie-keeping, no eighteenth-century naturalist contributed more to applied natural history than Daubenton. The voluminous and popular *Histoire naturelle* had focused attention on the zoological resources of faraway lands, and by the time Daubenton and Buffon ended their collaboration on that work in 1766, they had published exhaustive anatomical descriptions of the more than two hundred known quadrupeds. The *Histoire naturelle* served as a catalog of nature's bounty and raised the possibility that several, perhaps scores of, economically valuable exotic beasts could be relocated to France. Daubenton's studies of merino sheep, in particular, showed how these possibilities might be realized. A plan of the Spanish government to build its own factories for fine woolen production provoked the French to breed and rear sheep capable of meeting the needs of French industry.[9]

In the 1760s, about a year before the appearance of the *Histoire naturelle*'s last volume on quadrupeds, Daubenton accepted a commission from the French intendant of finance and commerce to explore ways to improve the quality of French wool. France's substantial industry in fine wool weaving purchased most of its raw wool from Spain; although France possessed many native flocks, they produced a coarse fleece fit mainly for sackcloth and cheaper woolen goods.

Daubenton experimented with breeding and shepherding practices for some fourteen years on the grounds of an abandoned church near Montbard, crossing varieties of sheep from Spain, Tibet, England, Morocco, and various regions of France. The Montbard operation was, in effect, a specialized menagerie, devoted to the scientific study of a single economically valuable species. The Montbard experiments demonstrated that exotic races could increase agricultural productivity and that zoological science could serve as a competent guide to agricultural practice. For those of enlightened sensibility, applied natural history marshaled the laws of nature to "civilize" the products of more primitive societies. Thus the exotic beast was imbued with valuable qualities as it was appropriated by the universal rationality of science.

Daubenton's true innovation was to rationalize shepherding practices and elevate their study to a scientific art. His major conclusion, that sheep raised in the open air were healthier and produced a finer, more abundant grade of wool than animals kept in poorly ventilated barns, had been suggested by trials in Normandy nearly a decade earlier. Nor was the keeping of foreign breeds of sheep a new idea, as exotic breeds had already been tried in several provinces of France.[10] But if science could lead the way, it could not force landowners to import new races of sheep and to embrace the principles of scientific husbandry. Daubenton attempted to convert skeptics to the scientific cause by establishing demonstration farms showing improved breeds maintained with open-air husbandry alongside domestic races raised in the traditional manner.[11] The stock of the Montbard menagerie multiplied prolifically and furnished sheep to two demonstration farms, one at the Jardin du Roi and another at the Alfort school of veterinary medicine, where Daubenton assumed the chair of rural economy in 1783. The great success of the Montbard experiment encouraged the government of Louis XVI to found a shepherds' school at Rambouillet with a herd of Spanish merinos, which increased in number from the original three hundred sixty in 1786 to nearly seven hundred animals by 1799.[12]

Encouraged by the success of his studies on merino sheep, Daubenton also wanted to investigate the acclimatization and domestication of the peccary, tapir, zebra, and other exotic animals.[13] These experiments required a park safe from poachers as well as sufficient funds for the purchase and maintenance of animals. By the time Daubenton had these requirements, he was nearly eighty years old, and the task of continuing research on the applied natural history of exotic animals was left to the next generation of scientists.

One of these younger men, Daubenton's colleague at the Jardin du Roi, the zoologist Bernard-Germain-Etienne de la Ville, Comte de Lacépède (1756–1825), referred to the Montbard menagerie as a new kind of institution dedicated to public utility and found only in a "very advanced civilization."[14] Although Daubenton and many other Jardin naturalists were sincere in their desire to place science in the service of the public good, they must have realized that it was also in their own best interests to stress the usefulness of their institution to the historical progress of France. Acclimatizing exotic animals for agricultural purposes seemed to be an appropriate means of demonstrating to the strengthening forces of liberalism that scientists and zoological science had practical value. As a result, an institution that had heretofore devoted itself mainly to the study of museum-based natural history assumed in 1793 the added charge of forming a collection of live animals for scientific, artistic, pedagogical, and agricultural purposes.

Applied Natural History
and Jacobin Science

The utility of science emerges as a central concern in the debates conducted in the revolutionary assemblies on the status of the Jardin du Roi. In 1790, when the National Assembly asked the officers of the Jardin du Roi to submit a plan for the institution's reform, the concept of utility was notoriously polyvalent. Members of the scientific community defined useful research in many different ways. There was of course the older Baconian idea of utility as power over nature, but many scientists made little or no reference to utility in this sense. Quite often "utile" was employed in an adjectival sense with no reference either to immediate usefulness or to the scientific improvement of technique. For the astronomer Pierre-Simon de Laplace (1749–1827), the calculus of probabilities embodied utility because it enabled humanity to avoid mistakes premised on a faulty view of nature. It enabled humankind to make the surest estimate of natural processes in an intellectual environment where final causes were seen as beyond the purview of science. The term "utile" also designated research conducted according to the standards of the scientific community. The industrial chemist Claude-Louis Berthollet (1748–1822) used the term in this sense, as did others who regarded "utile" as the very essence of Enlightenment science. For a substantial body of revolutionary scientists, then, "utile" was something that demarcated their own science from romantic misconceptions like Mesmerism and thus freed humanity of its prejudices.[15]

In the larger cultural arena, "science utile" denoted a scientific activity that improved daily life. This was what many revolutionary political reformers wanted. According to Charles C. Gillispie, this sense of utility was incorporated into a Jacobin philosophy of science that informed Jacobin scientific reforms. This philosophy revered natural history and the arts and crafts tradition, especially as these activities were portrayed by Diderot in the *Encyclopédie*. Gillispie describes the Jacobin philosophy of science as directed against highly theoretical science, which was held by the Jacobins to be insufficiently utilitarian. He identifies the Jacobin reform of science as a forerunner of the Marxist approach to science, characterizing it as a moralistic credo of liberal ideology and Baconian technology. More specifically, he argues that proponents of the philosophy found fault with the highly mathematical universe of Newton, seeking to replace it with an epistemology more intelligible to the common man, an organismic world view speaking in simple biological metaphors derived from the philosophy of Diderot and Rousseau. Thus the Jacobins vented their resentment at the analytical and metrological traditions of scientific research associated with mathematical physics and especially with the new chemistry of Antoine-Laurent Lavoisier (1743–1794), the tax-farmer, scientist, and civil servant who was guillotined in 1794. Gillispie describes the French scientific community as giving up "en masse" the crusade for science as pure inquiry, noting that people like the chemist Antoine-François de Fourcroy (1755–1809)—a member of both the Jacobin party and the Committee on Public Instruction—professed a "vulgarly utilitarian valuation" of science in speeches on the concept of utility.[16] Although Pietro Corsi, Roger Hahn, and other historians of French science have cautioned against attributing too much coherence to the Jacobin faction's view of science, the Convention did effect several important reforms in scientific organization, many of which were anti–intellectual in orientation. These reforms included the abolition of the Académie des Sciences and other bastions of scientific privilege and arrogance on 8 August 1793.[17]

Contrasting starkly with this image of institutional collapse and abuse heaped high on the physical and mathematical sciences is the favor the Jacobins bestowed on the practical arts and on natural history. The Jardin du Roi emerged from the Revolution much strengthened, transformed, and sanctified by the Jacobins as an institution of public utility. To be sure, the Jacobins sought to create a socially useful science, but they cared little for taxonomy and the major research traditions within natural history that, no less than mathematical physics, contained theoretical elements. Some revolutionary naturalists even attempted to recast natural history along the highly abstract and mathematical lines so distrusted by the Jacobins.[18]

A close reading of proposals made by politicians to the Convention concerning the fate of the Jardin du Roi reveals that natural history was not above suspicion. Natural history was given no quarter by some writers, who proposed doing away with it altogether. One proposal captured the essential anti–intellectualism of Jacobin thought in arguing that the greatest benefit to France could be realized by converting the Jardin du Roi into a field of potatoes. Other proposals were more moderate in scope, many suggesting that the Jardin du Roi be made more responsive to the needs of French agriculture and industry.[19]

What the more moderate members of the Convention admired about science in general, and natural history in particular, was the possibility of their application to concrete problems. A proposal for the reform of the Jardin du Roi, written by its officers, highlights the applied aspects of natural history. Presented to the National Assembly on 20 August 1790, it described the officers as currently "engaged in seeking or bringing together all truths and all objects useful to the natural sciences and, consequently, to agriculture, medicine, commerce, and the arts."[20] Although research and information gathering would continue at the new establishment, its principal goal would be the public teaching of natural history, taken in all its range.

The applied natural history of exotic animals, which entailed the appropriation and exploitation of the biotic wealth of foreign lands, was intended to assume central functions in the reconstituted institution. Daubenton and the ten other naturalists who signed the 1790 proposal intended to study "animals that degenerate by the cold or the heat; the influence of domesticity; the power of man to improve or maintain races and to acclimatize species from far-away lands."[21] A concern for practical pedagogy directed the officers in charge of the natural history of quadrupeds and entomology to focus their lectures on animals of immediate or potential economic value and to call attention to any "useful species, as yet unknown in France, which might be naturalized here."[22]

In 1792 Bernardin de Saint-Pierre, the Jardin du Roi's intendant, wrote a lengthy and elegant paper extolling the benefits of opening a menagerie in the Jardin du Roi, now renamed the Jardin national des plantes. Spurred on by the impending liquidation of the Versailles menagerie and playing on anti-royalist sentiment, Bernardin skillfully juxtaposed the image of dedicated, disinterested scientists laboring for the economic and social betterment of the nation against the Old Regime's excesses and corruption. The Versailles menagerie, argued Bernardin, "had only been a useless object of luxury and expense for the nation."[23] If, however, the animals could be transferred to the Jardin national des plantes, they could then serve the needs of public instruction and be studied by artists and scientists. There was no doubt, he continued, that once the Versailles animals became the property of the Jardin national des plantes, they would become "the most important part of natural history."[24]

Bernardin highlighted the economic benefits of a scientific menagerie and hinted that one day the menagerie might even furnish new industries for the colonies. His adroit weaving of the themes of economic progress and public utility, repeated time and again, was exactly what the Convention wanted to hear. France stood to gain a precious source of dye, for instance, by the introduction of exotic cacti and cochineal insects. Other new industries would result from the introduction of exotic silkworms, beaver, and reindeer.[25] Moreover, the general advance of scientific knowledge was better served, he claimed, by the simultaneous scrutiny of plants and animals, a method that would reveal the relationships between the two kingdoms.[26] Bernardin's project received the endorsement of the Société d'histoire naturelle de Paris, a body that had survived the revolutionary tumult by proclaiming its own utility, and it was sent to the Ministry of Public Instruction.[27]

When the Convention approved the transformation of the Jardin national des plantes into the Muséum national d'histoire naturelle in June 1793, it also endorsed the creation of a menagerie and established two new chairs of zoology. The botanist Jean-Baptiste-Pierre-Antoine de Monet de Lamarck (1744–1829) assumed the chair for invertebrates, insects, and microscopic animals, while Etienne Geoffroy Saint-Hilaire, a young mineralogist who had replaced Lacépède as a demonstrator of zoology, became director of the menagerie and took provisional charge of the chair for the study of quadrupeds, cetaceans, birds, reptiles, and fish. Shortly thereafter, Etienne Geoffroy Saint-Hilaire, still in charge of the menagerie, assumed teaching and research duties for the natural history of mammals and birds.

The Muséum menagerie, the first public zoo in France, was a true child of the Revolution. Its first animals arrived as a result of the Terror's attempts to keep public order. In the fall of 1793, the Paris police received a directive to clear the streets of all animal spectacles, a genre of entertainment thought to incite the mob to violence. The police rounded up about a dozen animals and their owners and took them to the Muséum, where the owners became salaried keepers of the beasts. Unfortunately, few of the animals collected by the police suggested even the remotest application for agriculture and industry.[28] Although Muséum professors were charged to perform work for the public good, no internal mechanism forced them to undertake applied research, which was held in low regard by the members of the Académie des Sciences.

The character of the new menagerie director presented another obstacle to establishing a viable program of applied natural history. Etienne Geoffroy Saint-Hilaire, who administered the Muséum menagerie for more than four decades, was a man with philosophical rather than practical interests. Muséum professors enjoyed nearly unlimited freedom in their choice of research priorities, and the French scientific community—despite the pressures of politics—tended to reward those who contributed to basic or pure scientific studies. Moreover, the Jacobins' ideology of anti–intellectualism and their program against theoretical science declined after the execution of Robespierre in the summer of 1794. Recent studies of Etienne Geoffroy Saint-Hilaire portray the naturalist as moving far from taxonomic concerns by 1805, and he lost interest in completing a catalog of the Muséum's collections of birds and mammals.[29]

Although Etienne and his family were of republican political inclinations, he did not devote himself to discovering agricultural or industrial applications for zoo animals, and the menagerie under his administration seems to have had no consistent collection policy. Gifts and exchanges accounted for most of the new acquisitions. Many animals came from countries engaged in significant diplomatic and commercial activities with France. The menagerie profited too from the new conquests of the French army; victories in Austria, Holland, and Algeria brought important additions to the collections.[30] The Enlightenment and revolutionary goal of creating a menagerie devoted to public utility persisted. But the way in which the live animal collection of the Muséum was built, and popular notions of the function of zoos, made it difficult to realize that goal. Most animal donors envisioned zoos as places of exotic encounter between humans and the most bizarre and different of beasts, and they only rarely captured or bought the domesticated animals of other lands. Yet it was these animals that were most suitable for immediate experimental application in French agriculture and industry.

Utilitarian Legacies
in the Nineteenth Century

The institutionalization of utilitarian research at the Muséum achieved at best mixed results. In terms of its subject matter—natural history—and its administrative structure and public teaching activities, the Muséum reflected a modified Jacobin ideology. The Muséum professors elected a director from within their ranks, and in an idealized sense this self-regulation of internal affairs was similar to the balanced and intelligible conception of nature promoted by Diderot and admired by Gillispie's Jacobins. Yet at another level, that of scientific practice, the application of zoology to agriculture and industry materialized only faintly within the confines of the Muséum. Even partisan biographers of Etienne Geoffroy Saint-Hilaire have had great difficulty in discerning any utilitarian social program in his scientific activities.[31]

If the assembly of Muséum professors had had its way, the menagerie might have more fully satisfied the pledge of public utility. In 1837 the professors' assembly decided to make the holder of a new chair of comparative physiology responsible for the menagerie. Frédéric Cuvier (1773–1838), who had served under Etienne Geoffroy Saint-Hilaire since 1804 as keeper of the menagerie, was the logical choice. Cuvier was engaged in research on the applied natural history of exotic animals, and he recommended the importation and domestication of the zebra and several other social ruminants, including the tapir, a hoglike mammal, and the vicuña, a close relative of the llama and alpaca. Cuvier suggested that the new chair concentrate on the investigation of the "nature of animals and their training." The minister of public instruction favored an even more utilitarian approach and expected the chairholder to teach a "Course of Applied Natural History for the Husbandry and Acclimatization of Animals."[32] Owing to Cuvier's premature death in 1838, control of the menagerie reverted back to Etienne Geoffroy Saint-Hilaire, who seized the opportunity to promote his son Isidore for the post.

Isidore Geoffroy Saint-Hilaire, who directed the Muséum menagerie from 1838 to 1861, would realize the creation of a menagerie devoted primarily to applied natural history. The odd twist of the story is that his dream was realized at a new institution, not the Muséum that the Jacobins had founded. Animated by theoretical convictions as well as practical goals, Isidore bemoaned the fact that most zoos still closely resembled those of the Old Regime. Like the Versailles menagerie, they existed purely for the entertainment of visitors. What was needed, he argued, was a more utilitarian mission for these storehouses of exotic faunal resources.[33] The two Geoffroy Saint-Hilaires were among the leaders of a group of naturalists who loosely followed Lamarck's evolutionary ideas. They argued that changes in animal morphology, as well as the forced adaptation of exotic animals to new environmental circumstances, could be effected by modifications in climate and diet. Isidore's interest in applied natural history was occasioned by the conviction that his father's *école philosophique*, and the transformist argument in general, needed more concrete examples of animals undergoing modification.[34]

At the beginning of his career, long before he had directed a menagerie, Isidore Geoffroy Saint-Hilaire envisioned in Baconian terms the ideal zoo. As described in the *New Atlantis*, this new kind of zoo was to be a multifunctional institution simultaneously serving to educate and amuse the public, to promote the advance of general zoology, and to provide assistance to agriculture by a reasoned selection of certain species "to replace advantageously our farm animals."[35] After two decades of service as director of the largest zoo in Europe, he reversed himself on this point and advocated specialized zoological institutions.

This shift in Isidore Geoffroy Saint-Hilaire's thinking toward specialization in institutions parallels the increasing tendency of practitioners of natural history to specialize in particular disciplines such as geology and ornithology during the early and middle years of the nineteenth century.[36] It also articulates with a major concern of French politics and biomedical theory of the middle third of the century—the problem of human settlement in colonial Algeria. Indeed, the appropriation of exotic beasts by French science and agriculture was embedded in a larger scientific discourse centering on theories of transformism and the appropriation and assimilation of exotic peoples and lands.[37] The transformist theory of Etienne and Isidore Geoffroy Saint-Hilaire argued that Europeans would eventually enjoy a healthy life in Algeria; only time and careful attention to diet and hygiene were required. But a coherent and practical theory of how to accomplish the forced adaptation of humans, plants, and animals eluded the French. To scientists and amateurs interested in exotic animal acclimatization in France and the health problems of Europeans in Algeria, research at the Muséum menagerie seemed woefully inadequate. Isidore Geoffroy Saint-Hilaire shared this frustration and proposed that like the French metropole itself, the menagerie had the right to form colonies to satisfy special needs. The menagerie needed to "disengage itself" from its multitudinous tasks and to streamline its operations; to accomplish these ends he proposed that a colony of the menagerie be built in eastern Paris in the Bois de Vincennes.[38]

Isidore Geoffroy Saint-Hilaire hoped that the Bois de Vincennes zoo would relieve the overcrowding at the Muséum menagerie and facilitate animal reproduction. The large and quiet spaces of the Bois de Vincennes would even allow Muséum naturalists to conserve some breeds and improve others.[39] In contrast to the Bois de Vincennes project, which was not realized until the present century, another of the zoologist's proposals—a plan to create a specialized zoo on the other side of Paris in the Bois de Boulogne—met with resounding success. The Jardin zoologique d'acclimatation opened in 1860, a creation of the Société zoologique d'acclimatation, which was founded by Isidore Geoffroy Saint-Hilaire in 1854. This zoo and scientific society embodied the best aspects of applied natural history and to a large extent realized Jacobin ambitions for the Jacobin vision of zoology. As an institution specializing in the practical exploitation of exotic animals, the Jardin zoologique d'acclimatation quickly displaced the Muséum's rather weak leadership in applied zoological studies. For its part, the Société zoologique d'acclimatation was a model of nonelite science. This band of naturalists, animal merchants, civil servants, bankers, and agriculturalists would become one of France's largest and most successful learned societies. Numbering more than two thousand members, the Société admitted anyone who could pay the membership fee.

How was it that this new voluntary scientific society could take over a function—even a neglected one—mandated in the Muséum's constitution? Furthermore why should an institution like the Jardin zoologique d'acclimatation emerge during the Second Empire? To be sure, Muséum naturalists of the Restoration era had evinced only sporadic interest in animal acclimatization studies. This indifference was countered most forcefully by the personal strategies of Isidore Geoffroy Saint-Hilaire, and by the changing political ecology of the French scientific establishment, with its fierce competition for resources and powerful patrons. Although Isidore viewed the Muséum as an inappropriate place for animal acclimatization, he was reluctant to surrender Muséum animals to other government institutions.[40] Hence in 1849, when the Ministry of Agriculture struck a firm blow for the applied natural history of exotic animals and created a farm for animal acclimatization at Versailles, the Muséum menagerie donated only two of its seven llamas. Most of the animals at the Versailles farm died, a special setback to applied natural history being the loss of thirty alpacas purchased from the king of Holland.[41] By creating a scientific society to work in acclimatization, one with the sponsorship of the French state, Isidore ensured that he would be able to keep control of his research program.

In addition to the speculative purity of Etienne Geoffroy Saint-Hilaire's research, which focused on the concept of a single morphological plan for all animals, factors internal to the Muséum itself made it difficult to sustain a program of applied natural history there. The period of Isidore's professorship (1841–1861) has been characterized as an era when the Muséum was "inhospitable to new departures in research."[42] This observation can be extended to include hostility to the revival of neglected research obligations, among them applied natural history.

The Muséum in midcentury moved only reluctantly toward an experimental program; and applied zoology, because it necessitated experiments and was associated with agriculture, appeared all the more marginal to the professors whose ambitions lay within specialized disciplines. Botany professor Adolphe-Théodore Brongniart (1801–1876), among others, remained resolutely suspicious of efforts to make the Muséum more responsive to agricultural needs. To the minister of public instruction, he suggested caution, "if we do not wish to cause the Muséum to lose its lofty scientific character, ... we must necessarily give very little coverage to applications."[43] Many Muséum professors shared Brongniart's attitude. This tradition of antipathy toward applied science, which Dorinda Outram has also detected among these professors, later resulted in a reactionary rejection of experimentalism on the part of the Muséum and a reorientation toward museology.[44]

By the 1850s, those Muséum zoologists who wanted to pursue applied studies began to look beyond the Muséum to fulfill their ambitions. It was a number of these men who banded together to form the Société zoologique d'acclimatation. Utilitarian in goal and overtly democratic in organization, the Société's growth was fueled by the growing fascination of the middle classes with the exotic and with the real and imitation luxuries of the Old Regime described by Leora Auslander.[45] Soon after its founding in 1854, the Société zoologique d'acclimatation began to encroach on the Muséum's access to exotic animals and on its role as a disseminator of useful zoological information.

Isidore Geoffroy Saint-Hilaire regarded the Société zoologique d'acclimatation and the Jardin zoologique d'acclimatation as two arms of the same organization. The Société zoologique d'acclimatation had been founded six years prior to the opening of the Jardin only because it was "less difficult for a new enterprise to assemble men than money."[46] As president of the Société zoologique d'acclimatation from 1854 to 1861, as well as director of the Muséum menagerie, Isidore Geoffroy Saint-Hilaire played the role of mediator. He intended that the Jardin specialize in the useful application of zoological theory. The Muséum would retain its role as France's center of theoretical zoology and collaborate with the Jardin in the selection of potentially useful species.[47] After the death of Isidore Geoffroy Saint-Hilaire, however, the Muséum virtually ceased to collaborate with the Jardin.

In keeping with the Jacobin view of the proper function of science, the Société elevated practice above theory and embraced the personage of Daubenton, the very symbol of Old Regime applied natural history. In the 1860s, Daubenton's supporters even erected a statue of him accompanied by a merino sheep at the Jardin. Most Société members required little theoretical explanation for their activities. They preferred to think of themselves as engaged in, or at least associated with, a practical art, where empiricism and technique would guide the way when theory faltered. In essence, many Société members believed that Isidore Geoffroy Saint-Hilaire was reviving the ideas of Daubenton and were unconcerned that Buffon's collaborator had maintained a static view of species not shared by their president, who saw the problems of exotic animal acclimatization and domestication as opportunities to study the limits of variation. The Jardin's honorary president, Prince Jérôme Napoleon, summed up the general approach as a desire to "exit the domain of theory to enter that of practice."[48]

After Napoleon III designated the Société as an institution "of public utility" in 1855, his supporters swelled the group's membership roster. The emperor's spokesman within the Société, his minister of foreign affairs, Edouard Drouyn de Lhuys (1805–1881), became a vice president in 1857 and succeeded Isidore Geoffroy Saint-Hilaire as president in 1862.

It is useful here to distinguish two threads of the scientific legacy of the Jacobins, for Napoleon III embraced one thread while he tried to break the other. The institutional Jacobinism of the Muséum worked against it because the emperor did not like the Muséum's tradition of self-governance. He tried to force the professors to accept as director his own appointee, and he made sure that the Muséum languished with an insufficient budget. In contrast, another current of Jacobinism—the scientific Jacobinism of applied natural history—found favor with Napoleon III. He and his entourage joined the Société, promoting it and investing money in the Jardin, which became a showpiece in the program for rebuilding Paris.

The political climate of the Second Empire, as well as the Muséum's own institutional frailties, help to explain the relative ease with which the Société assumed the tasks of applied natural history with the apparent acquiescence of the Muséum. This shift of responsibility is instructive because it shows that the Jacobin vision of applied natural history had failed to gain scientific respectability even within the Muséum although the institution owed its birth to Jacobin support.

We can distinguish three phases in the relationship between the Société and the Muséum during the Second Empire. Interaction, collaboration, and generally amicable relations characterized the period from the Société's inception in 1854 until 1859. A second phase, one of resentment and competition for animals and resources, is evident by the time of the opening of the Jardin in 1860 and coincides with Isidore Geoffroy Saint-Hilaire's term as director of the Muséum from 1860 to 1861. The third and final phase, one of overt conflict followed by nearly complete estrangement, began with the election of Henri Milne-Edwards (1800–1885) to the Muséum chair of mammals and birds and lasted through much of the Third Republic.

During the first phase of mutual assistance, the Société attracted as members about a third of the twenty-eight Muséum professors. Participation in the Société followed disciplinary lines, and Muséum zoologists accounted for nine of the Muséum's twelve Société members. An active core of Muséum personnel, six professors and three *aides-naturalistes*, became prominent among the more than two hundred thirty people who served as Société officers during the Second Empire. Of the Muséum professors, Isidore

Geoffroy Saint-Hilaire, the Société's president from 1854 until his death in 1861, and the zoologist Jean-Louis Armand de Quatrefages de Bréau (1810–1892), vice-president and committee member, were especially active. The conclusion would seem to be that although professors of natural history, applied physics, chemistry, and other disciplines were well disposed toward the project of applied natural history, they believed it should be pursued outside the confines of the Muséum.

The first phase in Société and Muséum relations found frequent mention of Société news in the meetings of the professors' assembly. In fact, the level of interaction between the Société and the Muséum, measured by the volume of letters, animals, and natural history objects exchanged, is the highest existing between the Muséum and any scientific society in this period. The Muséum assisted the Société by lending it samples of exotic wools, stuffed animals, and the like. These items and others, administered for the most part by Isidore Geoffroy Saint-Hilaire, were exhibited in Paris and London as examples of what the Société had collected.[49]

Collaboration between the Société and the Muséum blurred the lines demarcating each institution's corporate identity. Many correspondents wrote to the Muséum, only to have their requests answered by a representative of the Société.[50] By the time the Société opened its Jardin to the public in October 1860, it had already obtained the support of many scientific amateurs, agriculturalists, and colonial functionaries. Such figures, who had formerly looked to the Muséum for guidance and made its menagerie the object of their philanthropical attentions, now shifted their allegiance to the Jardin.

Owing to budgetary crises, by the late 1850s, gifts, exchanges, and births accounted for nearly all of the new additions to the Muséum menagerie. Isidore Geoffroy Saint-Hilaire's frustration with the situation was evident. Upon receiving a listing of a donation of Asian and African animals unsuited for agricultural and industrial uses, he wrote to a friend that he was "heartbroken to read such a list of animals. . . . The yak! The wild horse! I would give one of my fingers for each of these animals, which are . . . the ones I most desire to enrich our collections."[51] The gift-givers, most often foreign heads of state, diplomatic agents, or French military personnel, usually offered their animals to the emperor Napoleon III. Acting on whims of the moment, the emperor distributed the animals among his political supporters, the Muséum, and other applicants. The Muséum encouraged this arrangement since the emperor's budget, rather than its own, paid most costs.

A second phase in the relationship between the Muséum and the Société, evident by the late 1850s, is marked by a decline in the ability of Isidore Geoffroy Saint-Hilaire to mediate between the two bodies. Some professors resented what they perceived as an attempt to turn the Muséum in a more practical—and therefore less scientific—direction. In keeping with a vision of science as basic inquiry and descriptive activity, the professors rejected the application of Albert Geoffroy Saint-Hilaire, Isidore's son and the assistant director of the Jardin, to deliver lectures on applied zoology on Muséum premises.[52]

Isidore Geoffroy Saint-Hilaire's carefully nurtured ties between the two institutions began to unravel in October 1860, on the eve of the opening of the Jardin. In anticipation of the event, and in his capacity as director of the Muséum, he persuaded the professors' assembly to authorize a large exchange of animals with the Jardin.[53] Ultimately the minister of public instruction vetoed the measure and forced the Muséum once again to rely mainly on gifts to build its live animal collections. By this time Napoleon III had turned against the Muséum and, in addition to restricting its budget, was trying to make the directorship an appointive rather than an elective office.

An acrimonious dispute in 1862 between Milne-Edwards, Isidore Geoffroy Saint-Hilaire's successor at the Muséum, and Albert Geoffroy Saint-Hilaire tested the emperor's right of patronage and sealed the final divorce between the Muséum menagerie and the practical zoology of the Jardin. The Muséum professors had cleverly convinced the two kings of Siam to give a number of exotic animals to the emperor, who in turn, it was hoped, would offer them to the Muséum. But when Milne-Edwards met the shipment at Toulon, he encountered Albert Geoffroy Saint-Hilaire, who promptly claimed several animals for the Jardin.

The dispute over the animals escalated and reverberated back through the ranks of the Muséum and the Jardin. Each institution appealed to its friends and patrons in the government. Milne-Edwards summarized the divergent interests of the "two rival establishments" to Roulin, the minister of public instruction.[54] Since the Muséum had initiated and in part funded the shipment from Siam, reasoned Milne-Edwards, it deserved all the scientifically valuable animals. In his opinion, most of the animals fell into this category. But Napoleon III, acting through his minister and the president of the Société, Drouyn de Lhuys, reaffirmed the Jardin's claim to any animals given to him. Consequently, until the debacle of 1870 deposed the emperor, the Muséum menagerie languished as the directors of the Jardin carefully exercised this prerogative.

The controversy between the Muséum and the Jardin illuminates the low status of applied zoology within the elite of French zoology. Applied natural history, at least as it concerned exotic animals and was practiced at the Jardin, was not considered "scientific." Milne-Edwards denied that the Jardin had a real scientific role. In his view the menagerie deserved the emperor's animals, for scientific purposes: they completed pairs, they needed to be described or classified, or they represented species not presently owned by the Muséum.[55] This approach of course satisfied only the scientific obligation of the Muséum and left unfulfilled its revolutionary charge to assist agriculture and industry, a charge more actively pursued at the Jardin.

For Gillispie, the Jacobin philosophy of science cheapened the expectations of science and threatened to compromise it by surrounding it with enthusiasts who were "not very well qualified by temperament or nature of their interest to participate in the serious work of science."[56] For Milne-Edwards, the Jardin, which embodied the practical research tradition of natural history, was a threat to the Muséum and to properly conducted science. It existed "to the detriment of science, [and] no sensible person would ever dream of acclimatizing in France, in the interest of agriculture or public nutrition, most of the animals that the Jardin shows."[57] As I have tried to show, Gillispie's view—like that of Milne-Edwards in the nineteenth century—presents an unduly elitist conception of what constituted science. Enthusiasts were essential to science. From the Old Regime to the Third Republic, scientists and knowledgeable amateurs, including the diplomats and military men who collected exotic animals in foreign lands and the landowners who raised yaks and llamas on their estates, contributed to, and participated in, the continuing research tradition of applied natural history.

In spite of Milne-Edwards's assertion, hundreds of educated and presumably sensible people did dream of and attempt the appropriation of exotic animals for food, agriculture, industry, and aesthetic reasons. Although there was some irony in Napoleon III's support of a tradition once embraced by Jacobins, applied natural history had never been their exclusive property. Just as utilitarian ideals themselves were not exclusively Jacobin, and in the work of a figure like Daubenton antedated the Revolution, applied natural history had stood for enlightened progress. This aspect of the tradition, as well as the aristocratic veneer associated with exotic animal keeping, was embraced and promoted by Second Empire officialdom. The vogue of this tradition peaked during the Second Empire and lingered into the early years of the Third Republic, when the appreciation and cultivation of natural history, especially in its more accessible aspects of menagerie-keeping, collecting, attending lectures, and visiting zoos, had captured a wide public of nonscientists. The Muséum had done little to sustain a research program in utilitarian science from one revolution to another. Individuals such as Isidore Geoffroy Saint-Hilaire had kept alive a utilitarian vision of natural history, but they were frustrated in trying to realize that program within the institution itself. Thus Isidore Geoffroy Saint-Hilaire's personal research trajectory and Napoleon III's animus toward the Muséum and his crucial patronage of the Jardin combined to make the latter a cultural institution that reified utilitarian aspects of Old Regime practices. A sensibility for applied natural history, once revered in Jacobin rhetoric, had been inculcated in the people: not among the sansculottes but among members of a plethora of postrevolutionary scientific societies. People could now show their support for applied natural history by joining the Société and by visiting the Jardin, which contented itself with the public of workers and those with "small purses" once the Empire disintegrated into the Republic.[58]

7

After the Revolution: Recycling Ancien Régime Style in the Nineteenth Century

LEORA AUSLANDER

"Furniture is the clothing of life," Mazaroz, a great artist of the factory said to me one day. "One's furniture reveals one's taste and the quality of one's spirit. Furnishings are incorruptible witnesses, condemning or glorifying those who own them."[1]

If furniture reveals one's spirit, then the French bourgeoisie from the last quarter of the nineteenth century were inhabiting the souls of their ancien régime ancestors, for contemporary versions of prerevolutionary styles had come to dominate urban homes. Despite the efforts of some furniture makers and critics to promote new developments, including bentwood furniture, *style moderne*, *art nouveau*, and later *art déco*, these were largely rejected by consumers in favor of Henri II, Louis XIII, Louis XIV, Louis XV, and Louis XVI style furniture.[2] Although art historians tend to condemn these furnishings as bad copies of dead styles, they were in fact new inventions of a particular sort—historicist pastiche.[3] Furniture makers borrowed historical forms and altered their curves, angles, and colors, thereby inventing new furniture reminiscent of, although distinguishable from, the old.[4] These nineteenth-century versions were based on ideal types, rather than concrete embodiments, of particular ancien régime styles combined with contemporary form. Each historical style was understood to contain essential identifying characteristics—twisted columns, sculpture, and dark wood for Henri

II, dramatically curved forms for Louis XV, and extreme delicacy for Louis XVI, to cite a few—and all of the pastiches of those styles contained those elements, sometimes combined or assembled in startling ways. Exact reproductions were also made, but rarely. Late nineteenth-century furniture used a doubled visual vocabulary of the old and new, the historical and contemporary, but was labeled as simply historical. In short, this furniture "passed" as historically authentic discursively, but not visually.

This essay offers an alternative interpretation to the traditional historiographical, as well as contemporary, explanation for why historicist pastiche was the style of choice among the Parisian bourgeoisie from the end of the nineteenth century and into the twentieth. The view that the artisans were incompetent and the consumers cowardly or that the producers could not make innovative furniture and the public would not buy it is clearly insufficient.[5] A more adequate interpretation is, rather, that this particular form of historicist furniture was a uniquely appropriate response to the dilemmas facing French bourgeois society as a result of the complex interaction of the revolutionary legacy, the development of industrial capitalism, and the peculiar place of furniture in social representation.

Fascination with France's past in interior decor was not new in the 1880s. Although the Second Empire saw the invention of a distinct style, ancien régime style prevailed from 1815 to at least the First World War.[6] Earlier in the century individual prerevolutionary styles came in and out of fashion sequentially according to the needs for symbolic representation of the current political regime; the July Monarchy saw a strong revival of "Gothic," and the Second Empire of "Renaissance." At the end of the century, however, the makers and consumers of furniture reappropriated simultaneously the entire ancien régime, from the Middle Ages to the eve of the Revolution.[7]

The "making" of French history and society in furniture developed in both discursive and material practice; style was infinitely discussed and people made, acquired, used, and abandoned furniture. Consensus was reached by the 1860s that style was constitutive of the social order and therefore that furniture (like apartments, clothes, and tea sets) ought to represent aptly the social location of its owners.[8] Thus woods, colors, and monarchical styles received various (and contested) attributions as they served in this task of symbolically constituting the social order.[9] But the ownership of furniture was ambiguous; it was simultaneously familial and individual. In the bourgeois moment that was the late nineteenth century, when the individual, the family, the class, and the nation were perceived to be in need of simultaneous representation, this multiple ownership created contradictory representational tasks. And the story must be further complicated. For even if no social gap existed among members of a household, individuals invariably possessed more than one identity in need of representation. Individuals concurrently occupied several social locations. One could be at once Catholic, a woman, Alsatian petit bourgeois in origin, currently living in Paris, married to a doctor, and active in the women's movement.[10] Contemporaries disagreed among themselves concerning which identity, among the many that individuals possessed, was to be represented through furnishings. Some thought that how one earned a living was most important, others thought gender, social or geographic origin, or religious affiliation to be the most crucial, while a few even argued that individual expression itself was what was most at stake in choosing one's interior.[11] These disagreements, in addition to those concerning the appropriate symbolic representation of gender, class, and age, led to a profusion of competing "expert" discourses from the 1870s onwards.

Discussion of suitable furnishings was carried on in the decorating magazines and etiquette books that flourished in the period. Distributors also participated in this debate through their advertising materials while another site for discussion was provided by the world's fairs.[12] In addition, the administrators of the new institutions of the decorative arts, including libraries, museums, and trade schools, also participated in the debate.[13] Finally, novels and photographs both yield valuable insights into how contemporaries understood furnishings to function in the construction of the social order and helped to construct that reality.

These discourses sort out into identifiable strands with common themes. Those who earned their living directly from the sale of particular goods tended to make somewhat different arguments from those who had the luxury of assessing tastefulness from an administrative post within the government bureaucracy. Etiquette-book writers had different preoccupations than the organizers of world's fairs. The institutional and social site of the discourse, rather than either individual biography or identity of the author, was most salient in forming these discourses. As individuals moved from one discursive context to another, they took positions appropriate to their new location. I have therefore deprived my sources of their names, while I identify the social and temporal placement of the discourse that granted them speech.

Furthermore, certain discursive contexts produced great stability across a long period. Many fin-de-siècle texts are indistinguishable from texts of the 1930s, while others were more ephemeral. The period from 1880 to 1940 was marked by the production of a new bourgeois consumption regime. The texts produced in that period, within discursive genres invented for and by that regime, or colonized early (like decorating guides), tend to be relatively stable across time, although highly differentiated by their location in social space. Other more archaic or more resistant discourses, such as reports from the world's fairs, reveal in their chronological shifts the process of discursive transformation required by this bourgeois consumption regime. I move therefore with freedom among texts from relatively stable discursive fields and move with greater chronological specificity among texts from unstable fields, using seemingly anachronistic examples to mark the distinction between newly created discursive contexts or genres and the re-use of the old.

There was no one hegemonic discourse that consumers could obediently follow. The cacophony of competing expert discourses meant that there was never only one voice demanding to be heard and claiming authority. The frequent dissonance between individual and familial locations meant consumers were faced with contradictory tasks—being true to themselves and to their families. Lastly, the impossibility of choosing only one fragment of one's social being for self-representation meant that even being true to oneself was not really possible. Consumers appear to have made their way through the thicket of advice, admonition, and threat with varying degrees of aplomb. Grasping the processes of both the acquisition and the use of furnishings is essential to understanding the popularity of historicist pastiche in the late nineteenth century.[14] Exploring the discourses around furniture as well as how the objects were used therefore sheds light on the making of distinctions between and within classes, and on the peculiar ways in which the construction of class, gender, nation, and history coalesced in the chairs upon which people sat and the tables at which they ate.

Gender, Historicism, and the Bourgeoisie

The French bourgeoisie, in a manner unique in Europe, used the accumulated stylistic remains of previous epochs to produce new forms to consolidate its position. It used this symbolic repertoire in four ways: to represent its own internal diversity; as a medium in which to construct individual family histories where the reproduction of the class as a whole was to be assured; to differentiate itself from the aristocracy above and the working class below; and to lay claim to its role as the new heir of France's history and patrimony. The ancien régime became a source of the raw material for both a new bourgeois social order and a new bourgeois history. Although historicist pastiche was also popular in England, Germany, and the United States, styles of past historical epochs did not constitute a repertoire out of which the bourgeoisie could effect internal distinctions or create class distinctions, or make bourgeois history as they did in France.[15] For although by the late nineteenth century, France shared with England and Germany a similar moment of industrial capitalism, which produced the European fascination with the styles of a preindustrial age, the French experience of the Revolution was unique. The dramatic end of the ancien régime in France, combined with the particular course of history in the first seventy years of the nineteenth century, made the French manifestation of the general stylistic phenomenon of historicist pastiche distinctive.

Internal Differentiation through Style

The French bourgeoisie used various ancien régime styles to signify its own internal variations of gender, sexuality, generation, religion, social and geographic origins, and current locations. Although the gender coding was the most obvious, perhaps because it was seen as the most crucial and the most endangered, the task of simultaneously representing, through furniture, all of the factors of distinction created a singularly chaotic system.

By the 1880s, ancien régime reigns were defined as masculine or feminine depending on how far back in time they lay.[16] The earliest monarchies were defined as the most masculine; as one approached the Revolution they became increasingly feminine. Thus nineteenth-century furniture going under the name of "Louis XIII" and "Henri II" was unquestionably masculine, as was all furniture vaguely labeled "medieval" or "Gothic" or "Renaissance." [See illustrations 7.1 and 7.2.] "Louis XIV" and "Louis XV" styles were defined as intrinsically masculine, though potentially androgynous, while "Louis XVI" was held to exemplify femininity. [See illustrations 7.3, 7.4,

7.1 Nineteenth-century lithograph of a seventeenth-century cupboard (Armoire à deux corps) in the Louvre. It is identified as having been made during the reign of Louis XIII in the style of the "Ecole Française." Lithograph by E. Tomaszkiewicz in *L'Art pour tous: Encyclopédie de l'art industriel et décoratif* (15 October 1879), vol. 19, no. 464, p. 1853, plate 4114.

18ᵉ Année.   Nᵒ 464   15 Octobre 1879.

ABONNEMENT ANNUEL
France.....24 fr.
Étranger.....26 fr.
L'Année passée, 30 fr.

L'ART POUR TOUS
ENCYCLOPÉDIE DE L'ART INDUSTRIEL ET DÉCORATIF
Paraissant les 15 et 30 de chaque mois.

PUBLIÉ SOUS LA DIRECTION DE M. E. SAUVAGEOT | FONDÉ PAR M. ÉMILE REIBER, ARCHITECTE

Vᵉ A. MOREL & Cⁱᵉ
ÉDITEURS
13, rue Bonaparte
Paris.

XVIIᵉ SIÈCLE. — ÉCOLE FRANÇAISE.   ARMOIRE A DEUX CORPS, EN NOYER.

(ÉPOQUE DE LOUIS XIII.)   (AU MUSÉE DU LOUVRE, A PARIS.)

« C'est par une surabondance de décoration, par une richesse excessive que ce meuble se distingue et attire l'attention, et non par la pureté et l'élégance des formes. — Il n'est pas, néanmoins, dépourvu de tout mérite, et il devait faire bonne figure dans les anciennes salles de l'époque.

Dieser Schranken kann wohl durch seine überaus reichhaltige dekorative Ausschmückung die Aufmerksamkeit auf sich ziehen, aber ohne seine Formen weder rein noch elegant.

Dieses Mübel ist jedoch keineswegs werthlos, und hat sunächst zu seiner Zeit in den alten geräumigen Sälen seine Rolle gespielt.

This cabinet claims attention more for its superabundance of ornamentation and excessive gorgeousness than for purity and elegance of form.

It is not however devoid of merit, and made undoubtedly a grand figure in the large halls of the epoch.

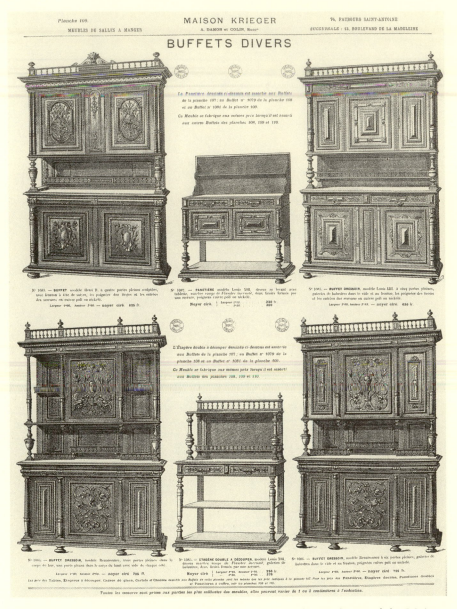

7.2 First page of three entitled "Buffets divers" from the catalogue of the Maison Krieger (Paris: A. Damon and Colin, n.d. [c. 1895]), plate 109. Krieger was a well-known furniture producer and distributor with stores at 74, rue du faubourg Saint-Antoine and 13, boulevard de la Madeleine. All of the buffets—an essential piece of dining room furniture—are identified to be in "medieval," "Renaissance," or "seventeenth-century" styles.

E.Maincent   Imp.Becquet fr. Paris   Chanat lith.

EXPOSITION DU TRAVAIL PARIS 1891

LIT & TABLE DE NUIT LOUIS XV

Exposés par la maison BERNOUX et Cⁱᵉ de Paris   médaille d'or en 1885

Publié par E. MAINCENT   rue de Lancry 2. Paris

D. GUILMARD fondateur

Droits de reproduction réservés

7.3 Bed and night table in "Louis XV" style from the Maison Bernoux. From the Exposition du travail in Paris, 1891. In *Le Garde-Meuble: Collection de meubles* (Paris: E. Maincent, n.d. [1892]), plate 1864.

and 7.5.] "Louis XVI" style was defined as "modest, alluring, indulgent, gracious, svelte, light, and varied."[17] Liminal styles could be altered to change their gender. According to the "taste professionals" of the late nineteenth century, furniture made in "Louis XIV," and especially "Louis XV," style could be specially modified for women to make it feminine.[18]

But the code of appropriate uses of different styles was complicated and often contradictory. The following advice in an 1895 etiquette book to a male customer trying to furnish his bedroom illustrates the complexity and fluidity of this system quite clearly:

As to the form of the bed—the most important issue to resolve— ideally one should seek the advice of the producer. . . . If the artisan

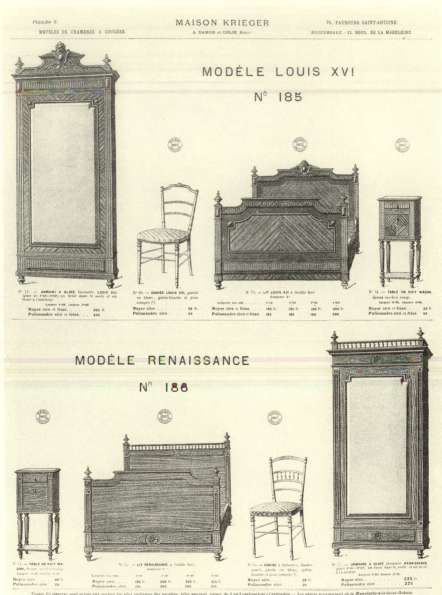

MODÈLE LOUIS XVI

N° 185

MODÈLE RENAISSANCE

N° 186

Nᵒ 71. — ARMOIRE A GLACE biseautée LOUIS XVI (glace de 1ᵐ20×0ᵐ60); un tiroir dans le socle et un tiroir à l'intérieur.

Largeur 1ᵐ08, largeur 2ᵐ40.

Noyer ciré et frisé. . . . 225 fr.
Palissandre ciré et frisé. . . 225

Nᵒ 69. — CHAISE LOUIS XVI, garnie en blanc, galon-lézarde et pose compris (¹).

Noyer ciré . . . . 26 fr.
Palissandre ciré . . . 34

Nᵒ 74. — LIT LOUIS XVI à double face.

Longueur 2ᵐ.

Largeurs du lit 1ᵐ10   1ᵐ30   1ᵐ45   1ᵐ60
Noyer ciré et frisé   183 fr.   185 fr.   196 fr.   200 fr.
Palissandre ciré et frisé   182   185   190   200

Nᵒ 73. — TABLE DE NUIT WAGON, dessus marbre rouge.

Largeur 0ᵐ40, hauteur 0ᵐ90.

Noyer ciré et frisé. . . . 55 fr.
Palissandre ciré et frisé.   55

Nᵒ 73. — TABLE DE NUIT WAGON, dessus marbre rouge.

Largeur 0ᵐ40, hauteur 0ᵐ90.

Noyer ciré . . . . 60 fr.
Palissandre ciré .   60

Nᵒ 75. — LIT RENAISSANCE à double face.

Longueur 2ᵐ.

Largeurs du lit 1ᵐ10   1ᵐ30   1ᵐ45   1ᵐ60
Noyer ciré . . . .   185 fr.   200 fr.   205 fr.   215 fr.
Palissandre ciré .   195   200   205   215

Nᵒ 70. — CHAISE à balustres, dossier gravé, garnie en blanc, galon-lézarde et pose compris (¹).

Noyer ciré . . . . 26 fr.
Palissandre ciré . . . 34

Nᵒ 77. — ARMOIRE A GLACE biseautée RENAISSANCE (glace 1ᵐ20×0ᵐ60); un tiroir dans le socle et un tiroir à l'intérieur.

Largeur 1ᵐ03, hauteur 2ᵐ40.

Noyer ciré . . . . 225 fr.
Palissandre ciré 225

Toutes les mesures sont prises aux parties les plus saillantes des meubles; elles peuvent varier de 1 ou 2 centimètres à l'exécution. — Les glaces proviennent de la *Manufacture de Saint-Gobain.*
(¹) Les prix des chaises entièrement terminées s'obtiennent en ajoutant aux prix ci-dessus la valeur de l'étoffe choisie pour la garniture. — Pour garnir les chaises nᵒˢ 74 et 69 il faut 0ᵐ95 d'étoffe en 1ᵐ30
de largeur et 0ᵐ65 d'étoffe en 1ᵐ60 de largeur.

Voir le Tarif de Literie à la suite des planches de Chambres à coucher.

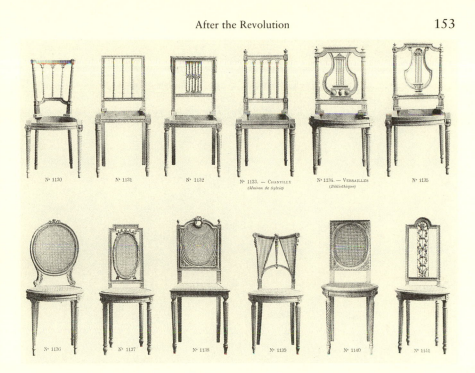

7.5 "Louis XVI" chairs from the catalogue of the Maison Schmit ([Paris, n.p., n.d.], p. 40, nos. 1130–1141). The Maison Schmit was located in the rue du faubourg Saint-Antoine in Paris. These "Louis XVI style" chairs include two exact reproductions with specific historical attribution while the rest represent what I am calling historicist pastiche.

7.4 Bedrooms number 185 ("Louis XVI") and 186 ("Renaissance") from the catalogue of the Maison Krieger (Paris: A. Damon and Colin, n.d. [c. 1895]), plate 8. These two bedrooms are in the style of Louis XVI and of the Renaissance—they do not pretend to be reproductions. Illustrations 7.3 and 7.4 demonstrate the relative arbitrariness of the gendering of ancien régime style. The "Louis XV" set shown in illustration 7.3 is at least as "feminine" in nineteenth-century terms as the "Louis XVI" shown in illustration 7.4, and it is difficult to see the "Renaissance" bedroom as especially "masculine."

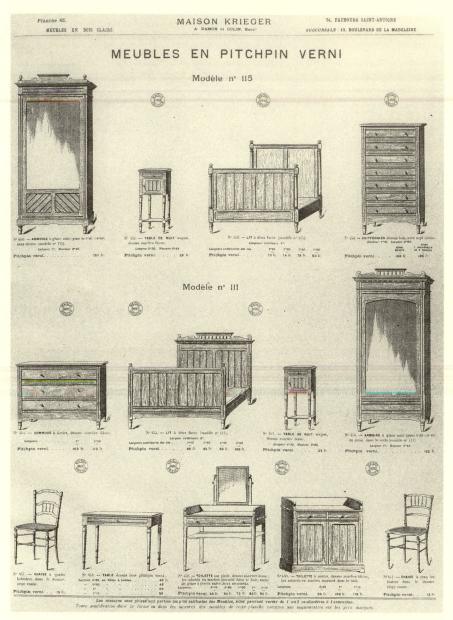

7.6 Maison Krieger, "Meubles en Pitchpin verni," from the catalogue of the Maison Krieger ([Paris: A. Damon and Colin, n.d. {c. 1895}], plate 65). This is an example of ahistorical, "styleless" furniture intended for consumers of small means.

was making a bedroom for someone of princely wealth . . . he would make a bedroom close to the style "Louis XIV"; if you, the customer, were a severe diplomat, a notary, or a magistrate, and slept alone in your room, he would certainly seek inspiration from the Renaissance or Louis XIII. On the other hand, the style "Louis XVI" would definitely be the thing if you were in the habit of sharing your room with your wife.[19]

According to this author, therefore, "Louis XIV" was a style suited to someone who could live like a prince in a republican age; "Louis XIII," a Renaissance style, was appropriate to those of high dignity and seriousness; while "Louis XVI," or feminine furniture, represented a necessary compromise if the bourgeois custom of separate bedrooms was broken. Knowing the "correct" style for a given social position within the bourgeoisie was not, therefore, a simple task. And although for men the critical issues were wealth, social position, and sexual habits, female consumers were supposed to consider their coloring and age as paramount when they furnished their apartments and especially their bedrooms. Another commentator suggested that brunettes should buy "Louis XV" and "Louis XVI," blondes "Louis XIV."[20] Thus other considerations could interfere with the gender code; "Louis XIV" was usually identified as masculine, but here it was attributed to women if they had hair of a certain shade. But age was important too: "If at forty years of age, you need to seek refuge in majesty, you have the choice between 'François I,' 'Henri II,' 'Louis XIII' and 'Louis XIV.' "[21] In this schema, in other words, the masculine, public styles became appropriate for a woman's room after she had passed the age of sexuality (at forty!).

The gendering of ancien régime style—Renaissance as masculine, late eighteenth century as feminine—was entirely a construction of the late nineteenth century. Clearly, people living in the periods when the original versions of this furniture were made did not consider it gendered by style. Furniture was made in each style during its period for all rooms of the house and for the use of both sexes. There was nothing intrinsically masculine about early furniture, nor anything essentially feminine about late eighteenth-century furniture. Even within the gendering of aesthetics in the late nineteenth century, the rococo of Louis XV style (full of curves, highly decorated and ornate) and even the elegance and exuberance of Louis XIV style could as easily have been dubbed feminine as masculine or variable. The gendered attributions had nothing to do with absolute aesthetic associations between certain forms and the masculine or feminine and everything to do with the gendering of the past and of history.[22] In the eyes of the late nineteenth century, the Renaissance was the epoch of robust, manly monarchs and the late eighteenth century the period of corrupt, effeminate kings.[23] The conservatism of this discourse—in the negative evaluation of the Revolution and the implicit causal explanation of the Revolution as an outcome of the corruption and effeminacy of Louis XV and especially Louis XVI—is fascinating, especially as it appears to have been unreflectively adopted by consumers and critics of all political persuasions.

This system was not completely divorced from the visual content of these styles, rather it was made possible by a coincidence between certain aspects of the styles and certain contemporary conceptions of femininity and masculinity. Decoration in the earlier styles was effected by carving the solid structural wood composing the object. Louis XV and Louis XVI, in contrast, were fundamentally veneer styles, where the structural elements of the piece were covered by thin sheets of carefully dyed and shaped wood, mother-of-pearl, or tortoise shell. Veneer could be dubbed feminine because it was ornamented through overlay; a frame was disguised (clothed, made-up) with decorative elements, including trompe l'œil and precious stones.[24] Sculpture, in contrast, transformed the essence of the form and the wood itself; it was done by penetrating the wood with a chisel and was the product of manly labor.[25] According to the assessment of the eighteenth-century furniture industry by a worker delegate to the World's Fair of 1867, "furniture became precious . . . [in the eighteenth century], it put on make-up and jewels. It was gallant, nonchalant . . . the pretty instead of the beautiful, the gracious instead of the heroic. The art of furniture from then on became more and more effeminized and dainty."[26] Selecting a wood when buying furniture was no simpler than choosing its style. This is apparent in an article in the 1882–1883 volume of the *Revue des arts décoratifs*, the elegant organ of the Union centrale des arts décoratifs:

> Among the woods suitable for a bed, there is oak, which is too male, too crude perhaps for a bedroom where a woman is to reign; walnut, a bit more delicate, which some sculpture should enhance; mahogany or rosewood which are both so graceful that any sculpture is unnecessary. If, however, we are discussing a young girl's room, a light or painted wood such as maple or pine, decorated with a colored wood or some inlay would be preferable.[27]

The gendering of style and material was mirrored in the division of space within the home by gender. The bourgeois home in the late nineteenth century was not the exclusively feminine, entirely private space often described by both contemporaries and historians.[28] Rather the home, like much other space in the period, was composed of feminine and masculine, private and public, and youthful and adult places. The records of the furnishings that the unremarkable bourgeois couple Victor and Clélie Dujardin brought into their marriage in 1876 reflect the distribution of tasks and space according to gender: Victor brought his mahogany, glass-doored bookcase "garnie de livres," a leather-topped mahogany desk, and a caned mahogany desk chair. He also had a gilded "Louis XV" picture frame, assorted statues, a barometer, and a bust of Voltaire. He did not bring his, or any other, bed; indeed, it was carefully noted that his iron bed remained with his parents. Clélie, in contrast, brought a mahogany bed, complete with bedding (which cost exactly the same amount as Victor's bookcase and books, 250 francs), matching curtains for the bed and bedroom window, chairs, wardrobe, bidet, mirror, armchair, bedside table for the bedroom, and a sewing basket and table as well as a sewing machine. She also brought a piano, a music stand, and a few things that might have been intended for a living room, such as shelves and their accompanying *objets*, a bentwood chair, and an inlaid bookcase. Victor's room, his space in the house, was clearly to be the study, which was furnished according to his taste and with his furniture. Her space was the bedroom and the salon. He had his bookcase "accompanied" by books, she had her shelves "accompanied" by knickknacks.[29]

Victor and Clélie's division of their apartment was commonplace. The gender-coding of rooms in the apartment had a necessary corollary, given the gender-coding of style, of specific styles for specific rooms. The most "public" of rooms, the dining room, was almost always furnished if not in "Henri II," then in "Louis XIII." Because "Henri II" and "Louis XIII" were explicitly defined as masculine, they were often seen in a study (by definition masculine), but very rarely in a bedroom or boudoir (by definition feminine).[30] Thus the potentially feminine "Louis XIV," "Louis XV," and always feminine "Louis XVI" were generally excluded from dining rooms. Bedrooms, especially women's bedrooms, were best furnished in "Louis XVI" style. It was therefore appropriate, in the dominant classification scheme, to furnish a living room (which was a liminal space) with the feminine version of "Louis XV." A hermaphroditic style was created for a relatively androgynous space.

Discursively, each person, each activity, each gesture, had a place and an appropriate piece of furniture. This image was mirrored in the bourgeoisie's dwelling practices. Bourgeois apartments generally contained a living room, a dining room, a boudoir with an attached bedroom for the mistress of the house, a study for the man and often a bedroom for him as well, rooms for the children, maids' rooms, and a kitchen. Besides these basic rooms, large bourgeois apartments or villas sometimes contained additional living rooms, music rooms, billiard rooms, libraries, antechambers, large front halls, multiple salons, and greenhouses, all of which had to be furnished appropriately.[31] As the scale of the apartment increased, the number of rooms expanded more dramatically than their size.

The specializations of style and of space were the product of the bourgeoisie's process of internal differentiation, which was effected in part to make the social code difficult for outsiders to learn. But they also ensured that every member of the family and of the class learned his or her place within the class. The ancien régime repertoire proved to be well suited to this task, as well as to that of helping to "write" family histories through furniture.

Making Family Histories

Not only did furnishings re-present history in their style, but assemblages of furniture constituted family histories. In the construction of those histories, one sees the ambiguous relationship between the nineteenth-century bourgeoisie and the past. Not only were bourgeois households filled with new "old" furniture, but the moment of marriage was marked by the creation of a new household filled with newly bought furniture. People usually did not want to be subjected to the past generation's taste nor to live surrounded by the un-mediated history of their own or their spouse's family. The horror with which a bourgeois woman married to a novelist described in her memoirs (published in 1894) the house of her husband's parents to which they moved after their marriage may be somewhat extreme, but it dramatically demonstrates the hideousness, to a young woman, of being tied to the past of things and people dead and gone:

> On the ground floor was the dining room with a few chairs lined up along the walls, a large dining table dancing on three legs, a piano whose strings sang a melancholy melody during damp weather, and a desk on which were scattered newspapers received since 1830. Then there was M. Feuillet's study, which he had not used since he had taken to his bed. This room was inhabited by many books entombed under dust, scientific instruments, and a headless statue sitting in the middle of the mantel.

On the first floor was the living room, furnished with the aridness and the stiffness of the First Empire. Everything there was faded, dusty, torn; it all reflected the depression and discouragement of the master of the house. The lampshades disappeared under spiderwebs, the mirrors no longer reflected, only the clock, covered by its dome, was preserved from the ravages of time.

An enormous room, which was supposed to be mine, came after the living room. This room had belonged to my husband's mother. It had not been opened since her death. The wallpaper, succumbing to the cold dampness, was falling off the walls. The "swan's neck" mahogany furniture now listed. Only a painting of Boucher retained its charming freshness.[32]

This text deploys a depiction of the house and of the furniture to evoke a sense of entombment and a loss of identity following marriage. But not accidentally, the only objects that are described as having withstood the passage of time are the eighteenth-century objects—the domed clock and the canvas by Boucher. Although in this case it is real eighteenth-century artifacts that are admired, their privileged exclusion from the general horror of the more recent nineteenth-century past again underlines the bourgeoisie's desire to create links with the prerevolutionary past. But even if the memoirist found the eighteenth-century relics less revolting than the others, she was disinclined to take over the ancestral home. The idea of taking the place of her husband's mother in this animate house where the piano played mournful tunes without human assistance was not attractive. The quotation is full of illness, death, and decay. The description clearly implied, with its insistence on the details of the interior, that the house and its furnishings symbolized the marriage. In moving into a house that was not one's own, furnished with the moldy goods of another generation, the crucial contract between two families did not happen, no new family was formed, and history ended. In contrast, the ideal was to create a new household with earmarked money received from both sides of the family, out of which a new/old story could be constructed. That ideal was well embodied in historicist pastiche, leavened perhaps with a few genuinely old and new objects.

Money for the purchase of furniture was often a nuptial gift. The account books of Jean Pariset show the contributions of various of his relatives, designated for specific purchases, upon the occasion of his marriage in 1873. The largest contribution, 31,500 francs in cash, was from his future wife's family. His father provided three thousand francs for furniture, one uncle gave him one hundred and fifty francs for knives, and his grandmother provided two hundred francs for decorative objects for the mantel over the fireplace. Several people identified only by name gave him large sums: two thousand francs for a bedroom; five hundred and fifty francs for bronzes; two hundred additional francs for ornamenting the mantel. The account books in the following months record the purchases made with this money.[33] By giving money allocated for particular pieces of furniture, but not the furniture itself, relatives asserted the importance of the home, claimed their own place in that home—the new couple would remember who had paid for what—but at the same time allowed the new generation to establish itself. Not only would the couple remember and perhaps tell their children the source of their possessions, but also the account books recorded for posterity the continuity of capital, and of the family. So allocated monetary gifts protected both the future of the family and the integrity of the new couple.[34] Bourgeois families, through the purchasing of objects and the keeping of accounts, were writing their own family histories, creating a legitimate bourgeois past, uniting on paper families joined through marriage. Just as the cohabitation of objects from both sides of a new family testified to the separate past histories and joint future history of the family, so too the accounts recorded the details and history of that merger for all time. The account books reveal bourgeois acceptance of individual mortality and the assumption of familial immortality. They acknowledge that although every marriage was to end in one way or another, the family would endure.

Inheritance of furnishings occurred ideally (and in fact) later in life.[35] Bourgeois families did often inherit furnishings from their parents or other relatives; when couples took over their parents' or relatives' homes, they generally also acquired the contents.[36] Heirs did not feel obliged to keep all of their relatives' furniture, and given the absence of primogeniture, they rarely inherited a complete household.[37] Upon the death of a relative, the heirs or their lawyer would draw up a room-by-room inventory of the contents of the house, often with approximate values in the margins. The heirs would then go through the house, each claiming goods of comparable worth.[38] The old was assessed in monetary terms, divided, dispersed, fragmented, and recombined. The bourgeois world of the late nineteenth century deeply understood the cultural and economic capital provided by the old.

The bourgeois home in late nineteenth-century Paris was neither a refuge nor a place of certainty. It was rather a location filled with desires, needs, and expectations. The making of interiors in the second half of the nine-teenth century was an individual, familial, class, regional, and national project constructing the present, past, and future. Furniture reflected and produced the social standing of the family and served as a space in which individuals tried to make themselves at ease. Interiors were to help create the unity of the family, and yet the space within them was divided by usage and by gender. They were to provide a material basis for the history of the family, and yet the furniture was dispersed with every generation. Consum-ers were simultaneously urged to buy new, innovative furniture and told the right way to use nineteenth-century pastiches. Women were told that the home was to represent their personality, but homes also served to constitute families, groups, and the nation. Women were best represented by "Louis XVI" style, unless they were blond, over forty, or under twenty-one. The world was supposed to be divided in binary opposition, yet there were hermaphroditic styles and androgynous spaces. The home was not simply a private, feminized space; it was also a masculine, public space. Thus the home was always simultaneously inside and outside, part of a private narra-tive, and part of a public one as well. Its public quality was, however, social rather than political. As a mixed feminine/masculine, private/public space, it had its own temporality and relation to history. And, not least, this space outside of capital was constructed with capital and used to reproduce it.

Bourgeois apartments were characterized by a preoccupation with the creation of a specialized, complete, and apparently enclosed and self-contained world. Yet in its fragmentation and specialization, the haven emulated the world it claimed it was trying to exclude. This world was further inhabited by furnishings that were named after and resembled those of France's past but were in fact new. Through the complexities of elaborate combinations and contradictory codings, interior decoration served to cre-ate boundaries against interlopers from within and from the classes beneath and to forge links with the past while insisting on the importance of the present. Thus each object was intended to go with every other object, but unlike eighteenth-century aesthetics, where the ideal was contemporaneous-ness, rationality, and symmetry, the aesthetic basis of nineteenth-century interiors was complex pastiche. In these interiors the old world and the new were to meet, the generations were to be brought together and reconciled, hidden rationality and overt sentimentality were to merge. The price of every object in these apartments was known, recorded, and calculated, but remained invisible; on the surface all was cozy and protected.

It is not surprising then that many bourgeois commentators on taste should have accepted and even embraced and used the middling classes' commitment to ancien régime styles while unanimously condemning the same taste in the working class and regretting the bourgeoisie's reluctance to support new styles. The elaboration of systems of internal differentiation through style was deemed appropriate for the bourgeoisie, while the working class was defined as an undifferentiated mass with no individual or collective history.

Class-making through Style

In the last quarter of the nineteenth century, how and if class difference was to be marked by furniture style became an issue in a new way. In the eighteenth and early nineteenth centuries, cost made furniture that resembled that of the wealthy inaccessible to the laboring classes, so the only possible style slippage across class came between the nobles and very wealthy commoners.[39] The elaboration of systems of distribution, the increasing availability of credit, the expansion of outwork, and mechanization in the nineteenth century made many cheap versions of ancien régime furniture available.[40] By the 1850s the prospect was imminent enough to worry critics, and by the 1880s even some workers could have purchased furniture in the style of kings. This was perhaps not very high quality "royal" furniture but nonetheless furniture whose forms echoed those of the courtly society of the ancien régime and, equally important, furniture that mirrored the styles acquired by the owners' wealthy neighbors.[41] This possibility of the class blurring of interior furnishings, at the same time that divisions between classes were deepening in other ways, raised the question of where social boundaries were to fall and how they were to be marked.

The availability of furniture in the style of the ancien régime at a price the working class could afford was viewed with deep distrust and chagrin by both conservative and socialist commentators; the former argued that the working class should have furniture appropriate to its station that would encourage good and moral behavior, while the latter hoped for furniture that would assist in the building of class solidarity.[42] The conservatives argued that furnishings in courtly style would lead to unreasonable expectations and a dangerous sense of social entitlement, while the socialists thought they would contribute to false consciousness. The following quotation, from an etiquette book published just before the First World War, perpetuated a point of view common thirty years earlier: "Today, the display of false and imitation [furniture] has given to modest households the ambition of elegance and the vanity of appearances. This failing would be moving, if it did not damage the most serious of interests, for it on the one hand exaggerates coquetry and on the other leads to extravagant spending."[43]

Other critics thought that it was also wrong for the bourgeoisie to live in prerevolutionary interiors, but the logic of their complaint was different. The bourgeoisie who acquired courtly furniture were judged unfaithful to their age and class and lacking in courage, whereas members of the working class who chose courtly furniture were thought deceitful in their tastes.[44] The discourses concerning appropriate representation of the working class combined in complicated ways paternalist concern for working-class welfare and a preoccupation with the construction of class boundaries. The ancien régime style furniture offered to workers was itself judged not only inappropriate but also deceptive because inexpensive versions of luxury furniture required cost-cutting—usually in materials and workmanship—and it was claimed that the furniture was often not sound.[45] This admonition from the World's Fair of 1855 in Paris documents this double preoccupation: "Therefore instead of that furniture known under the name of *camelotte* that apes luxury by elaborate forms and fraudulent appearance and offers only illusory good value, woodworkers who would really like to work with intelligence and success for the middling and laboring classes should present furniture in domestic woods, solid, practical and elegant in its simplicity, and above all perfectly adapted to the service that it will provide."[46] If the working class were to buy this furniture that pretended to be something it was not, they would themselves not only pretend to be something they were not, but would also be cheated.[47] The working class was now to live in specially designed working-class dwellings, with working-class furniture.[48] No commentators thought that ancien régime style of any description was appropriate for the working class.

The working class, in this discourse, was saturated with its class position. Although members of a bourgeois household were to be carefully distinguished, within and between households, by their precise status, location, gender, age, and religion, interior working-class space was undifferentiated. The cramped space of working-class dwellings limited the possibilities of elaborate subdivisions, but the working class could, nonetheless, have had furniture marked by gender, age, and religion, rather than simply by class. But the fundamental functions of working-class furniture were to keep the man of the house at home rather than out on the street and to represent the social order.[49] For although the bourgeoisie perceived itself as

highly differentiated and stratified, it believed the working class to be a
basically unified entity, internally segmented only with respect to bourgeois
images of what it ought to be. The bourgeoisie thus drew only one line of
demarcation within the working class—between the domesticated and the
untamed.[50] Cleanliness, practicality, and solidity were to take priority over
aesthetic pleasure for the working class, and all members of that class were
to have interiors in which all the space looked identical. Furthermore, in
this schema, the working class was to have no opportunity to construct its
continuity with a national past through the appropriation of objects with
history, nor was the project of establishing a familial past or an individual
past through objects considered of relevance. The furniture recommended
to the working class was to be practical for everyday use; it was not the
stuff from which dreams, or history, or individuality were to be made.

This project was neither instantaneously realized nor monolithic, however. The class boundaries in these discussions solidified only slowly in the
second half of the nineteenth century. The following quotation, from a
report on the World's Fair of 1867 in which "legitimate" or "illegitimate"
labor, rather than working-class or bourgeois social location, was the most
crucial divide, was already somewhat anachronistic when it was written:

> Here is . . . the horoscope of Parisian furniture. For the worker, the
> artist, the lawyer, the doctor, the scientist, the man of letters, [choose]
> oak—the strong, robust wood—and solid walnut, or their analogues.
> For wealthy households, sculpted furniture in the dining room, the
> living room, and study; veneered furniture from Boutung or Godin
> [stores that sold expensive, fashionable furniture] in the bedroom. For
> châteaux and palaces, elaborate furniture: mantelpieces, canopy beds,
> bookcases, filing-cabinets, wardrobes. . . . For the dubious profes-
> sions, for shady opulence, for boudoirs that are really salesrooms, junk
> (la camelotte). Birds of a feather should flock together. [*Qui se
> ressemble doit s'assembler.*][51]

According to this author, workers, doctors, scientists, and lawyers all did
honest work and were therefore entitled to solid, strong, robust wood. Those
who were wealthy (and the author implies that they were wealthy by birth
rather than by labor) were best represented by highly ornamented pieces.
Those who performed dishonest labor were to possess fraudulent furniture.

Discussions grouping individuals of diverse social class in stylistic categories would become much rarer as the century neared its end. By the late

1860s, a more conservative commentator would have been careful to distinguish between the appropriate representation of a man who labored with his hands and that of a man of letters. So, although the route to class boundaries marked by style was long and somewhat torturous, by the end of the century such distinctions were firmly in place (at least in the minds of bourgeois commentators). Even if all could have lived in the style of kings, this was not to be, and distinctions on the basis of consumer goods were as evident as in the ancien régime.

The vast documentation provided by the Parisian World's Fairs of 1855, 1867, and 1889 offers a window onto these changing conceptions of how social class was to be represented through furniture. Various classification schemes were tried: honest versus dishonest laborers; producers versus consumers; and finally, working class versus the bourgeoisie. These taxonomies demonstrate that the later exclusion of working-class consumers from the ancien régime repertoire of representation was not inevitable; an outcome in which people of all classes would be united in their role as consumers was considered.

It was not obvious to the organizers of the fair of 1855 that class should be the most salient element in how people were addressed in these fairs. This early fair divided producers from consumers of all classes, rather than opposing the owners of the means of production to wage-earners or even the wealthy to the poor. The next major fair in 1867 grouped working-class consumers and producers into one category, separate from the middling classes, and that categorization was maintained through the end of the century.

The creation of the "Galerie de l'économie doméstique" at the Parisian World's Fair of 1855 marked the first step towards a bourgeois consumption regime, but its form indicates that that regime was yet to arrive. The purpose of the *Galerie* was to inform consumers of the sound furniture and other domestic items available and to encourage producers to make such goods.[52] But all consumers except the exceedingly wealthy were targeted by the Galerie, not simply the working class. The organizers shifted the emphasis of the fair from a locus for the producers to show off their art and skill through a presentation of masterpieces in the ancien régime tradition—with the retail cost of prize-winning furniture equivalent to several times a well-paid bourgeois's yearly salary—to an effort to improve consumer taste and provide a bridge between producers and consumers. Economic differences were not completely obscured, however; consumers were divided into a four-tier hierarchy. At the bottom were the poorest, who had little choice but were limited to necessities. Next came those who could afford to be more selective but who were still limited by economic and practical considerations; then came those who could "add to the useful that which was practical and agreeable."[53] Last, and not expected to attend this exhibit, were those for whom money was no object. But the identity of "consumer," which bridged social difference, was central to this organization of the fair. Consumers of different wealth were to have different furniture, but they were all addressed by the fair as consumers in search of self-representation and good taste. By 1867 this classification no longer existed in this form, and working-class consumers had joined working-class producers in their own autonomous world as anthropological objects of bourgeois curiosity rather than as social actors: "This [display] . . . no longer contains only *inexpensive objects*, but also includes exhibits on the methods and materials used in elementary schooling, folk costumes, the work techniques and products of master artisans, and housing blueprints and models. In brief, as the . . . title given to the whole of group indicates, it concerns all of the *objects specially displayed with a view to improving the physical and moral condition of populations*."[54] The bourgeois rather than mass nature of this consumption regime had been established.[55]

The world had come to be divided into wealthy consumers and people who were part of a population in need of amelioration. The effort to build a stylistic wall between a supposedly homogeneous, ungendered working class without history and a highly internally differentiated bourgeoisie with history was fully mobilized. Although in 1855, all were to partake in symbolic social enfranchisement through participation as consumers, by 1867 and especially by the 1880s, the workers' fundamental social role in production was firmly reestablished discursively. Even at midcentury the poor and the rich were not to have the same furniture, but at least the laboring classes were understood to be internally differentiated. Ironically, it was under the Third Republic that some of the dreams of social equality of the Revolution and of the First and Second Republics ran most firmly aground as social boundaries rigidified. The role of the working class as consumers was elided, while the aristocrats were understood to own the real, the archaic, the valuable, and the obsolete. "I knew an old, somewhat decrepit castle lost in the forest of Haute Saône; at the lightest breeze the roof tiles fell on one's head. But what an idyllic interior! The duchesse de Marmie sat in an armchair the likes of which even Wildenstein [a famous collector of the period] does not have; she warmed her feet on a footstool chiseled by Gouthière [an eighteenth-century sculptor]."[56] The aristocratic furniture may have been real and the interior idyllic, but the castle was lost in the depths of the woods, a relic of the past. The workers meanwhile were to possess the furniture linked to neither time nor space, while the bourgeoisie claimed for itself French history as well as the only properly nineteenth-century style.

In fact, efforts by fair organizers in 1855, 1867, and 1889 to influence working-class consumption appear to have failed; few producers were willing to display their goods in the exhibits devoted to the working class, and working-class consumers, like their bourgeois counterparts, were fondest of pastiche ancien régime furniture.[57] The evidence from working-class furniture retailers as well as that yielded by sociological investigations and that derived from novelistic and photographic evidence reinforces this image.[58] Working-class stores sold largely cheap pastiche of ancien régime style (although the style was often even less determinate than that from more expensive stores), and there is evidence that the furniture sold in open-air markets was also generally historicist.[59]

The dreams of the bourgeois taste-enforcers could never have worked, for families and individuals were far more complex and far more sophisticated than the taste-enforcers appear to have been willing to grant. The social location of the family (of any class) emerged from a complex calculus of the origins of the husband and wife, their current position in life, and the social trajectory upon which they were embarked. For social positions were not stable and access to the bourgeoisie or to a particular stratum within the bourgeoisie could be acquired either through a job change (generally on the part of the man) or through the transformation of the interior (generally through the woman's labor). The choice of wife and of interior by M. Rougon (a character in Zola's novel *Son Excellence Eugène Rougon*) vividly demonstrates one facet of this phenomenon:

Mme. Rougon, in three months, had brought a sober atmosphere to the house in the rue Marbeuf, where a licentious mood had dominated before. Now, the rooms—a little cold and very clean—reflected an honorable life. The furniture was methodically arranged, the drapes allowed only a small glimmer of daylight to penetrate, carpeting smothered all noise. The room was dominated by the almost-religious austerity of a convent sitting-room. One even felt that these things were old, that one had entered into a dwelling permeated by a patriarchal odor.

Rougon smiled when complimented on his home. He insisted on saying that he had married following the advice and the choice of his friends. His wife delighted him. He had wanted a bourgeois interior for a long time, an interior that would be a material proof of his honesty and upright character. That was all that was needed to separate him completely from his dubious past, to place him with respectable people.[60]

Zola's Rougon makes a shift from one location within the bourgeoisie to another by way of his furniture. Paul Nizan's novel *Antoine Bloyé* demonstrates the possibilities (and perhaps the costs) of social mobility by a simultaneous change in job and interior. Bloyé climbs the social ladder from laborer to the height of supervisor in the SNCF, the national railroad company.[61] Bloyé's wife consolidates their class position through her newly acquired "Louis XV" living room set that her husband's new job has made materially and imaginatively possible. His continued success in that job may in fact depend to some degree upon the appearance of the room. Nizan makes it clear, however, that the style of the room makes Bloyé feel that he is living a masquerade: "The Bloyés' salon was done in Louis XV style. The chairs, the armchairs, the divan were of polished oak covered with green patterned velvet. In the corner was an Empire card table in mahogany with gilded copper inlays, bought at a sale. Antoine never passed in front of this table without being reminded that he could play neither chess, nor backgammon, nor whist, but only rummy, which he had learned in the depot roundhouses."[62]

Although this example is drawn from a novel intending to document the evils of class betrayal through social mobility, the depiction of class positioning through representation (and its gendering) can be generalized beyond the particularly eloquent example. It was understood that men acquired a class position for their family through their relation to the means of production while women were to realize that possibility through symbolic representation.

The place of a wife, from the 1860s onwards, in class-making through the acquisition and deployment of objects appropriate to the social position of her husband in combination with a parallel emphasis on the importance of the individual, individual expression, and the experience of inhabiting a home authentic to one's inner being, made interior decoration the site of much dissonance.[63]

Revolutionary Effects

The story of the gendered and class meanings attributed to furnishings and spaces in the second half of the nineteenth century and of the use the

Parisian bourgeoisie made of furniture in the construction of personal and national narratives is now told. The question, however, of why consumer goods and why especially pastiche of ancien régime furniture should have been central in this process has not yet been fully resolved. Why, in the late nineteenth century, resurrect the entire ancien régime, rather than specific reigns? And why did commentators seek to exclude the working class from this system? Why furniture? How did these processes of class-, gender-, and history-making happen differently through architecture, clothing, or some other consumer item? Although definitive answers to these questions are as yet impossible, I would like to propose an explanation in which the Revolution plays a crucial role.

The French Revolution of 1789 irrevocably divided the eighteenth century from the nineteenth, inaugurating the latter and inventing the ancien régime. The invention of the ancien régime meant that it was no longer an earlier part of ongoing history but rather a part of the dead past, to be understood, analyzed, and reused as needed by the present. Not only did the Revolution disrupt the flow of history from one reign to the next; it also dissolved ancien régime court culture, thereby creating the possibility of a consumer society in France. For although courtly life was re-created under Napoleon and other nineteenth-century leaders, it never regained the hegemonic position it had held under the ancien régime. Innovation no longer served the same purpose, and social and political legitimacy could better be acquired through historical referents than through novelty.

From the second half of the seventeenth century to the Revolution, courtly consumption was constitutive of power. The essential purpose of royal consumption was to demonstrate the creative and economic strength of the monarch and the loyalty of his court.[64] This could best be done through extremely elaborate and often-changed interiors that would exemplify wealth and power. Furthermore, the cultural hegemony of the royal court was intimately interconnected with the system of guilds and royal manufacturers, all of which were abolished during the Revolution. Critical characteristics of the prerevolutionary courtly consumption regime had been the valorization of stylistic novelty and the denigration of continuity and historicity. Because monarchs acquired legitimacy through inheritance, intrigue, or war, there was no desire or need to imitate the styles of recent or distant regimes; on the contrary, each royal regime used style to differentiate itself from the preceding reign.[65] Everyone in court society participated in this system, with the less powerful reproducing a version of a courtly interior appropriate to their station. Because of the place of interiors in the constitution of power and position in the present, style in interior decoration could not play a significant role in the construction of national or individual narratives across time. And because social and political continuity and legitimacy were provided by a hereditary monarchy and a system of lineages, it did not have to.[66]

Parallel to this system of courtly, patronage-based consumption were the beginnings of bourgeois consumer culture. Distinctive patterns of consumption separate from the court in clothing, accessories, and small items of decoration, including porcelain, flatware, and linen, appeared in France as well as in England and Germany. But although Britain had a highly developed bourgeois and perhaps even petit-bourgeois culture by the second half of the eighteenth century, the same was not true of France.[67] In France, people of all social positions inhabited furnished interiors in ancien régime society, but only those who participated in courtly life had access to "style." There was no specifically bourgeois culture—capable of producing autonomous style—separate from that of the court, and certainly no urban object-based proletarian culture.[68] Political and cultural representation went together, and so devoid of one, the individual or group was excluded from the other. There was the king's style, and then there were scaled-down versions of the king's style, and then there was no style.[69] The people's present and past could not be constructed through objects under this courtly consumption regime.[70]

Revivals and pastiche, which would become the norm of design in the nineteenth century, were unimaginable in this world of courtly consumption. When there was borrowing from the past it was from the very distant past and was perceived as a reclamation of the timeless truths of classical aesthetics. Thus even the neoclassical revival in the mid-eighteenth century, which would appear to be a clear moment of temporal and spatial pirating, was understood in other terms by contemporaries. Eighteenth-century neoclassicism was defined as a reappropriation of abstract principles of aesthetics simply codified or discovered (and not invented) by the ancient Greeks. It was, therefore, not perceived as an instance of borrowing but rather as an enlightened appropriation of transhistorical, universal, aesthetic principles.[71] Likewise, borrowings from distant cultures, including the incorporation of actual elements of Chinese furniture into French pieces, were considered to be complete appropriation rather than a sign of succumbing to the influence of another culture.[72] All of this changed with the Revolution.

Revolutionary efforts to transform thoroughly the staging of everyday life happened more slowly and painfully than efforts in other domains, because they were dependent on a new infrastructure of production and distribution and perhaps because history-making centered in the home was considered of secondary importance to history-making in the public sphere.[73] Developments in interior decoration during the revolutionary moment both resembled and differed from other transformations of the system of representation. The new festivals, calendars, and clothing regulations all served to break with the past and to create novel temporal and ritual cycles.[74] Although few of these innovations were to prove durable even to 1799 and fewer still would survive into the First Empire, they—along with the regicide, new political institutions and discourses, and the abolition of the system of guilds and royal manufacturers—had the enduring effect of breaking the rhythm and seeming inevitability of history.[75] Nineteenth-century historians would be preoccupied with understanding the place of the Revolution within the traditional history of France, with explaining its causes and its consequences. Thus, despite continuities in the organization of manufacturing and of courtly regimes across the revolutionary divide, the Revolution definitively destroyed essential features of an old order of cultural production and consumption. Society was now constituted through the symbolic coding of commodities, which were freed by the Revolution of sumptuary regulation and were now more widely available.[76]

The nineteenth century saw the development of a laissez-faire organization of production and distribution, of an internally stratified, socially uncertain bourgeois society and vociferous demands from nonelite groups for a social place and a political voice. The century inaugurated by the Revolution was crucially marked by new participants in social and political life claiming representation and history as part of the French nation in all domains, including the cultural and symbolic. The Revolution of 1848 continued the task started in 1789 of establishing working-class people as members of society with a claim to representation of all kinds. The battle over the form that representation would take in everyday life would start under the Second Empire. That regime both patronized monumental architecture and encouraged manufacturers to find "appropriate" representations of private life and family history. The expansion of industrial capitalism, the need for the French luxury trades to cope with competition from England, Germany, and the United States, the changing boundaries between public and private spheres, and the increasingly prominent voices of bourgeois women and the working class were all critical in pushing the Second Empire to try to revitalize consumer industries. This complex, diverse, and unruly society was unrepresentable by one unified style; social heterogeneity was represented and constituted through style.

Creating new, sufficient forms of style was a complicated task, for the French were not, in their own eyes, by any means alike and were becoming increasingly unlike as the century neared its end. All the French were to go to school, but they were not all to receive the same schooling. Even in public schools, pedagogical practices and the content of the knowledge taught were adjusted at least as much to the class and gender of the students as to their intellectual potential. Likewise, there was a perceived need for a style adequate to represent the century and the nation, and yet women and men, the bourgeoisie and the working class, Parisians and provincials were not to be represented and reproduced in their homes in the same way. One solution was to appropriate the entire ancien régime past, to represent the bourgeois present and past by excluding other groups from that history, but until the late nineteenth century, that recuperation was problem-ridden.

The recuperation of the entire ancien régime in the late nineteenth century was possible only because it was clear that France would never again have a monarchy. From the 1880s, the Republic was solidly enough settled that reuse of the late ancien régime repertoire became less problematic.[77] The new relative stability of republicanism freed the culture to reappropriate its past more playfully, while at the same time new needs arose for a historical narrative and aesthetic forms adequate to republicanism and to the social structures produced by industrial capitalism.

Thus, although the Revolution played a critical role in the creation of the repertoire, the dynamic of capitalism was essential in producing the need for that repertoire, for it was the result of a shift to a consumer society. The period from 1880 to 1940 was marked by the creation of a bourgeois consumer society; true mass consumption was only to arrive in France after the Second World War. Although by the 1860s, systems of production and distribution would have allowed the working class access to "style"—in certain consumer goods—at prices they could afford, efforts were made to exclude the working class from social representation through style, at least in interior decoration. They were to have their own unique "styleless" goods; the possibilities for elaborate working-class style in consumer durables only emerged after the Second World War. Until the 1950s, if a working-class family acquired objects with style, it left its class to migrate into the petite bourgeoisie. I have been concerned here primarily with the birth of this bourgeois consumer society; the story of its reproduction and transformation in the twentieth century must be left to another occasion, and although many consumer goods could be used to tell the story of the transition from a courtly to a bourgeois to a mass consumer society, my choice has been to focus on furniture.

Furniture was a peculiarly expensive and intensely symbolic consumer good throughout the period. The acquisition of a piece of furniture, for consumers of all classes, represented something different from the purchase of a new spring suit. Its purchase was done more deliberately, with less possibility of frivolity than was the purchase of more perishable goods. Furniture, unlike food and clothing, was often intended to be kept for more than one generation. In buying furniture one was building the family's future. This was not simply a matter of cost. Working-class families waited until they could afford a bed before marrying, even though a bed was not in material terms a necessity of life. Furniture came to constitute the social unit in a unique way.

Part of the symbolic weight of furniture derived from its location at a particular point in the border between public and private lives, a location very different from that of clothing. One could have different outfits and different personalities for various occasions and various interlocutors, but one had at most only one dining room. Thus one's interior was a much less fluid vision and representation of oneself than was clothing.[78] Furniture was considerably more private, and especially more private in nineteenth-century Paris. One did not invite just anyone into one's home, whereas one could be seen by anyone when dressed in a new suit. So the representation through furnishings was more rigid, but the eyes that participated in the vision were more controllable. Thus although the particular puzzle this essay attempts to solve is one concerning taste in furniture, solving that puzzle requires not only coming to terms with the impact of the Revolution on matters of representation and the problem of history, but also grasping the dynamic of the succession of consumption regimes from the courtly consumption of the ancien régime to a bourgeois consumption regime, which was in its turn overtaken by mass consumption.

In the nineteenth century, interiors served to create not only contemporary identities but also historical narratives for a new, much larger society of consumers. The home became one locus where the self, the family, the group, the class, the region, and the nation were imagined, constituted, represented, and reproduced in the past and in the present. The placement of the home in so many different simultaneous social locations generated potential contradictions. The locations did not nest, with an individual contained within a family, which was in turn contained within a group, then within a class, and so on. Most stylistic repertoires were inadequate to the complex project of history-making and representation demanded by this postmonarchical, early commodity culture. The solution was a particular form of historicist design in interior decoration and architecture. Ancien régime style became the dominant and discursively sanctioned style for the middling classes and bourgeoisie, while the laboring and aristocratic classes were to be excluded from this means of participation in the body social.

Nineteenth-century style was not characterized then by bad pastiche, nor by art nouveau, and the style did in fact suit the century. The Revolution dissolved ancien régime court culture (patronage-based) and thereby created the space for the expansion of an already nascent consumer culture (market-based). Furthermore, the Revolution caused an epochal rupture, leaving to the future a newly indeterminate past from which to construct intelligible historical narratives. The Revolution, in destroying the monarchy, killed the old order and invented the "ancien régime" as an historical period now definitively in the past. The ancien régime was incarnated, then, as a symbolic repertoire available for the representation and production of the present and the past.

Lastly, the Revolution inaugurated new contests over the form and meaning of representation. Not only was the definition of who represented the nation politically destabilized, but the Revolution also created the opportunity for claims to cultural and social representation by previously less visible groups. The breaking of historical continuity and the elaboration of industrial society left the French bourgeoisie of the late nineteenth century deeply preoccupied by the problems of historicity, of boundaries, and of categories. The ancien régime repertoire was used to express those internal tensions, to make a claim to a particular relation to the nation's history, and to mark thicker boundaries between men and women of the bourgeoisie and between the working, petit bourgeois, bourgeois, and aristocratic classes. In the process, history became gendered in a new way, with a masculine, heroic, ancient past and a feminized, fragile, more recent past. And although these distinctions made of the bourgeoisie the visible representation of history and nation, they made of the working class a single category, whose lack of differentiation followed from what was assumed to be an inherent incapacity for aesthetic taste.

Notes

List of Abbreviations

AD   Archives départementales
AM   Archives municipales
AN   Archives nationales
BHVP   Bibliothèque historique de la ville de Paris
BM   Bibliothèque municipale
BN   Bibliothèque nationale

Introduction

1. François Furet, "The Revolution is Over," in *Interpreting the French Revolution* (Cambridge: Cambridge Univ. Press, 1981), 1–79. For two recent debates that discuss Furet's contribution to the historiography of the Revolution, see *French Historical Studies* 16 (1990): 741–802. Participants include William Doyle, Michel Vovelle, Colin Lucas, Lynn Hunt, Donald Sutherland, Claude Langlois, David D. Bien, and François Furet.

2. Where revisionists do see significant long-term consequences of the Revolution for French society, these are judged to be largely negative in character. In the controversial *A Critical Dictionary of the French Revolution*, ed. François Furet and Mona Ozouf, trans. Arthur Goldhammer (Cambridge: Harvard Univ. Press, 1989), 715, 789, the Revolution is said to have anticipated the totalitarian politics of the twentieth century. For Anglophone scholars this new direction taken by the *Critical Dictionary* necessarily evokes J. L. Talmon's classic argument about the totalitarian character of Rousseauism (*The Rise of Totalitarian Democracy* [Boston: Beacon Press, 1952]). What its implications will be for the historiography of the Revolution is not yet clear, although it seems likely to revive the Left-Right polemics that Furet originally claimed he was laying to rest.

3. For a clear analysis of the history of the historiographical debate over the French Revolution, see Sarah Maza, "Politics, Culture, and the Origins of the French Revolution," *Journal of Modern History* 61 (1989): 704–723.

4. Even Michel Vovelle, the holder of the traditionally Marxist chair of the French Revolution at the Sorbonne, now declines to defend all aspects of the classical interpretation. In a recent article, he stated, "In the end, one wonders if it is still

appropriate to maintain such shrunken, ambiguous, and above all reductionist terms received from the past, or whether it would not be best to get rid of the labels 'Jacobin' and 'revisionist' altogether. Rather than crushing the opposing point of view under the weight of polemics or under the scorn of a carefully nurtured silence, it would perhaps be preferable to recognize that no hegemonic interpretation of the Revolution exists today and that this is undoubtedly a very good thing" ("Reflections on the Revisionist Interpretation of the French Revolution," trans. Timothy Tackett and Elisabeth Tuttle, *French Historical Studies* 16 [1991]: 749–755, esp. 755). There are, however, a number of historians who continue to do interesting work in the classical mode. See, for example, Florence Gauthier, ed., *La Guerre du blé au XVIIIᵉ siècle: La Critique populaire contre le libéralisme économique au XVIIIᵉ siècle* (Paris: Passion, 1988); Guy Lemarchand et al., *Les Campagnes françaises: Précis d'histoire rurale* (Paris: Messidor, 1983); Claude Mazauric, *Jacobinisme et Révolution: Autour du bicentenaire de 1789* (Paris: Messidor, 1984).

5. The seminal "revisionist" texts are Alfred Cobban, *The Social Interpretation of the French Revolution* (Cambridge: Cambridge Univ. Press, 1964); Colin Lucas, "Nobles, Bourgeois, and the Origins of the French Revolution," *Past and Present*, 60 (1973): 84–126; George V. Taylor, "Types of Capitalism in Eighteenth-Century France," *English Historical Review* 79 (1964): 478–497; Taylor, "Noncapitalist Wealth and the Origins of the French Revolution," *American Historical Review* 72 (1967): 469–496; and most recently, William Doyle, *Origins of the French Revolution* (Oxford: Oxford Univ. Press, 1980).

6. See Lynn Hunt, *Politics, Culture, and Class in the French Revolution* (Berkeley: Univ. of California Press, 1984)

7. See, for example, Keith Michael Baker, *Inventing the French Revolution* (Cambridge: Cambridge Univ. Press, 1990); Hunt, *Politics, Culture, and Class*; Mona Ozouf, *Festivals and the French Revolution*, trans. Alan Sheridan (Cambridge: Harvard Univ. Press, 1988).

8. Furet, *Interpreting the French Revolution*, esp. 12–17.

9. *Ibid.*, 72.

10. Baker, *Inventing the French Revolution*, 4. In this study, Baker traces two distinct lines of origin for the term "political culture"—the first deriving from the political science tradition associated with Gabriel Almond, Lucian Pye, and Sidney Verba and the other drawing "in eclectic fashion" on the work of theorists such as Michel Foucault, the "Cambridge" school of the history of political discourse, Marshall Sahlins, and others (*ibid.*, 307–308, n. 8).

11. Hunt, *Politics, Culture, and Class*, 10. See also *The New Cultural History*, ed. Lynn Hunt (Berkeley: Univ. of California Press, 1989).

12. Hunt, *Politics, Culture, and Class*, 10.

13. Furet, *Interpreting the French Revolution*, 48.

14. The essays in this collection have been influenced to some degree by the work of Michel Foucault. For a clear discussion of the usefulness of Foucault's approaches

and theories for historians, see Patricia O'Brien, "Michel Foucault's History of Culture," in *The New Cultural History*, 25–46.

15. There have been a few very important studies done in this field, however. See especially William H. Sewell, Jr., *Work and Revolution in France: The Language of Labor from the Old Regime to 1848* (Cambridge: Cambridge Univ. Press, 1980).

16. Furet, *Interpreting the French Revolution*, 6.

17. For two fascinating discussions that evaluate the current tendency to question the relevance of the Revolution, see Isser Woloch, "On the Latent Illiberalism of the French Revolution," *American Historical Review* 95 (1990): 1452–1470; Eric J. Hobsbawm, *Echoes of the Marseillaise: Two Centuries Look Back on the French Revolution* (New Brunswick: Rutgers Univ. Press, 1990).

18. Hobsbawm, *Echoes of the Marseillaise*, 110.

1. "Constitutional Amazons"

I would like to thank Dena Goodman and Lynn Hunt for their helpful comments on earlier versions of this paper.

1. AD Doubs L2879, *Vedette*, 2 November 1792; AD Doubs L2880, *Vedette*, 18, 22, and 25 January 1793; AD Doubs L2881, *Vedette*, 1 and 15 March 1793; AD Doubs L2845, *Feuille hebdomadaire*, 22 February 1793, and Description de la Fête de la Raison, 20 November 1793; AD Doubs L2890, *Feuille hebdomadaire*, 15 March 1793 and 5 April 1793, and Réponse de C. Legrand à Dormoy, 3 February 1793. Above all, see Henriette Perrin, "Le Club de femmes de Besançon," *Annales révolutionnaires* 9 (1917): 629–653 and 10 (1918): 37–63, 505–532, 645–672, esp. 10:40–56. As Perrin explains, the battle between the female club and the male Jacobins and their journalists became embroiled in a rivalry between leading male revolutionaries over control of local political opinion.

2. Joan Landes, *Women and the Public Sphere in the Age of the French Revolution* (Ithaca: Cornell Univ. Press, 1988), esp. chap. 4. For recent critiques of Landes, see Dena Goodman, "Public Sphere and Private Life: Toward a Synthesis of Current Historiographical Approaches to the Old Regime," *History and Theory* (February 1992: 58–77); Benjamin Nathans, "Habermas's 'Public Sphere' in the Era of the French Revolution," *French Historical Studies* 16 (1990): 620–644, esp. 634–636.

3. Lynn Hunt, "The Unstable Boundaries of the French Revolution," in *A History of Private Life*, vol. 4, *From the Fires of Revolution to the Great War*, ed. Michelle Perrot (Cambridge: Harvard Univ. Press, 1990), 12–45, esp. 12–20, 44–45. Nancy Fraser, "Rethinking the Public Sphere: A Contribution to the Critique of Actually Existing Democracy," *Social Text* 25–26 (1990): 56–80, offers helpful insights into the changing definitions of the private.

4. Revolutionary women's clubs existed in the following fifty-six towns or villages. In the north or northwest: Bréteuil, LeMans, Lille, Saint-Omer; in the center or Paris basin: Blois, Creil, Cusset, Melun, Montargis, Orléans; in the east or Burgundy: Avallon, Besançon, Châlons-sur-Marne, Colmar, Dieuze, Dijon, Gevrey, Montcenis, Nancy, Plombières, Tonnerre; in the southeast: Alès, Arles, Castellane (Basses-Alpes), Clermont-Ferrand, Eguilles, Grasse, Grenoble, Lyon, Marseille, Montpellier, Saint-Zacharie, Yssingeaux; in the southwest: Angoulême, Auch, Aulnay, Bayonne, Beaumont (Dordogne), Bordeaux, Caraman, LeCarla, Casteljaloux, Civray (Vienne), Cognac, Condom, Damazan, Limoges, Montauban, Pau, Rodez, Ruffec, Saint-Junien (Haute-Vienne), Saint-Sever-Cap, Tonneins, Tulle, Vic-en-Bigorre. Fleeting or less clearly organized clubs may also have existed in Boulogne, Honfleur, Rouen, and Toulouse. This list does not include royalist women's clubs, nor "sociétés fraternelles des deux sexes." More research will no doubt turn up other women's clubs. This list is compiled from archival sources in Besançon, Bordeaux, Dijon, and Lyon, and from Georges Fournier, "Les Femmes dans la vie politique locale en Languedoc pendant la Révolution française," in *Les Femmes et la Révolution française*, ed. Marie-France Brive (Toulouse: Presses Univ. de Mirail, 1989), 115–122; Dominique Godineau, *Citoyennes tricoteuses: Les Femmes du peuple à Paris pendant la Révolution française* (Aix-en-Provence: Alinéa, 1988), 113–114; Michael Kennedy, *The Jacobin Clubs in the French Revolution: The First Years* (Princeton: Princeton Univ. Press, 1982), 88–99; Yvonne Knibiehler, "Femmes de Provence en Révolution," in *Femmes et la Révolution*, ed. Brive, 149–155; and especially Marc Villiers, *Histoire des clubs de femmes et légions d'amazones* (Paris: Plon-Nourrit, 1910), 109–221.

5. *Annales patriotiques et littéraires de la France*, 2 March 1790; AD Gironde 12L19, Lettre des Amies de la liberté et de l'égalité aux citoyens frères et président de la section Guillaume Tell, 22 July 1793. (Versions of this same appeal to the sections and men's popular societies to accept the Constitution of 1793 also appear in AM Bordeaux I68 and I78, dated between July and September 1793.) Kennedy, *Jacobin Clubs*, 96; BM Dijon, *Journal patriotique du département de la Côte-d'Or*, 12 July 1791.

6. Henri Giroux, "Les Femmes clubistes à Dijon," *Annales de Bourgogne* 57 (1985): 23–45, esp. 25, 31–33; Knibiehler, "Femmes de Provence," 149; Abbé Laborde, *La Société des amies de la Constitution de Pau* (Pau: Lescher-Moutoué, 1911), 7; Geneviève Langeron, "Le Club de femmes de Dijon," *La Révolution en Côte-d'Or* 5–7 (1929): 5–71, esp. 18–20; Perrin, "Femmes de Besançon," 9:646–649; R. Roger Tissot, *La Société populaire de Grenoble pendant la Révolution* (Grenoble: Imprimerie Léon Aubert, 1910), 69; "Registre de la Société des amies des vrais amis de la Constitution à Ruffec," published by M. Chauvet, *Bulletin historique et philologique* 3 and 4 (1902): 528–530 (also published without membership list in *Révolution française* 46 [1904]: 247–278). Most of the members provide only names and no information about their social occupation or that of their husbands or

fathers. AD Gironde 12L19, Lettre des Amies de la liberté et de l'égalité aux citoyens frères et président de la section Guillaume Tell, 22 July 1793. Louis de Combes suggests that the second women's club of Lyon, named "Société populaire des citoyennes amies de la Constitution," was founded by women of a more popular class, who found little appeal in the "patriotisme de bon ton" of the "Association des citoyennes dévouées à la patrie et à la loi" (*Clubs révolutionnaires des Lyonnaises* [Trévoux: Jeannin, 1908], 5). The largest women's club in Bordeaux also claimed to have as members "a large number of wives of your [the Recollets] society members" (AD Gironde 12L19, Lettre des Amies de la liberté et de l'égalité séante à l'Intendance aux Recollets, 2 May 1793).

7. Kennedy, *Jacobin Clubs*, 89–93; Villiers, *Histoire des clubs de femmes*, 109–110. Throughout chapter 5, Villiers provides examples of limited female participation in Jacobin men's clubs.

8. BM Dijon, Fonds Milsand 2040, Discours prononcé à la Société des amies de la Constitution de Dijon par Madame Masuyer, 6 September 1791; *Journal patriotique de la Côte-d'Or*, 20 September 1791, Lettre des Amies de la Constitution de Dijon aux sociétés populaires de chefs-lieux des départements. These two documents also appear in AD Doubs L2843, showing that they had been received at least by the Jacobin society of Besançon. Inaugural oaths and speeches often reveal clues to the major goals and motivations of women's clubs. In June 1791 the women of Bordeaux, for example, swore their loyalty to "Nation, Law, and King," promised to "maintain the Constitution with all [their] power," and to "neglect nothing to inspire [their] children with the love of liberty and of the laws." Oath taken by "Amies de la Constitution," 28 June 1791, as quoted in Aurélien Vivié, *Histoire de la Terreur à Bordeaux* (Bordeaux: Feret et fils, 1877), 95–97.

9. Laborde, "Amies de la Constitution à Pau," 7–10; Kennedy, *Jacobin Clubs*, 93–95; Perrin, "Femmes de Besançon," 9:647; *Journal patriotique de la Côte-d'Or*, 7 June 1791; Giroux, "Clubistes à Dijon," 25; *Annales patriotiques*, 10 December 1790, 31 December 1790, 16 March 1791. Carra's most extensive praise of women's clubs appears on 8 October 1791.

10. *Journal patriotique de la Côte-d'Or*, 3 May 1791, 7 June 1791, 12 July 1791, 20 September 1791, Lettre des Amies de la Constitution de Dijon aux sociétés populaires de chefs-lieux des départements; Louis Hugueney, *Les Clubs dijonnais sous la Révolution, leur rôle politique et économique* (Dijon: Jobard, 1905), 103–104; Kennedy, *Jacobin Clubs*, 95; "Registre de la Société des amies à Ruffec," 260; Villiers, *Histoire des clubs de femmes*, 150; "Etta Palm d'Aelders Proposes a Network of Women's Clubs to Administer Welfare Programs in Paris and Throughout France," in *Women in Revolutionary Paris, 1789–1795*, ed. Darline Gay Levy, Harriet Branson Applewhite, and Mary Durham Johnson (Urbana: Univ. of Illinois Press, 1979), 68–69.

11. Knibiehler, "Femmes de Provence," 151.

12. Sobry also provided for three male officers and a "superior general" to "inspire

respect"; women had to have the permission of their husbands or fathers to join. This Lyonnais club was unusual in that it had male officers. BM Lyon, Fonds Coste 4027, Règlement de l'Association des citoyennes dévouées à la patrie, 1 October 1791, and Institution de l'Association des citoyennes devouées à la patrie, discours par M. Sobry, président du comité central des 31 sociétés populaires de Lyon.

13. Règlement des Sœurs de la Constitution de Bréteuil, 8 août 1790, as reproduced in R. Anchel, "Les Sœurs de la Constitution à Bréteuil," *Révolution française* 56 (1909): 531–536, esp. 531–534.

14. Discours par M. Pille à l'inauguration des Amies de la Constitution de Dijon, 30 May 1791, in *Journal patriotique de la Côte-d'Or*, 7 June 1791.

15. Perrin suggests that one reason for the developing animosity between the men's and women's clubs of Besançon was the women's persistent attachment to Catholicism, which became problematic as male anticlericalism grew in 1792–1793 ("Femmes de Besançon," 9:652–653). In Bordeaux, when the "Amies de la liberté et de l'égalité" (formerly of Saint-André) urged the reluctant Recollets men's club in August 1793 to allow Constitutional clergy to say mass in the hospitals, they assured the male Jacobins that the women would guard against counterrevolutionary clergy (AD Gironde 12L19, Lettre des citoyennes Amies de la liberté et de l'égalité séante à la ci-devant Intendance au citoyen président [des Recollets], 4 August 1793).

16. AM Bordeaux D86, Procès-verbaux des délibérations municipales de Bordeaux, 27 and 28 June 1791; Discours par Mlle. Mantegués de Grasse, printed in *Annales patriotiques*, 28 September 1791; AM Bordeaux I78, Lettre de Mlle. Elisabeth Lé au président des Surveillants, 3 March 1792.

17. Knibiehler, "Femmes de Provence," 152; *Journal patriotique de la Côte-d'Or*, 7 June 1791; BM Dijon, MSS 1660, Louis Benigne Baudot, *Notes des événements révolutionnaires et mouvements politiques qui ont eu lieu principalement à Dijon pendant la Révolution*, 88–89. Baudot also describes the more conservative women's zealous reaction to prevent parish suppressions and to protect nonjurors (39–40). AM Dijon, 1D1/2, Délibérations de la municipalité de Dijon, 16 August 1791; Procès-verbaux des séances de l'assemblée législative, 25 December 1791, as quoted by Hugueney, *Clubs dijonnais*, 128; Lettre de M. Gros, 22 June 1792, in Abbé L. Jarrot, *Dijon du 1er janvier 1790 au 23 janvier 1793: Lettres à un émigré*, special volume of *Mémoires de la Société bourguignonne de géographie et d'histoire* 16 (1900): 91–268. Langeron suggests that the women supporting the nonjurors may even have had a women's organization of their own ("Femmes de Dijon," 11–15, 41–42).

18. BM Lyon, Fonds Coste 4027, Institution de l'Association des citoyennes.

19. Discours par Françoise Sanson, Avis aux dames portées pour la contre-Révolution, as quoted by Villiers, *Histoire des clubs de femmes*, 127–128; AM Bordeaux I78, Discours prononcé par Veuve Brillat, Amie de la Constitution de Saint-André, n.d. (c. spring 1792).

20. References to the participation of women in varied revolutionary ceremonies are

pervasive. See especially Kennedy, *The Jacobin Clubs*, 97–98; Villiers, *Histoire des clubs de femmes*, chap. 5; Giroux, "Femmes clubistes à Dijon."

21. *Révolutions de Paris*, 16–23 February 1793, Réponse de la citoyenne Blandin-Desmoulins de Dijon au citoyen Prudhomme, 10 February 1793; *Annales patriotiques et littéraires*, 8 October 1791; BM Dijon, Fonds Juigné, no. 58, recueil 112, P. Baillot, "Chant de la Côte-d'Or pendant la guerre de la liberté"; AD Doubs L2877, *Vedette*, 13 January 1792.

22. *Journal de Provence*, July 1791, 28:279, as cited by Knibiehler, "Femmes de Provence," 150; Villiers, *Histoire des clubs de femmes*, 139; Péricaud, *Tablettes chronologiques*, 22 June 1791, as quoted in Albert Metzger and Joseph Vaesen, *Lyon en 1791*, vol. 4 of *Bibliothèque lyonnaise: Révolution française*, 11 vols. (Lyon: Georg., 1882–1888), 4:53; *Journal de Lyon*, 9 January 1793.

23. In various instances throughout France, male Jacobins and local authorities objected when women sought to organize women-only festivals or, above all, when they sought to bear arms, even in a ceremonial fashion. See, for example, Laborde, *Amies de la Constitution de Pau*; AM Bordeaux D95, Déliberation du corps municipal de Bordeaux, 28 June 1792; *Journal patriotique de la Côte-d'Or*, 20 December 1791; Giroux, "Femmes clubistes à Dijon," 36–37; AN C162 (359), Lettre de la Société des dames de la Constitution de Lille aux législateurs, 18 August 1792.

24. *Journal patriotique de la Côte-d'Or*, 3 May 1791, records a recent session of the Société des amis de la Constitution; see also the 30 May 1791 speech by President Pille in the 7 June 1791 issue; Claude Hollier, "Discours sur les bienfaits de la Constitution envers les femmes," 10 October 1791, as quoted in Villiers, *Histoire des clubs de femmes*, 152–153; AD Doubs L2844, vol. 62, no. 1167, Discours de H. F. Robert, vicaire-supérieur et président de la Société des amis de la Constitution, 19 May 1792; BM Lyon, Fonds Coste 4027, Règlement de l'Association des citoyennes, and Institution de l'Association des citoyennes. Sobry also wrote several pamphlets on the proper ceremonial dress of both male and female patriots.

25. Lynn Hunt, *Politics, Culture, and Class in the French Revolution* (Berkeley: Univ. of California Press, 1984), 31, 61–66; Elke Harten and Christian Harten, *Femmes, Culture, et Révolution*, trans. B. Chabot, J. Etore, and O. Mannoni (Paris: des Femmes, 1989), 38–45; Marie Hélène Huet, *Rehearsing the Revolution: The Staging of Marat's Death, 1793–1797*, trans. Robert Hurley (Berkeley: Univ. of California Press, 1982), 35–38; Landes, *Women and the Public Sphere*, 162–167.

26. On Besançon: AD Doubs L2880, *Vedette*, 1 January 1793 and 1 February 1793, Lettre des Amies de la liberté et de l'égalité aux curés et officiers municipaux des communes du département de Doubs; AD Doubs L2845, Règlement pour les hospitalières de l'hôpital Saint-Jacques de Besançon, 1793; Perrin, "Femmes de Besançon," 10:647–653, 656–670. On Bordeaux: AM Bordeaux I75, Adresse de la Société des amies de la Constitution à leurs concitoyens sur la nécessité de former des listes de souscription où les veuves et les filles s'engageront à soigner les malades dans les hôpitaux, n.d. (c. early 1792). See also I72, Registre des délibérations de la

Société patriotique des surveillants de la Constitution, 7 March 1791 to 6 July 1792, and I73, Registre des délibérations de la Société patriotique des surveillants zélés, 19 July 1792 to 19 frimaire an II (9 December 1793). On Dijon: AM Dijon 1D1/2, Délibérations de la municipalité de Dijon, 5 August 1791; 1D1/6, Délibérations du conseil général de la commune de Dijon, esp. 24 May 1792, 3 July 1792, 21 September 1792, 31 December 1792, 1D1/3, Délibérations de la municipalité de Dijon, esp. 21 January 1792, 23 October 1792, 8 November 1792; Langeron, "Femmes de Dijon," 47–54; *Journal patriotique de la Côte-d'Or*, 5, 12, and 26 July 1791.

27. Fournier, "Femmes en Languedoc," 121; Alan Forrest depicts the confused and often sad results of the revolutionary attempt to overhaul care of the poor and sick (*The French Revolution and the Poor* [New York: St. Martin's, 1981], esp. chaps. 3–5). On charitable work as the acceptable extension of maternity from the family to society, see Harten and Harten, *Femmes, Culture, et Révolution*, 28–31.

28. *Annales patriotiques*, 8 October 1791.

29. On transparency, see Hunt, *Politics, Culture, and Class*, 44–46; Jean Starobinski, *Jean-Jacques Rousseau: Transparency and Obstruction*, trans. Arthur Goldhammer (Chicago: Univ. of Chicago Press, 1988).

30. Landes, *Women and the Public Sphere*, chap. 4.

31. "Registre de la Société des amies à Ruffec," ed. M. Chauvet.

32. BM Dijon, Fonds Delmasse 1551, Discours prononcé par M. André Brès aux Dames dijonnaises peu de jours après le serment fédératif de la troisième année de la liberté française; *Révolutions de Paris*, 16–23 February 1793, Réponse de la citoyenne Charton de Lyon au citoyen Prudhomme, 15 February 1793.

33. *Révolutions de Paris*, 16–23 February 1793, Réponse de la citoyenne Blandin-Desmoulins de Dijon au citoyen Prudhomme, 10 February 1793.

34. *Journal patriotique de la Côte-d'Or*, 20 September 1791, Lettre des Amies de la Constitution de Dijon aux sociétés populaires de chefs-lieux des départements; Adresse de la Présidente Chedaneau, 11 August 1791, "Registre de la Société des amies à Ruffec," ed. M. Chauvet, 250.

35. In Bordeaux, for example, one of the women's clubs renamed itself "Amies de la République une et indivisible" after the Federalist revolt to assert loyalty to a centralized, Montagnard republic. The signatures make clear that this club had been the "Amies de la Constitution," then "de la liberté et de l'égalité"; the club originated in the Saint-Dominique parish of Bordeaux (AD Gironde 12L19, Lettre de la Société des amies de la République une et indivisible aux législateurs, 15 October 1793).

36. AD Doubs L2880, *Vedette*, 18 January 1793; Villiers, *Histoire des clubs de femmes*, 191–192. See also *Annales patriotiques*, 6 June 1791, Lettre des Amies de la Constitution de Grenoble, 31 May 1791; Discours prononcé à la Société des amis de la Constitution de Grenoble, 29 June 1791, par Mme. B . . . , as excerpted in M. Maignien, *Bibliographie historique du Dauphiné pendant la Révolution*, 3 vols. (Grenoble: Imprimerie Dauphinoise, 1891), 2:60.

37. Perrin, "Femmes de Besançon," 10:529–532. Their vocal stance and repeated

petitions earned them the unending enmity of the market women, but also enabled them to win municipal backing for their demands. BM Dijon, Fonds Delmasse 1724, Arrêté pris en commun par les deux sociétés des Amies et Amis de la Constitution, à Dijon, sur l'usage du sucre et du café, and Lettre des quatre commissaires à l'Assemblée nationale, 12 February 1792. The ten-page letter accompanying the petition amounted to a veritable political program, addressing every issue from foreign policy to the viability of a republic. On the grain riot, see BM Dijon, MSS 1660, Baudot, *Evénements révolutionnaires*, 188–189; AM Dijon 1D1/6, Délibérations du conseil général de la commune de Dijon, 1 December 1792.

38. AN F⁷3686 (6), Affiche des citoyennes de Lyon, September 1792, Extrait de registres des délibérations du Conseil général de Lyon, 18 September 1792, Lettre du Laussel (procureur général) au Ministre de l'intérieur Roland, 22 September 1792; *Procès-verbaux des séances des corps municipaux de la ville de Lyon*, 13–22 September 1792; *Procès-verbaux des séances du conseil général du département de Rhône-et-Loire, 1790–1793*, ed. Georges Guigue, 2 vols. (Trévoux: Jeannin, 1895), 1:131–133 (17–20 September 1792); Villiers, *Histoire des clubs de femmes*, 178–180; Maurice Wahl, *Les Premières années de la Révolution à Lyon (1789–1792)* (Paris: Armand Colin, 1894), 604–612.

39. Godineau emphasizes that Parisian female political activism should not be viewed as centering merely on subsistence issues (*Citoyennes tricoteuses*, 160, 208). The same point holds true for the provinces.

40. AM Bordeaux I78, Adresse aux représentants du peuple français des Amies de la liberté et de l'égalité, n.d. (c. February 1793); "Adresse de la Société des femmes républicaines de Besançon aux administrateurs et au peuple du Jura," 4 August 1793, as quoted in Perrin, "Femmes de Besançon," 10:59–60; AD Gironde 12L19, Lettre des citoyennes Amies de la liberté et de l'égalité aux représentants en mission Ysabeau et Baudot, 25 August 1793, Lettre des représentants aux Amies, 7 September 1793, Lettre des citoyennes Amies au citoyens [des Récollets?], 17 September 1793, Lettre des citoyennes Amies de la République une et indivisible aux législateurs, 15 October 1793; AM Bordeaux I78, Lettre des représentants du peuple aux citoyennes Amies de la liberté et de l'égalité à Bordeaux, 28 August 1793; Lettre des Amies de la liberté et de l'égalité à Bordeaux à la Convention nationale, 28 September 1793. The women's clubs from the parishes of Saint-André and Saint-Dominique are represented here. On the struggle for control of Bordeaux between the Girondins and Montagnards, and the involvement of the deputies, see Alan Forrest, *Society and Politics in Revolutionary Bordeaux* (Oxford: Oxford Univ. Press, 1975), esp. chap. 9.

41. Godineau, *Citoyennes tricoteuses*, 144–145; Perrin, "Femmes de Besançon," 9:633; BM Poitiers S22, Elisabeth-Bonaventure Lafaurie, *Discours sur l'état de nullité dans lequel on tient les femmes, relativement à la Politique*, 16 May 1791, (Dax, 1791); AD Gironde 12L19, Lettre des Amies de la liberté et de l'égalité aux législateurs, 14 April 1793.

42. Godineau, "Autour du mot citoyenne," *Mots* 16 (1988): 91–110. This theme of citoyennes without citizenship is also discussed in *Citoyennes tricoteuses*, esp. 263–284. See also Darline Gay Levy and Harriet Branson Applewhite, "Women and Militant Citizenship," in *Femmes et la Révolution*, 63–69.

43. AM Bordeaux I74, Projet d'adresse aux épouses et mères de famille par C. Morin, 10 October 1791; Discours du citoyen Moisard, 10 November 1793, as quoted in Camille Bloch, "Les Femmes d'Orléans pendant la Révolution," *La Révolution française* 43 (1902): 49–67, esp. 61.

44. Linda K. Kerber, *Women of the Republic: Intellect and Ideology in Revolutionary America* (New York: W. W. Norton, 1980), chap. 9.

45. "Registre de la Société des amies à Ruffec," ed. M. Chauvet, 248, 258–259; Villiers, *Histoire des clubs de femmes*, 124, 141–142 ("Arrêté des Dames et demoiselles patriotes de Nantes").

46. AM Bordeaux I78, Discours de Mlle. Dorbe à la Société des amies de la Constitution pour l'anniversaire du grand homme Mirabeau, 10 April 1792.

47. AD Doubs L2880, Discours d'Emilie Tardy, in *Vedette*, 11 January 1793; Lettre de la citoyenne Maugras, c. March 1793, as quoted in Perrin, "Femmes de Besançon," 10:42–43.

48. On the revolutionaries' depiction of aristocratic, feminine, and dissimulating qualities in opposition to transparency and masculine qualities, see Lynn Hunt, "The Many Bodies of Marie-Antoinette: Political Pornography and the Problem of the Feminine in the French Revolution," and Sarah Maza, "The Diamond Necklace Affair Revisited (1785–86): The Case of the Missing Queen," both in *Eroticism and the Body Politic*, ed. Lynn Hunt (Baltimore: Johns Hopkins Univ. Press, 1991). See also Dorinda Outram, "'Le Langage mâle de la vertu': Women and the Discourse of the French Revolution," in *The Social History of Language*, ed. Peter Burke and Roy Porter (Cambridge: Cambridge Univ. Press, 1987), 120–135, esp. 124–126.

49. Discours de Grosjean à la société populaire de Baume, 20 October 1791, as quoted in Perrin, "Femmes de Besançon," 641.

50. Lettre des Amies de la Constitution de Dijon à leurs frères de la Société des amis, *Journal patriotique de la Côte-d'Or*, 20 December 1791; AD Doubs L2880, Discours de la citoyenne Guillemet, *Vedette*, 4 December 1792; *Révolutions de Paris*, 16–23 February 1793, Réponse de la citoyenne Blandin-Desmoulins de Dijon au citoyen Prudhomme, 10 February 1793; Discours de Madame Challan, 21 March 1790, as quoted in Villiers, *Histoire des clubs de femmes*, 193.

51. Discours de Monestier du Puy-de-Dôme, as quoted in Villiers, *Histoire des clubs de femmes*, 158, also see 192–193; "Registre de la Société des amies à Ruffec," ed. M. Chauvet, 258.

52. Discours des citoyennes d'Avallon, armées de piques, aux Amis de la Constitution, prononcé par Madame Peutat, spring 1791, reprinted in *Les Femmes dans la Révolution*, 3 vols. (Paris: Edhis, 1982), vol. 1.

53. AM Bordeaux I78, Lettre des Amies de la liberté et de l'égalité aux Surveillants, 9 November 1792; AD Gironde 12L19, Lettre des Amies de la liberté et de l'égalité aux Recollets, 24 April 1793; *Procès-verbaux des séances de la Société populaire de Rouen*, ed. Chardon, as quoted by Villiers, *Histoire des clubs de femmes*, 121–122.

54. Discours de la citoyenne Vigoureux aux Amis de la Constitution de Rouen, 28 December 1791, as quoted by Villiers, *Histoire des clubs de femmes*, 121–122; *Annales patriotiques et littéraires de la France*, 8 October 1791.

55. National Convention, session of 9 brumaire an II (30 October 1793), and General Council of the Commune of Paris, session of 27 brumaire an II (17 November 1793), in *Women in Revolutionary Paris*, 212–220; Godineau, *Citoyennes tricoteuses*, 163–176.

56. *Révolutions de Paris*, 19–26 January 1793.

57. AD Doubs L2881, "Lettre d'un abonné," *Vedette*, 12 March 1793; Malot, Poème sur la prise de l'église Saint-Julien, as cited in Michelle Sabanadze, "Les Femmes et la Révolution française en Bourgogne," in *Femmes et la Révolution*, 157–166, esp. 161.

58. AM Bordeaux I78, Lettre des frères Surveillants aux sœurs Amies de la liberté et de l'égalité, 20 February 1793.

59. Haize, *Saint-Servan pendant la Révolution*, as quoted by Villiers, *Histoire des clubs de femmes*, 132; *Déclaration des droits de femmes* (Lyon, 1791), as quoted in Wahl, *Premières années de la Révolution à Lyon*, 365–366n, and Combes, *Clubs révolutionnaires de Lyonnaises*, 12; BM Lyon, Fonds Coste 4027, Règlement de l'Association des citoyennes and Institution de l'Association des citoyennes. M. Sobry most probably wrote these regulations; at the very least, his suggestions had a definitive influence on their essential qualities. For further satires of the "chaotic" women's club of Lyon, see *La Mère Duchesne à Lyon*, reproduced in Alphonse Balleydier, *Histoire politique et militaire du peuple de Lyon pendant la Révolution française (1789–1795)*, 3 vols. (Paris, 1846) 3:xvii–xxvi; Abbé Guillon de Montléon, *Mémoires pour servir à l'histoire de la ville de Lyon pendant la Révolution*, 3 vols. (Paris: Baudouin frères, 1824), 1:90. Combes provides further discussion of the mockeries of the women's clubs of Lyon; however, he (and Balleydier) misquote the "Règlement" by attributing the power of silencing discord to a female rather than male president (*Clubs révolutionnaires de Lyonnaises*, 10–12).

60. AD Doubs L2880, *Vedette*, 28 December 1792; Discours par Jacques Boileau à la société populaire d'Avallon, 1792, in M. Leger, *Les Représentants du peuple dans l'Yonne*, 88–89; Amar, Session of National Convention, 30 October 1793, as quoted in *Women in Revolutionary Paris*, 216; François Poullain de la Barre, *De l'excellence de l'homme contre l'égalité des sexes* (1675), unpublished translation by Natalie Zemon Davis.

61. Règlement des Sœurs de la Constitution de Bréteuil, 8 August 1790, as reproduced in Anchel, "Sœurs de la Constitution à Bréteuil," 531–534; AN F⁷3686 (6),

Lettre de Laussel au Ministre de l'intérieur Roland; Lettre de Boileau, *La Bouche de Fer*, 1:341, as quoted in Villiers, *Histoire des clubs de femmes*, 204; BM Dijon, Fonds Delmasse 1551, Discours prononcé par M. A. Brès. On Besançon, see n. 1.

62. Laborde, *Amies de la Constitution de Pau*, especially his quotes of *Courrier des 83 départements*, 40, and of the anonymous pamphlet, *Réponse au discours de Pauline Siro, présidente de la Société des amies de la Constitution séante à Pau*, 42–43; Chaumette, Session of Paris Commune, 17 November 1793, in *Women in Revolutionary Paris*, 219.

63. Amar, Session of National Convention, 30 October 1793, as quoted in *Women in Revolutionary Paris*, 216.

64. *Journal patriotique de la Côte-d'Or*, 24 May 1791.

2. Rural Political Activism

I would like to thank Gail Bossenga, Geraldine Friedman, Lynn Hunt, Ted W. Margadant, and Dennis J. McEnnerney for their helpful suggestions on earlier versions of this essay. The research was made possible thanks to support from the Bourse Chateaubriand and the University of California, Berkeley.

1. Keith Michael Baker, ed., *The Old Regime and the French Revolution* (Chicago: Univ. of Chicago Press, 1987), 239.

2. All population figures for this study are taken from a census made in year III and appear in AD Somme Lᵃ460, District d'Abbeville; Lᵃ461, District d'Amiens; Lᵃ462, District de Doullens; Lᵃ463, District de Montdidier; Lᵃ464, District de Péronne. The documents concerning Roye-sur-le-Matz are in AN D VI 53, Comité de Finances.

3. See AN series D VI, Comité de Finances. Contenant lettres, mémoires, et réclamations concernant la répartition et perception de l'impôt, des octrois, et autres droits. See also AN series D XIV, Comité de Droits féodaux. Lettres suppliques, réclamations, et mémoires au sujet des droits féodaux, personnels ou réels, dîmes et champarts, rentes foncières, adressées soit par les communautés d'habitants, soit par des particuliers, 1789–1791. Each of these is classified alphabetically by department.

4. The literature on the early modern tax revolt is vast. For an excellent synthesis covering insurrections throughout Europe, see Yves-Marie Bercé, *Revolt and Revolution in Early Modern Europe*, trans. Joseph Bergin (New York: St. Martin's Press, 1987). For Bercé's work on the French case, see *Histoire des Croquants: Etude des soulèvements populaires au XVIIᵉ siècle dans le sud-ouest de la France*, 2 vols. (Paris: Droz, 1974); *Croquants et Nu-pieds: Les Soulèvements paysans en France du XVIᵉ au XIXᵉ siècle* (Paris: Gallimard, 1974). For a provocative analysis of the reasons why there were so few revolts in the late-seventeenth and the eighteenth centuries, see Emmanuel LeRoy Ladurie, "Révoltes et contestations rurales en France de 1675

à 1788," *Annales: Economies, Sociétés, Civilisations* 29 (1974): 6–22. For the Vendée revolt during the Revolution, see Charles Tilly, *The Vendée* (Cambridge: Harvard Univ. Press, 1964).

5. Eugen Weber, *Peasants into Frenchmen: The Modernization of Rural France, 1870–1914* (Stanford: Stanford Univ. Press, 1976).

6. See Karl Marx, *Class Struggles in France, 1848–1850* (New York: International Publishers, 1964).

7. Georges Lefebvre, *Les Paysans du Nord pendant la Révolution française* (Paris: F. Rieder, 1924); Pierre de Saint-Jacob, *Les Paysans de la Bourgogne du Nord au dernier siècle de l'ancien régime* (Paris: Société des Belles Lettres, 1960).

8. Hilton Root, *Peasants and King in Burgundy: Agrarian Foundations of French Absolutism* (Berkeley: Univ. of California Press, 1987); François Hincker, "Un Micro-climat politique: Les Paysans du Causse de Villeneuve (Aveyron) pendant la Révolution," in *Les Paysans et la politique: 1750–1850,* ed. Roger Dupuy, a special volume of *Annales de Bretagne* 89 (1982): 167–183.

9. Pierre Goubert, "Aspects sociaux des manufactures picardes et beauvaisiennes au temps de Louis XIV," *Bulletin de la Société de l'histoire moderne* 52 (1953): 10–15, esp. 11.

10. Pierre Deyon, "Les Progrès économiques et les sociétés provinciales," in *Histoire de la Picardie,* ed. Robert Fossier (Toulouse: Privat, 1974), 261–289, esp. 264–265.

11. AD Somme L^a467, Statistique. Renseignements demandés par Thévenet, député de l'Assemblée nationale, sur les récoltes et le commerce du département; réponses des cinq districts, 1792.

12. Victor Daline, *Gracchus Babeuf à la veille et pendant la Grande Révolution française, 1785–1794,* trans. Jean Champenois (Moscow: Éditions du Progrès, 1976), 82–86. Originally published as V. M. Dalin, *Grakkh Babef; Nakanune i vo vremia Velikoi Frantsuzkoi revolutsii (1785–1794)* (Moscow: Akademie Nauk, 1963).

13. R. B. Rose, *Gracchus Babeuf 1760–1797, the First Revolutionary Communist* (Stanford: Stanford Univ. Press, 1978), 56.

14. For a clear discussion of the feudal system, feudalism, and seigneurialism, see François Furet, "Feudal System," in *A Critical Dictionary of the French Revolution,* ed. François Furet and Mona Ozouf, trans. Arthur Goldhammer (Cambridge: Harvard Univ. Press, 1989), 684–693. Also helpful is J.Q.C. Mackrell, *The Attack on "Feudalism" in Eighteenth-Century France* (London: Routledge, 1973).

15. For a narrative of the history of the Somme during the Revolution, see François-Irénée Darsy, *Amiens et le département de la Somme pendant la Révolution,* 2 vols. (Amiens: A. Douillet, 1878–1883).

16. Georges Lefebvre, *The Great Fear of 1789: Rural Panic in Revolutionary France,* trans. Joan White (Princeton: Princeton Univ. Press, 1973).

17. François Furet, "Night of August 4," in *Critical Dictionary,* 107–114. Also see P. M. Jones, *The Peasantry in the French Revolution* (New York: Cambridge Univ. Press, 1988), 81–85.

18. Baker, *The Old Regime and the French Revolution*, 228–231.

19. Jones, *The Peasantry in the French Revolution*, 81–85.

20. R. B. Rose, "Jacquerie at Davenescourt in 1791: A Peasant Riot," in *History from Below: Studies in Popular Protest and Popular Ideology in Honour of George Rudé*, ed. Frederick Krantz (Montreal: Basil Blackwell, 1985), 141–158.

21. AN D VI 53, Finances.

22. AN D XIV 10, Droits féodaux.

23. AD Somme L³375, Evénements de police dans les communes, 1791. Rose gives a complete account of this riot ("Peasant Riot," 141–142) and the subsequent court case ("Peasant Riot," 154–155).

24. Daline, *Babeuf*, 63.

25. Rose, *Babeuf*, 28.

26. Rose, "Peasant Riot," 158.

27. AN D XIV 10, Droits féodaux.

28. *Ibid.* For an account of the legislation regarding the redemption of seigneurial dues, see J.-N. Luc, "Le Rachat des droits féodaux dans le département de la Charente-Inférieure (1789–1793)," in *Contributions à l'histoire paysanne de la Révolution française*, ed. Albert Soboul (Paris: Editions sociales, 1977), 309–352, esp. 311–313.

29. AN D XIV 10, Droits féodaux.

30. *Ibid.*

31. *Ibid.*

32. For more on the politics of the departmental Directory and the political cleavages in the Somme, see my "Rural Political Culture in the Department of the Somme during the French Revolution," (Ph.D. diss., Univ. of California, Berkeley, 1988).

33. AN D XIV 10, Droits féodaux. It is interesting to note that the same week that the circular was published, the Directory of the Somme incensed liberal and moderate revolutionaries by sending Louis XVI a letter in support of his flight to Varennes. The letter caused a national scandal and was even reprinted in the *Moniteur universel*. The Constituent Assembly called the administrators to Paris to explain why they had written such a letter, then relieved most of them of their positions.

34. AD Somme L³375, Evénements de police.

35. *Ibid.*

36. Luc, "Le Rachat des droits féodaux," 311–313. Jones also provides a good summary of this legislation (*The Peasantry in the French Revolution*, 86–94).

37. AN F³§II Somme 1, Organisations communales.

38. Luc, "Le Rachat des droits féodaux," 312–313.

39. André Castaldo, *Les Méthodes de travail de la Constituante: Les Techniques délibératives de l'Assemblée nationale, 1789–1791* (Paris: Presses Univ. de France, 1989), 292.

40. *Moniteur universel*, 18 December 1789.

41. Marcel Marion, *Histoire financière de la France depuis 1715*, 5 vols. (Paris: Rousseau, 1919), 2:35.

42. Marion, *Histoire financière*, 2:8.

43. For an excellent overview of royal taxes in France, see Gail Bossenga, "Taxes," in *Critical Dictionary*, 582–603. For a brief, but thorough, overview of the complicated system of taxation in the Old Regime, see François Hincker, *Les Français devant l'impôt sous l'ancien régime* (Paris: Flammarion, 1971). For a detailed examination of taxes under the Old Regime and into the modern period, see Marcel Marion, *Histoire financière*.

44. Rose, *Babeuf*, 58.

45. M. S. Romaineville, *Mémoire sur la Picardie, contenant les doléances de la généralité d'Amiens* (Cap de Bonne-Espérance, 1789), 2.

46. Rose, *Babeuf*, 61.

47. AN AD XVI 77, Histoires de la Somme pendant la Révolution. Compte-rendu par André Dumont.

48. Rose, *Babeuf*, 61–62.

49. Marion, *Histoire financière*, 2:91.

50. AN F^{11}221, Documents divers sur les subsistances.

51. Ted W. Margadant has demonstrated that analogous calls to equalize the tax burden were made by small towns that sought to eliminate tax advantages enjoyed by larger cities: "The Rhetoric of Contention: Conflicts between Towns during the French Revolution," *French Historical Studies* 16 (1989): 284–308, esp. 298.

52. Cited by Marion, *Histoire financière*, 2:91.

53. For an account of Babeuf's role in the tax revolt, see Gérard Walter, *Babeuf, 1760–1797, et la Conjuration des Egaux* (Paris: Payot, 1980), 36–47.

54. See especially Daline, *Babeuf*, 170–220. Daline attacked Gérard Walter's study of Babeuf because Walter "tried to depreciate the importance of Babeuf's activities." In his polemical critique, Daline takes Walter to task for a chapter subhead entitled, "Au Service des cabaretiers de Roye." This "Leninist" position considers it anathema even to suggest that Babeuf was but a part of a larger sociopolitical movement. Albeit from a more moderate stand, Rose basically takes the same point of view: "Babeuf was careful to explain the political principle which lay behind the use of the right of petitions itself. In this way the inhabitants of the remote villages and working-class faubourgs of Picardy were introduced to the same principles of direct democracy on which the advanced revolutionaries of Paris districts were currently basing their campaign for political autonomy" (*Babeuf*, 68).

55. AN D VI 53, Finances.

56. Marion, *Histoire financière*, 2:85–89, 237.

57. *Ibid.*, 2:225.

58. For a balanced treatment of the tensions caused by fiscal privileges within rural communities during the Old Regime, see Jones, *The Peasantry in the French Revolution*, chap. 2.

59. Marion, *Histoire financière*, 2:34.

60. AN D VI 53, Finances.

61. *Ibid.*

62. *Ibid.*

63. Marion, *Histoire financière*, 2:35; AN D VI 53, Finances.

64. AN D VI 53, Finances.

65. *Ibid.*

66. *Ibid.*

67. Camille Bloch, ed., *Procès-verbaux du Comité des finances de l'Assemblée constituante* (Rennes: Imprimerie Oberthur, 1922), 34–35, 52, 58, 64–65.

68. Marion, *Histoire financière*, 2:36–38; Bloch, *Comité des finances*, 65.

69. This study fits into a larger literature by scholars who are providing empirical evidence of the politicization of rural inhabitants during the Revolution. See, for example, John Markoff, "Peasant Grievances and Peasant Insurrection: France in 1789," *Journal of Modern History* 62 (1990): 445–476; Markoff, "Peasants Protest: The Claims of Lord, Church, and State in the *Cahiers de Doléances*," *Comparative Studies in Society and History* 32 (1990): 413–454; Melvin Edelstein, "La Place de la Révolution française dans la politisation des paysans," *Annales historiques de la Révolution française* 280 (1990): 135–149.

70. For two compelling analyses of rural politics in the twentieth century, see Suzanne Berger, *Peasants against Politics: Rural Organization in Brittany, 1911–1967* (Cambridge: Harvard Univ. Press, 1972); Laird Boswell, "Rural Communism in France, 1920–1939: The Example of the Limousin and the Dordogne," 2 vols. (Ph.D. diss., Univ. of California, Berkeley, 1988).

3. Revolutionary Audiences

This article was made possible through the support of the American Council of Learned Societies and the John M. Olin Program for the Study of Political Culture at the University of Chicago. I wish to thank Elisabeth C. Bartlet, Steven Englund, and Caroline C. Ford for their comments and suggestions.

1. Paul d'Estrée [Paul Quentin], *Le Théâtre sous la Terreur (Théâtre de la peur) 1793–1794* (Paris: Emile-Paul Frères, 1913), 52–53; Aurélien Vivié, *Histoire de la Terreur à Bordeaux*, 2 vols. (Bordeaux: Feret et fils, 1877), 2:111–120. The offending lines of Pedro Calderón de la Barca's *La Vida es sueño* (1636), which appeared in French translation in 1733, come in the third act, when supporters of the reigning king Basilio attempt to prevent his son Sigismundo from overthrowing him.

Although there is no reason to doubt d'Estrée's account of Arouch and his execution, I have been unable to find additional references to the actor in the press or in secondary literature. Vivié's *Histoire de la Terreur* lists the man as a victim of the guillotine but gives no circumstances of arrest.

2. Molé was away from his home, Naudet was traveling in Switzerland, and Dessartes was in Barèges when the police rounded up their colleagues. Noted for his obesity in many dramatic roles, Dessartes reportedly suffered an attack of apoplexy and died the moment he learned of the arrests.

For descriptions of the *Pamela* incident, see Georges Duval, *Souvenirs thermidoriens*, 2 vols. (Paris: Victor Magen, 1844), 1:278–288; *Almanach des spectacles*, 1794, 1:122–125; *Moniteur universel*, 5 September 1793; Marvin Carlson, *The Theater of the French Revolution* (Ithaca: Cornell Univ. Press, 1966), 159–161; d'Estrée, *Le Théâtre sous la Terreur*, 18–20. See also François de Neufchâteau, *Pamela, ou la Vertu récompensée* (Paris: Barba, an III).

3. *Le Modéré*, which premiered 28 October 1793, portrayed the necessary arrest of "M. Modératin" as a victory for the Republic ([J.- B.- Henri Gourgault, *dit* Dugazon], *Le Modéré* [Paris: Maradan, an II]). The formal complaint against Dugazon was that he "dared to commit the guiltiest antics and jokes against Marat" (*Feuille du salut public*, 31 October 1793).

4. A 1790 performance of *Iphigénie en Aulide*, for instance, was temporarily halted when the duchesse de Biron stood up to demand a repeat of the chorus "Chantons, célébrons notre reine" and was promptly showered with fruit from the parterre below. By 1792, both revolutionary and counterrevolutionary songs were often the instruments of war between factions in the theaters. See August von Kotzebue, *Paris en 1790: Souvenirs de voyage* (Paris: n.d.), 16–17; Adélaïde de Place, *La Vie musicale en France au temps de la Révolution* (Paris: Fayard, 1989), 59; Laura Mason, "*Ça ira* and the Birth of the Revolutionary Song," *History Workshop* 28 (1989): 22–38.

5. Carlson, *The Theater of the French Revolution*, 114–115.

6. D'Estrée, *Le Théâtre sous la Terreur*, 19–20.

7. Quoted in *Almanach des spectacles*, 1794, 1:124.

8. "Extrait d'une lettre écrite par les représentants du peuple à Bordeaux au ministre de l'intérieur," published in *Moniteur universel*, 13 December 1793.

9. "Extreme sensitivity creates mediocre actors; mediocre sensitivity creates the multitude of bad actors; and an absolute lack of sensitivity prepares sublime actors" (Denis Diderot, *Paradoxe sur le comédien* [Paris: Flammarion, 1981], 133). For a discussion of eighteenth-century attitudes toward the actor's place in the fiction of the drama, see Martine de Rougemont, *La Vie théâtrale en France au XVIIIᵉ siècle* (Paris: H. Champion, 1988), 84–90, 205–212; Angelica Goodden, *'Actio' and Persuasion: Dramatic Performance in Eighteenth-Century France* (Oxford: Oxford Univ. Press, 1986).

10. *Journal des spectacles*, 15 August 1793.

11. A round of applause went through the audience when a character in *La Chêne patriotique* wearing a liberty bonnet walked onto the stage, for example; *Tarare*, an

opera by Salieri and Beaumarchais, invariably provoked shouting matches and even a few fistfights as the Asian king swore his oaths on an altar of liberty, decreed the dissolution of (Buddhist) monasteries, and liberated African slaves (*Chronique de Paris*, 12 July 1790, 5 August 1790, 10 August 1790; Béatrice Didier, *Ecrire la Révolution 1789–1799* [Paris: Presses Univ. de France, 1989], 161–169).

12. *Chronique de Paris*, 12 July 1790.

13. *Ibid.*

14. *Ibid.*

15. *Journal de Paris*, 14 July 1790.

16. *Ibid.*

17. *Ibid.*, 28 August 1793.

18. *Journal des spectacles*, 28 August 1793.

19. *Moniteur universel*, 30 August 1793.

20. *Journal des spectacles*, 28 August 1793.

21. Joseph Fiévée, *Les Rigueurs du Cloître* (Paris: Imprimerie de l'Auteur, n.d.), 37; *Almanach des spectacles*, 1791.

22. Emmet Kennedy provides yearly statistics for the period 1789–1799 that show that the performance of plays with "nonrevolutionary" titles far outnumbered the performance of plays with "revolutionary" titles. In 1792 there were 665 plays with revolutionary titles staged as compared to 6,544 with nonrevolutionary titles; in 1794, when the numbers were the closest, the nonrevolutionary still outnumbered the revolutionary by 4,872 performances to 2,443. Kennedy's general point is valid, but only with the caveat that it is extremely difficult to judge whether a work bore revolutionary references by its title alone. See Emmet Kennedy, *A Cultural History of the French Revolution* (New Haven: Yale Univ. Press, 1989), 396. For similar statistics and conclusions regarding the low percentage of plays with political overtones before 1793 in boulevard theaters, see Michèle Root-Bernstein, *Boulevard Theater and Revolution in Eighteenth-Century Paris* (Ann Arbor: UMI Research Press, 1984), 219–229, 248–250.

23. Quoted in Elisabeth C. Bartlet, "Etienne Nicolas Méhul and Opera During the French Revolution, Consulate, and Empire: A Source, Archival, and Stylistic Study," 5 vols. (Ph.D. diss., Univ. of Chicago, 1982), 1:275.

24. D'Estrée, *Le Théâtre sous la Terreur*, 6; Place, *La Vie musicale en France*, 109.

25. *Feuille du salut public*, 7 brumaire an II (28 October 1793).

26. *Moniteur universel*, 2 December 1793.

27. D'Estrée, *Le Théâtre sous la Terreur*, 193.

28. *Moniteur universel*, 16 May 1794; see also Henri Welschinger, *Le Théâtre de la Révolution, 1789–1799* (Paris: Charavay Frères, 1880), 479–492.

29. "Three hundred persons were on the stage when the curtain rose," the spectator writes. "At the stanza beginning with the verses 'Amour sacré de la patrie,' the people and the warriors knelt, lowered their lances, and with an adagio this hymn that had been so sublimely martial assumed a religious character. Suddenly, when the

choir sounded the terrible battle cry, 'Aux armes citoyens,' the three hundred men, women, and children rose spontaneously to the sound of the tocsin and of the drums beating. . . . Everyone flew into combat, waving armor, bonnets, and banners in the air. This magical outburst was unlike all else; nothing could be more skillfully combined than this disorder that so genuinely communicated the enthusiasm simulated on the stage to the hall." Quoted in Jean Mongrédien, *La Musique en France des Lumières au Romantisme, 1789–1830* (Paris: Harmoniques Flammarion, 1986), 43–44.

30. Welschinger, *Le Théâtre de la Révolution*, 271, 306, 327–329.

31. The tumult began when someone shouted, "Down with the Jacobins!" Several fights broke out inside the hall, and, hearing the commotion within, a crowd from the surrounding quarter soon gathered outside "to vindicate the patriots." The fighting spilled out onto the sidewalk and several local women were dragged through the mud before the municipal guard was able to quell the riot. See *Chronique de Paris*, 27 February 1792.

32. *Ibid.*

33. *Ibid.*, 15 May 1792.

34. *Ibid.*

35. D'Estrée, *Le Théâtre sous la Révolution*, 4.

36. *Feuille du salut public*, 31 August 1793.

37. *Ibid.*

38. *Journal des spectacles*, 2 October 1793.

39. *Almanach des spectacles*, 1794, 1:119; d'Estrée, *Le Théâtre sous la Terreur*, 288.

40. D'Estrée, *Le Théâtre sous la Terreur*, 8, 288.

41. Quoted in Elisabeth C. Bartlet, "From *Académie Royale de Musique* to *Opéra National*: The Republican 'Regeneration' of an Institution," unpublished manuscript quoted by permission of the author, 36.

42. *Journal de Paris*, 9 November 1793; Pierre Caron, *Paris pendant la terreur. Rapports des agents secrets du ministre de l'intérieur*, 6 vols. (Paris: Picard, 1910), 1:317.

43. Welschinger, *Le Théâtre de la Révolution*, 144–146.

44. *Feuille du salut public*, 3 floréal an II (22 April 1794).

45. *Ibid.*, 25 vendémiaire an II (16 October 1793).

46. *Révolutions de Paris*, 5–12 November 1793, quoted in Beatrice F. Hyslop, "The Parisian Theater During the Reign of Terror," *Journal of Modern History* 17 (1945): 332–355, esp. 343.

47. Letter signed Aristide Valcour, in *Journal des spectacles*, 9 September 1793.

48. *Ibid.*; d'Estrée, *Le Théâtre sous la Terreur*, 90.

49. This fusion of state and society took many diverse forms as republican virtue reshaped the language, altered the calendar, redefined fashions, and created a generation of babies with such names as Brutus, Gracchus, and Cato. See Lynn Hunt,

Politics, Culture, and Class in the French Revolution (Berkeley: Univ. of California Press, 1988), 56–57, 72; *idem.*, "The Unstable Boundaries of the French Revolution," in *A History of Private Life*, vol. 4, *From the Fires of Revolution to the Great War*, ed. Philippe Ariès and Georges Duby, trans. Arthur Goldhammer (Cambridge: Harvard Univ. Press, 1990).

50. See Keith Michael Baker, "Sovereignty," in *A Critical Dictionary of the French Revolution*, ed. François Furet and Mona Ozouf, trans. Arthur Goldhammer (Cambridge: Harvard Univ. Press, 1989), 844–859.

See also " 'Jacobin': Fortune et infortunes d'un mot," in Mona Ozouf, *Ecole de la France* (Paris: Gallimard, 1984), 83: "The essence of Jacobinism is in the impossibility of conceiving a divided popular will, a frontier between minority and majority, between the public and private spheres. The world of Jacobinism is that of the declaration, of the vision of Saint-Just that each year at the Temple each man should name his friends, announce his associations and give the reasons for his separations; where the inner conscience is itself criminal. This ideal of perfect social and psychological visibility is the essence of Jacobinism."

51. Caron, *Paris pendant la Terreur*, 1:169, 374.

52. Barré, Léger, and Rosières, *L'Heureuse décade* (Paris: Librairie de la Vaudeville, n.d.), 30.

53. Welschinger, *Le Théâtre de la Révolution*, 145–146.

54. Caron, *Paris pendant la Terreur*, 3:88.

55. See Jean-Jacques Rousseau, *Lettre à M. d'Alembert sur son article Genève* (Paris: Flammarion, 1967); Jean Starobinski, *Jean-Jacques Rousseau: Transparency and Obstruction*, trans. Arthur Goldhammer (Chicago: Univ. of Chicago Press, 1988), esp. 92–97; David Marshall, "Rousseau and the State of Theater," *Representations* 13 (1986): 84–114; Carol Blum, *Rousseau and the Republic of Virtue: The Language of Politics in the French Revolution* (Ithaca: Cornell Univ. Press, 1986).

Lynn Hunt has written on the relationship between the dangers of private interest and revolutionary transparency: "In France in the 1790s, factional politics was synonymous with conspiracy, and 'interests' was a code word for betrayal of a nation united. Nothing particular (and all 'interests' were by definition particular) was supposed to divide the general will. Constant vigilance and the publicity of all politics were the ways to prevent the emergence of particular interests and factions. Behind these notions was the revolutionary belief in the possibility and desirability of 'transparency' between citizen and citizen, between the citizens and their government, between the individual and the general will. Accordingly, there should be no artificial manners or conventions separating men from each other and no institutions blocking free communication between citizens and their delegates" (*Politics, Culture, and Class*, 44).

56. This was precisely how revolutionary festival planners described audiences. Two examples must suffice to stand for the many rich parallels between revolutionary dramatic experience and the disposition among citizens that festival planners hoped

to encourage: De Moy defined a festival as "a sort of drama, as it were, in which the celebrants [*fêtans*] are the actors"; Merlin articulated the same ideal, writing that at festivals the people are at once "spectator, actor, and spectacle." See Charles-Alexandre de Moy, *Des Fêtes, ou Quelques idées d'un citoyen français relativement aux fêtes publiques* (Paris: Garnery, an VII), 6; Antoine Christophe Merlin, *Opinion de Merlin (de Thionville) sur les fêtes publiques* (Paris: Imprimerie Nationale, 9 vendémiaire an III [30 September 1794]), 2. See also Mona Ozouf, *Festivals and the French Revolution*, trans. Alan Sheridan (Cambridge: Harvard Univ. Press, 1988).

57. *Feuille du salut public*, 9 brumaire an II (30 October 1793).

58. Rousseau raised a version of this complaint against the hypocrisy of actors: "Of what does the actor's skill consist? It is the art of counterfeit, of assuming a character other than one's own, of appearing different than one actually is, of speaking passionately in cold blood, of saying the things one does not believe as naturally as the things one does, and of ultimately forgetting one's own place for having taken on that of another" (*Lettre à d'Alembert*, 163).

59 François Furet, *Interpreting the French Revolution*, trans. Elborg Forster (Cambridge: Cambridge Univ. Press, 1978), 53–57.

60. Letter to *Journal de la Montagne*, reprinted in *Journal des spectacles*, 9 September 1793.

61. Quoted in Arthur Pougin, *La Comédie-Française et la Révolution*, (Paris: Gaultier, Magnier, 1902), 116.

62. The play was still running in December, when a press notice remarked favorably upon the "loud, happy acclaim" it continued to elicit (*Moniteur universel*, 3 December 1793).

63. *Journal des spectacles*, 9 September 1793.

64. *Feuille du salut public*, 20 September 1793.

65. D'Estrée, *Le Théâtre sous la Terreur*, 90–91.

66. Caron, *Paris pendant la Terreur*, 2:324.

67. D'Estrée, *Le Théâtre sous la Terreur*, 36; Bibliothèque de l'Arsenal, Fonds Rondel, Rt. 720, "Extrait des registres des arrêtés du Comité de Salut Public de la Convention nationale," 5 messidor an II (23 June 1794).

68. *Moniteur universel*, 15 July 1794.

69. Welschinger, *Le Théâtre de la Révolution*, 102.

70. Quoted in d'Estrée, *Le Théâtre sous la Terreur*, 43–44; see also Root-Bernstein, *Boulevard Theater and Revolution*, 229–233. Mona Ozouf describes the same dissatisfaction with inauthenticity among festival audiences: some found the mountains and altars inappropriately artificial, others claimed that the actresses were prostitutes made up to look like virtuous women, still others found the ritual oaths and declarations hollow recitations (*Festivals and the French Revolution*, 27–32).

71. Letter from "Polyscope," in *Décade philosophique*, 30 floréal an III (19 May 1795); see also *Paris pendant la réaction thermidorienne et sous le Directoire*, ed. A. Aulard, 3 vols. (Paris: Léopold Cerf, 1898), 1:492.

72. See Georges Duval, *Souvenirs thermidoriens*, 1:354–355; Aulard, *Paris pendant la réaction thermidorienne*, 1:350.

73. *Journal des théâtres et des fêtes nationales*, 10 vendémiaire an III (1 October 1794).

74. *Ibid.*, 22 brumaire an III (12 November 1794).

75. *Moniteur universel*, 4 August 1795.

76. Quoted in Aulard, *Paris pendant la réaction thermidorienne*, 1:492.

77. For plot summaries, see *Moniteur universel*, 14 November 1794, 21 December 1794, 7 April 1795, 24 January 1796, 30 March 1796.

78. *Feuille de la République* (formerly *Feuille du salut public*), 5 sans-culottide de l'an II (21 September 1794).

79. The correspondent clinched his point with an elaborate analogy that, while forced, is strangely appropriate to the ostentation that followed Thermidor: "Doesn't anyone have the good sense to realize and the good faith to show us that the abuse of the poetic arts is much like the abuse of the art of cooking, and that theatrical relevance and a fancy stew are often an artificial and ruinous resource for apathetic souls and exhausted palates?" (Letter from "Votre concitoyen, Alceste" to *L'Abréviateur universel*, 4 September 1794, quoted in Aulard, *Paris pendant la réaction thermidorienne*, 1:82).

80. *Moniteur universel*, 26 December 1795. Crying was widespread among musical audiences in the 1770s and 1780s but was criticized during the Revolution as contrary to "strong republican morals." Louis-Sebastien Mercier, for instance, wrote "Gluck has come, and I now know the charms of music. . . . I have at last felt myself shedding tears as I never have in this place of enchantment" (*Tableau de Paris*, 12 vols. [Paris: n.p., 1782–1788], 7:272). See also *Journal des spectacles*, 15 July 1793.

81. *Moniteur universel*, 30 January 1795; Aulard, *Paris pendant la réaction thermidorienne*, 4:619. The lines in *La Famille américaine*, "Qu'il est heureux qu'il y ait des âmes bienfaisantes parmi tant de méchants!" similarly occasioned anti-Jacobin displays in early 1796, as did the lines "Renverser le tyran et non la tyrannie" in *Epicharis et Néron* (Aulard, *Paris pendant la réaction thermidorienne*, 3:7).

82. Despite the explosive atmosphere that the "Marseillaise" produced whenever it was sung in theaters, the Directory decreed in early January 1796 that it and other songs "dear to republicans" be played before all performances in Paris theaters. Precisely why the decree was issued is not clear, since audiences had by then begun to enjoy a measure of calm by simply avoiding both the "Réveil" and the "Marseillaise," although it was probably related to the Directory's attempt to master events from above by a combination of education and control. Whatever the motivations, the decree brought a new storm of protests. Whistles and shouts typically covered the obligatory singing, although certain spectators responded more creatively: some turned their backs to the stage, others applauded deliriously only at the lines "tremblez, tyrans," still others entered loudly only after the "Marseillaise" had been sung.

At the Feydeau large numbers of the audience took to blowing their noses "with affectation" to cover the singers' voices, and at the Vaudeville two prostitutes interrupted the "Marseillaise" with "immodest laughter and indecent gestures" (for which they were carted off to the police station). By March, however, only scattered protests remained among a more general indifference, and theaters simply dropped the songs. See Laura Mason, "Songs: Mixing Media," in *Revolution in Print*, ed. Robert Darnton and Daniel Roche (Berkeley: Univ. of California Press, 1988), 252–269, esp. 268; Aulard, *Paris pendant la réaction thermidorienne*, 2:639, 641, 644, 711, 729; 3:21–23.

83. Dorval, *Souvenirs thermidoriens*, 1:355.

84. *Moniteur universel*, 27 January 1795; *Journal des théâtres et des fêtes nationales*, 10 vendémiaire an III (1 October 1794).

85. *Journal de Paris*, 30 July 1796.

86. J. B. Poncet, who was present at the performance, relates that after the announcement the choir sang "with transport" the chorus "Poursuivons jusqu'au trépas l'ennemi qui nous outrage" and the audience "felt and applauded" their enthusiasm ("Notes sur les spectacles et les musées de Paris en l'an VII et en l'an VIII" [Extraits du journal de J.-B. Poncet], in *Bulletin de la société de l'histoire de Paris et de l'Ile-de-France, 1891*, ed. Edouard Forestié [Paris: H. Champion, 1891], 60).

87. Mona Ozouf, "Thermidor ou le travail de l'oubli," in *L'Ecole de la France*, 93. See also Bronislaw Baczko, *Comment sortir de la terreur: Thermidor et la Révolution* (Paris: Gallimard, 1989), esp. 164–177.

4. Anthropological Medicine

The research for this article was supported by the Department of History, Oklahoma State University; the Oklahoma Foundation for the Humanities; and the National Science Foundation.

1. The older literature on the medical revolution is typified by Erwin Ackerknecht, *Medicine at the Paris Hospital, 1794–1848* (Baltimore: Johns Hopkins Univ. Press, 1967). The shift in perspective attributable to Michel Foucault stems from his two works of the early 1960s: *Folie et déraison: Histoire de la folie* (Paris: Plon, 1961), trans. Richard Howard under the title *Madness and Civilization: A History of Insanity in the Age of Reason* (New York: Vintage Books, 1965), and *Naissance de la clinique* (Paris: Presses Univ. de France, 1963), trans. A. M. Sheridan Smith under the title *The Birth of the Clinic: An Archaeology of Medical Perception* (New York: Vintage Books, 1973). See also Robert Castel, *L'Ordre psychiatrique: L'Age d'or de l'aliénisme* (Paris: Minuit, 1976); Marcel Gauchet and Gladys Swain, *La Pratique de l'esprit humain: L'Institution asilaire et la révolution démocratique* (Paris: Gallimard, 1980);

Dorinda Outram, *The Body and the French Revolution: Sex, Class, and Political Culture* (New Haven: Yale Univ. Press, 1989).

2. See Jean-Pierre Goubert, "Introduction," *La Médicalisation de la société française, 1770–1830* (Waterloo, Ont.: Historical Reflections Press, 1982), 3–13; Jacques Léonard, *Les Médecins de l'Ouest au XIXème siècle*, 3 vols. (Lille: Atelier Reproduction des Thèses. Université de Lille III, 1971), 1:197–252; Matthew Ramsey, *Professional and Popular Medicine in France, 1770–1830: The Social World of Medical Practice* (New York: Cambridge Univ. Press, 1988), 122–125; Jan Goldstein, *Console and Classify: The French Psychiatric Profession in the Nineteenth Century* (New York: Cambridge Univ. Press, 1987), 28–40; David M. Vess, *Medical Revolution in France, 1789–1796* (Gainesville: University Presses of Florida, 1975), 3–9.

3. Raymond Williams, *Keywords: A Vocabulary of Culture and Society* (New York: Oxford Univ. Press, 1976), 9–24.

4. Max Weber, *Economy and Society: An Outline of Interpretive Sociology*, ed. Guenther Roth and Claus Wittich, 2 vols. (New York: Bedminster Press, 1968), 1:214.

5. For a discussion of Foucault's importance for medical history, see Ramsey, *Professional and Popular Medicine*, 7–9; see also in this volume Catherine J. Kudlick, "The Culture of Statistics and the Crisis of Cholera in Paris, 1830–1850," 98–124; Goldstein, *Console and Classify*; Castel, *L'Ordre psychiatrique*; Gauchet and Swain, *La Pratique de l'esprit humain*; William R. Albury, "Experiment and Explanation in the Physiology of Bichat and Magendie," in *Studies in History of Biology*, ed. William Coleman and Camille Limoges (Baltimore: Johns Hopkins Univ. Press, 1977), 47–131; and "Heart of Darkness: J. N. Corvisart and the Medicalization of Life," in Goubert, *La Médicalisation de la société française*, 17–31. For a later period, see Robert A. Nye, *Crime, Madness, and Politics in Modern France: The Medical Concept of National Decline* (Princeton: Princeton Univ. Press, 1984).

6. Foucault, *Birth of the Clinic*, esp. chaps. 2–4, 5, 7, and *Madness and Civilization*, esp. chaps. 2, 9. For Foucault's later reflections on the concept of power, see *Power/Knowledge: Selected Interviews and Other Writings, 1972–1977*, ed. and trans. Colin Gordon (Hassocks, Eng.: Harvester Press, 1980), esp. 55–62, 109–165.

7. Marcel Mauss, *The Gift: Forms and Functions of Exchange in Archaic Societies*, trans. Ian Cunnison (New York: W. W. Norton, 1967), 63–81.

8. Jan Goldstein, "Foucault among the Sociologists: The 'Disciplines' and the History of the Professions," *History and Theory* 23 (1984): 170–192.

9. Gerald Geison, *Professions and the French State, 1700–1900* (Philadelphia: Univ. of Pennsylvania Press, 1983), 2. On the failure of French doctors to achieve professional autonomy, see Goldstein, *Console and Classify*, 35–40; Ramsey, *Professional and Popular Medicine*, 77–105.

10. See, for example, George D. Sussman, "Etienne Pariset: A Medical Career in Government under the Restoration," *Journal of the History of Medicine and Allied*

Sciences 26 (1971): 52–74; Dora B. Weiner, "Public Health under Napoleon: The Conseil de Salubrité de Paris, 1802–1815," *Clio Medica* 9 (1974): 271–284; Matthew Ramsey, "The Politics of Professional Monopoly in Nineteenth-Century Medicine: The French Model and its Rivals," in Geison, *Professions and the French State*, 225–305; Léonard, *Médecins de l'Ouest*, 263–302, 416–430, 607–610; Vess, *Medical Revolution in France*; George Weisz, "The Politics of Medical Professionalization in France, 1845–1848," *Journal of Social History* 12 (1978–1979): 3–30, and "Constructing the Medical Elite in France: The Creation of the Royal Academy of Medicine, 1814–1820," *Medical History* 30 (1986): 419–443.

11. See the sources cited in n. 5. See also Allan Megill, *Prophets of Extremity: Nietzsche, Heidegger, Foucault, Derrida* (Berkeley: Univ. of California Press, 1985), 240–252; Léonard, "L'Historien et le philosophe: A propos de *Surveiller et punir: Naissance de la prison*," in *L'Impossible prison: Recherches sur le système pénitentiaire au XIXe siècle*, ed. Michelle Perrot (Paris: Seuil, 1980), 14–16.

12. Goubert, *La Médicalisation de la société française*, 9.

13. Albury, "Heart of Darkness," 28.

14. Foucault, *The Archaeology of Knowledge*, trans. A. M. Sheridan Smith (New York: Harper Colophon, 1972), 120; Goldstein, "Foucault among the Sociologists," 171–172.

15. On the problem of the canon, see the special issue of *Critical Inquiry* 10 (1983), ed. Robert von Hallberg.

16. On prestige and related sociological concepts, see William J. Goode, *The Celebration of Heroes: Prestige as a Social Control System* (Berkeley: Univ. of California Press, 1978). On the charismatic leader, see Weber, *Economy and Society*, 1:241–245.

17. See, for example, the discussion of Claude Bernard, who is said to have been endowed with "creative genius in science," in Harry Paul, *From Knowledge to Power: The Rise of the Science Empire in France, 1860–1939* (New York: Cambridge Univ. Press, 1985), 60–92, esp. 77.

18. Bruno Latour, *The Pasteurization of France*, trans. Alan Sheridan and John Law (Cambridge: Harvard Univ. Press, 1988).

19. Albury, "Heart of Darkness," 28.

20. Camille Limoges, "The Development of the Muséum d'Histoire Naturelle of Paris, c. 1800–1914," in *The Organization of Science and Technology in France, 1808–1914*, ed. Robert Fox and George Weisz (New York: Cambridge Univ. Press, 1980), 211–212; Charles C. Gillispie, "The *Encyclopédie* and the Jacobin Philosophy of Science," in *Critical Problems in the History of Science*, ed. Marshall Clagett (Madison: Univ. of Wisconsin Press, 1969), 255–289. For a full discussion of the perceived utility of natural history, see in this volume Michael A. Osborne, "Applied Natural History and Utilitarian Ideals: 'Jacobin Science' at the Muséum d'Histoire Naturelle, 1789–1870," 125–143.

21. On tissue theory, see Russell C. Maulitz, *Morbid Appearances: The Anatomy of*

Pathology in the Early Nineteenth Century (New York: Cambridge Univ. Press, 1987), 9–59. On statistics, see William Coleman, *Death is a Social Disease: Public Health and Political Economy in Early Industrial France* (Madison: Univ. of Wisconsin Press, 1982), 124–141; Paul Delaunay, "Les Doctrines médicales au début du XIXe siècle: Louis et la méthode numérique," in *Science, Medicine, and History: Essays on the Evolution of Scientific Thought and Medical Practice Written in Honour of Charles Singer*, ed. E. A. Underwood, 2 vols. (London: Oxford Univ. Press, 1953). On the materia medica, see John Lesch, *Science and Medicine in France: The Emergence of Experimental Physiology, 1790–1855* (Cambridge: Harvard Univ. Press, 1984), 125–134.

22. There are useful bibliographies in Ronald Primeau, ed., *Influx: Essays on Literary Influence* (Port Washington, N.Y.: Kennikat Press, 1977).

23. Harold Bloom, *The Anxiety of Influence: A Theory of Poetry* (New York: Oxford Univ. Press, 1973).

24. On the bureaucracy, see the sources cited in n. 10; on the numbers of practitioners, see Léonard, *Médecins de l'Ouest*, 221, 416–420. On the medical monopoly, see Ramsey, "Politics of Professional Monopoly." On the role of the hospital, see Ackerknecht, *Medicine at the Paris Hospital*. On medical periodicals and societies, see Pierre Astruc, "Les Sociétés médicales françaises de 1796 à 1850," *Le Progrès médical* (10 January 1950): 28–30. On medical manuals, see Jacques Léonard, *Archives du Corps: La Santé au XIXe siècle* (Rennes: Ouest-France, 1986).

25. On the lack of professional autonomy, see Weisz, "The Politics of Medical Professionalization." On cameralism, see George Rosen, "Cameralism and the Concept of Medical Police," *Bulletin of the History of Medicine* 27 (1953): 21–42, Goubert, *Médicalisation*, 5. On the numbers of doctors, see Léonard, *Médecins de l'Ouest*, 416–430, and on the comparison with lawyers, *ibid.*, 502. On the ascendancy of experimental physiology, see Lesch, *Science and Medicine*.

26. On the general shift in valorization of social roles, see E. J. Hobsbawm, *Echoes of the Marseillaise: Two Centuries Look Back on the French Revolution* (New Brunswick: Rutgers Univ. Press, 1990), 1–31, esp. 23.

27. Jacques Léonard, *La Médecine entre les pouvoirs et les savoirs: Histoire intellectuelle et politique de la médecine française au XIXe siècle* (Paris: Aubier, 1981), 68–73, 106–109. See also Ramsey, *Professional and Popular Medicine*, 9, 69–70, 124.

28. Goubert, *Médicalisation*. Ramsey uses the term "heroic age" in discussing these dates (*Professional and Popular Medicine*, xii–xiii).

29. On the Société Royale de Médecine, see Caroline C. F. Hannaway, "Medicine, Public Welfare, and the State in 18th-Century France: The Société Royale de Médecine of Paris (1776–1793)" (Ph.D. diss., Johns Hopkins Univ., 1974); Charles C. Gillispie, *Science and Polity in France at the End of the Old Regime* (Princeton: Princeton Univ. Press, 1980), 194–203.

30. Toby Gelfand, *Professionalizing Modern Medicine: Paris Surgeons and Medical*

Science and Institutions in the Eighteenth Century (Westport, Conn.: Greenwood Press, 1980).

31. Coleman, *Death Is a Social Disease*; Ann F. LaBerge, "Public Health in France and the French Public Health Movement, 1815–1848" (Ph.D. diss., Univ. of Tennessee, 1974).

32. Goubert, *Médicalisation*, 3.

33. For the term "usufructory," see George Armstrong Kelly, *Victims, Authority, and Terror: The Parallel Deaths of d'Orléans, Custine, Bailly, and Malesherbes* (Chapel Hill: Univ. of North Carolina Press, 1982), 10–12. On the ancien régime conception of monarchy as "a spiritual function" and challenges to it, see Keith Michael Baker, *Inventing the French Revolution: Essays on French Political Culture in the Eighteenth Century* (New York: Cambridge Univ. Press, 1990), 113–117.

34. Jean-Louis Alibert, "Discours sur les rapports de la médecine avec les sciences physiques et morales," *Mémoires de la Société Médicale d'Emulation* 2 (an VII), iv.

35. Foucault, *Birth of the Clinic*, 197.

36. On the importance of vitalism to the generation of doctors who made the medical revolution, see Henri Gouhier, *La Jeunesse d'Auguste Comte et la formation du positivisme*, 3 vols. (Paris: J. Vrin, 1933–1941), 2:191–200.

37. P.-J.-G. Cabanis, *Rapports du physique et du moral de l'homme*, in *Œuvres philosophiques de Cabanis*, ed. Claude Lehec and Jean Cazeneuve (Paris: Presses Univ. de France, 1956), esp. 1:165–234 (the phrase cited appears on 1:239). Xavier Bichat, *Physiological Researches upon Life and Death* (Philadelphia: Smith and Maxwell, 1809), pt. 1, esp. 69–94; François Chaussier, "Leçons de physiologie de M. Chaussier," Bibliothèque de la Faculté de Médecine, Paris, MSS 5520.

38. Kathleen M. Grange, "Pinel and Eighteenth-Century Psychiatry," *Bulletin of the History of Medicine* 35 (1961): 442–453, esp. 448.

39. For a fuller treatment of this subject, see Elizabeth A. Williams, *The Physical and the Moral: Anthropology, Physiology, and Philosophical Medicine in France, 1750–1850* (New York: Cambridge Univ. Press, forthcoming).

40. Cabanis, *Œuvres*, 1:168.

41. *Ibid.*, 1:174–178.

42. This view was elaborated by the Ideologues' heir François-Joseph-Victor Broussais in *De l'Irritation et de la folie: Ouvrage dans lequel les rapports du physique et du moral sont établis sur les bases de la médecine physiologique* (Brussels: Librairie Polymathique, 1828).

43. It was these addresses that were collected and published together as the *Rapports du physique et du moral*. On their delivery and reception, see Martin S. Staum, *Cabanis: Enlightenment and Medical Philosophy in the French Revolution* (Princeton: Princeton Univ. Press, 1980), 174–177.

44. L. Brodier, *J.-L. Alibert, médecin de l'Hôpital Saint-Louis* (Paris: A. Maloine, 1923).

45. Alibert, "Discours," i-cxii.

46. *Ibid.*, iv.

47. *Ibid.*, lxviii.

48. *Ibid.*, lxxxiii.

49. *Ibid.*, xc-xci.

50. *Ibid.*, xcv.

51. *La Décade philosophique, littéraire et politique*, no. 29 (20 messidor an VII): 29.

52. Philippe Pinel, *Nosographie philosophique, ou la méthode d'analyse appliquée à la médecine* (Paris: Crapelet, an VI), i–xxxviii; Jacques-Louis Moreau de la Sarthe, "Encore des réflexions et des observations relatives à l'influence du moral sur le physique, et à l'emploi médical des passions, des affections et des émotions," *Décade philosophique* (20 and 30 nivôse an IX), 69–75, 134–141. On Hallé, see Staum, *Cabanis*, appendix E, 381–382.

53. Ramsey, *Professional and Popular Medicine*, 73–74; Léonard, *La Médecine entre les pouvoirs et les savoirs*, 12–21; Foucault, *Birth of the Clinic*, 32; Gillispie, "The *Encyclopédie* and the Jacobin Philosophy of Science." After Thermidor, articles in the *Décade philosophique* portrayed the Jacobins as merciless persecutors of men of science; see, for example, "Eloge de Vicq d'Azyr" (vendémiaire-frimaire an III): 513–520 and (nivôse-ventôse an III): 1–10; "Eloge de Bailly" (nivôse-ventôse an III): 321–330.

54. A. M. Eymar, Review of P.-J.-G. Cabanis, *Du Degré de certitude de la médecine*, *Décade philosophique* no. 34 (an VI): 385–395, esp. 393.

55. Quoted in Charles Coury, "The Teaching of Medicine in France from the Beginning of the Seventeenth Century," in *The History of Medical Education*, ed. C. D. O'Malley (Berkeley: Univ. of California Press, 1970), 121–172, esp. 148.

56. See A. Prévost, *La Faculté de Médecine de Paris: Ses Chaires, ses annexes et son personnel enseignant de 1794 à 1900* (Paris: Maloine, 1900).

57. On Thouret, see *Dictionnaire des sciences médicales: Biographie médicale* 7 vols. (Paris: C.-L.-F. Panckoucke, 1820–1825), 7:328–336. Staum discusses Thouret's work with Cabanis in *Cabanis*, 132–135.

58. A. Proust, "L'Evolution de l'hygiène et l'histoire de la chaire d'hygiène de la faculté," *Gazette des Hôpitaux* (25 April 1895): 485–488; Pierre Huard and Marie Imbault-Huart, "Structure et fonctionnement de la Faculté de Médecine de Paris en 1813," *Revue d'histoire des sciences* 28 (1975): 139–168, esp. 156, n. 15.

59. Coury, "Teaching of Medicine," 149.

60. Staum, *Cabanis*, 132–135. It is important to recognize this Cabanisian dimension of the inauguration of clinical teaching because the establishment of the clinic is too often seen purely as a conquest for pathological anatomy. It was only after the passage of the new autopsy law (1798) that dissection on a large scale even became possible and later still that significant results began to be obtained. Seen in this light, the material conditions for the development of pathological anatomy were made

possible by the prior gains in medical authority achieved by the proponents of anthropological medicine.

61. Ramsey, *Professional and Popular Medicine*, 76.

62. *Mémoires de la Société médicale d'Emulation*, 1–5 (1797–1803).

63. Ramsey, *Professional and Popular Medicine*, xiii.

64. Weiner, "Public Health."

65. Coury, "Teaching of Medicine," 165.

66. For a discussion of Bonaparte's favoritism to certain doctors, see Léonard, *Médecins de l'Ouest*, 1:254–256. On the relations between Bonaparte and the Ideologues and on the closing of the Second Class of the Institute, see Georges Gusdorf, *Les Sciences humaines et la pensée occidentale*, vol. 8, *La Conscience révolutionnaire: Les Idéologues* (Paris: Payot, 1978), 315–330.

67. Coury, "Teaching of Medicine," 152.

68. On antagonisms between the church and the medical establishment during the Restoration, see L. S. Jacyna, "Medical Science and Moral Science: The Cultural Relations of Physiology in Restoration France," *History of Science* 25 (1987): 111–146.

69. Louis Liard, *L'Enseignement supérieur en France (1789–1893)*, 2 vols. (Paris: Armand Colin, 1888, 1894), 2:88–178.

70. Coury, "Teaching of Medicine," 156.

71. Weisz, "Constructing the Medical Elite," 435–442.

72. Jacyna, "Medical Science and Moral Science," esp. 130–137.

73. On the campaign against "materialists," see *ibid.*

74. [C.-C.-H.] Marc, "Prospectus," *Annales d'hygiène publique et de médecine légale* 1 (1829): v–xxxix.

75. LaBerge, "Public Health," 355–365, 382.

76. Goldstein, *Console and Classify*, 179–184.

77. Frédéric Dubois (d'Amiens), "Nouvelles inductions philosophiques appliquées à l'étude de l'idiotisme et de la démence," *Mémoires de l'Académie royale de médecine* 5 (1836): 553–576.

78. See Nye, *Crime, Madness, and Politics.*

5. The Culture of Statistics

Special thanks to Marjorie Beale, Alice Bullard, Joshua Cole, Lawrence Glickman, Patricia O'Brien, Andrea Rusnock, and Herbert Sloan for their helpful comments on earlier drafts.

1. See Howard M. Solomon, *Public Welfare, Science, and Propaganda in Seventeenth-Century France* (Princeton: Princeton Univ. Press, 1972) for an account of

early ideas on this aspect of government in France. For the history of statistics and the hygienists in France, see Jean-Claude Perrot, *L'Age d'or de la statistique régionale française (an IV-1804)* (Paris: Société des Etudes Robespierristes, 1977); Theodore Porter, *The Rise of Statistical Thinking* (Princeton: Princeton Univ. Press, 1986); Stuart Woolf, "Contribution à l'histoire des origines de la statistique, France, 1789–1815," in Ecole des Hautes Etudes en Sciences Sociales, *La Statistique en France à l'époque napoléonienne* (Brussels: Centre Guillaume Jacquemyns, 1980); William Coleman, *Death is a Social Disease* (Madison: Univ. of Wisconsin Press, 1982), esp. 124–148; Ann Fowler LaBerge, "Public Health in France and the French Public Health Movement" (Ph.D. diss., Univ. of Tennessee, 1974); Louis Chevalier, *Laboring Classes and Dangerous Classes in Paris During the First Half of the Nineteenth Century*, trans. Frank Jellinek (Princeton: Princeton Univ. Press, 1973); Joan Scott, "A Statistical Representation of Work: la Statistique de l'industrie à Paris, 1847–1848" in her *Gender and the Politics of History* (New York: Columbia Univ. Press, 1988); Hilde Rigaudias-Weiss, *Les Enquêtes ouvrières en France entre 1838 et 1848* (Paris: F. Alcan, 1936).

2. Much of the following is digested from William Coleman's elegant synthesis in *Death is a Social Disease*, 139–146.

3. Chevalier, *Laboring Classes*, 44. The *Recherches* explored these matters in greater depth, listing figures for stillborn vs. natural children, intentional vs. unintentional suicides, an indication, according to Chevalier, of the census compiler's naive rigor.

4. For a more general discussion of the history of graphic display, see Edward R. Tufte, *The Visual Display of Quantitative Information* (Cheshire, Conn.: Graphics Press, 1983).

5. Erwin Ackerknecht, "Hygiene in France, 1815–1848," *Bulletin of the History of Medicine* 22 (1948): 117–155; Coleman, *Death is a Social Disease*, 128–130. For the influence of the census and the social investigations on literature, see Louis Chevalier, *Laboring Classes*; Thomas Laqueur, "Bodies, Details, and the Humanitarian Narrative," in *The New Cultural History*, ed. Lynn Hunt (Berkeley: Univ. of California Press, 1989), 176–204.

6. Matthew Ramsey, *Professional and Popular Medicine in France, 1770–1830: The Social World of Medical Practice* (Cambridge: Cambridge Univ. Press, 1988); Toby Gelfand, *Professionalizing Modern Medicine: Paris Surgeons, Medical Science, and Institutions in the 18th Century* (Westport, Conn.: Greenwood Press, 1980).

7. For a more detailed account of this intellectual history, see Coleman, *Death is a Social Disease*; Anne Fowler LaBerge, "Public Health in France."

8. Porter, *The Rise of Statistical Thinking*, 27–30.

9. AD Seine VD⁶669, Epidémies du choléra, Commissions d'hygiène, 1831–1832.

10. See *Annales d'hygiène publique* for numerous examples of the genre of articles published by the urban investigators.

11. By contrast, investigators later in the century would measure progress less exclu-

sively in terms of mortality rates by adding employment rates, consumption habits, and literacy to their definition. See, for example, Robert A. Nye, *Crime, Madness, and Politics in Modern France: The Medical Concept of National Decline* (Princeton: Princeton Univ. Press, 1984); Joshua Cole, "The Power of Large Numbers: Population and Politics in Nineteenth-Century France" (Ph.D. diss., Univ. of California, Berkeley, 1991).

12. François Marc Moreau, *Histoire statistique du choléra-morbus dans le quartier du Faubourg St.-Denis* (Paris, 1833), 1–3.

13. A. Bazin, *L'Epoque sans nom: Esquisses de Paris*, 2 vols. (Paris, 1833), 2:266–267.

14. Before the cholera epidemic, the French press used tables to present qualitative data on trade figures and votes in the National Assembly, but this did not represent an ongoing part of daily life in the same way as the bulletins du choléra. Moreover, such tables had been far more common in the *Moniteur universel*, the official organ, than they were in more popular papers such as the *Journal des débats*, *La Quotidienne*, or *Le National*, to name but a few.

15. For a history of the press under the July Monarchy, see Charles Bellanger, Jacques Godechot, and Pierre Guiral, *Histoire générale de la presse française*, 5 vols. (Paris: Presses Univ. de France, 1969–1976), esp. vol. 2; Eugène Hatin, *Histoire politique et littéraire de la presse en France*, 8 vols. (Paris: Poulet-Malassis et de Broisse, 1859–1861), esp. vol. 8. For a more eclectic, provocative discussion, see Richard Terdiman, *Discourse/Counter-Discourse: the Theory and Practice of Symbolic Resistance in Nineteenth-Century France* (Ithaca: Cornell Univ. Press, 1985), esp. chap. 5.

16. *L'Entracte*, 28 April 1832, "Une Correspondance."

17. *Le Corsaire*, 4 April 1832.

18. *Le Globe*, 1 April 1832.

19. *L'Entracte*, 4 April 1832.

20. *Le National*, 2 April 1832.

21. *La Révolution*, reprinted in *La Quotidienne*, 3 April 1832.

22. *Le Bonhomme Richard*, 16 April 1832.

23. *Rapport sur la marche et les effets du choléra dans Paris et les communes rurales du département de la Seine* (Paris: Imprimerie nationale, 1834), 43–44.

24. AD Seine, Public Health Minutes, VD^{6}274, VD^{6}354, VD^{6}361, VD^{6}537, VD^{6}669, VD^{6}689, VI^{5}1.

25. *Journal des débats*, 30 March 1832.

26. *Le National*, 31 March 1832.

27. *Moniteur universel*, 9 April 1832.

28. See, for example, the Saint-Simonian paper, *Le Globe*, 1 April 1832.

29. Louis Blanc, *L'Histoire de dix ans*, 5 vols. (Paris, 1867), 3:202.

30. *Moniteur universel*, 2 April 1832.

31. *Ibid.*, 5 April 1832.

32. See, for example, *ibid.*, 14 May 1832.

33. *Le Corsaire*, 16 June 1832.

34. *Ibid.*, 22 June 1832.

35. Bazin, *L'Epoque sans nom*, 2:267.

36. *Moniteur universel*, 10 April 1832.

37. F. A. Duchesne, *Histoire statistique du choléra-morbus dans le XIᵉ arron- dissement de Paris* (Paris: Baillière et fils, 1849), 3.

38. François Marc Moreau, *Histoire statistique du choléra-asiatique de 1849 dans le Vᵉ arrondissement municipal de Paris* (Paris: Labé, 1850), 2.

39. *Courrier français*, 29 March 1849.

40. See Berranger et al., *Presse française*, vol. 2.

41. *Moniteur universel*, 22 March 1849.

42. See, for example, *Courrier français*, 28 March 1849, 29 March 1849, 31 March 1849.

43. *Union médicale de Paris*, 13 March 1849, 3:121.

44. *Ibid.*, 15 May 1849, 3:231.

45. *Gazette médicale*, 19 May 1849, 375.

46. *Gazette des hôpitaux*, 26 June 1849. This move was somewhat arrogant, given the fact that the paper had been in the throes of a controversy with editors of the *Union médicale*, who had criticized its lack of accuracy and large number of typo- graphical errors. The *Gazette*'s 16 June response had essentially warned its adversar- ies not to expect perfection in this kind of work.

47. *Union médicale*, 15 May 1849, 3:231.

48. *Gazette des hôpitaux*, 3 April 1849.

49. Paul Caffe, *Notice sur le choléra* (Paris, 1849), 2–3.

50. *Ibid.*

51. *Gazette médicale*, 17 March 1849, 202.

52. *Union médicale*, 14 June 1849.

53. *Journal du peuple*, 18 July 1849.

54. *Journal des débats*, 8 June 1849. The *Moniteur universel* complained that the public imagination exaggerated figures (8 June 1849, 9 June 1849).

6. Applied Natural History

I wish to thank Andrew J. Butrica, Jean Dhombres, Charles C. Gillispie, Anita Guerrini, and Paul Sonnino for comments and assistance.

1. Paul L. Farber, "Research Traditions in Eighteenth-Century Natural History," in *Lazzaro spallanzani e la biologica de settencento*, ed. W. Bernardi and A. La Vergata (Florence: Leo S. Olschki, 1982), 397–403.

2. Michael A. Osborne, "The *Société zoologique d'acclimatation* and the New French Empire: The Science and Political Economy of Economic Zoology during the Second Empire" (Ph.D. diss., Univ. of Wisconsin, Madison, 1987), 1–61; André J. Bourde, *Agronomie et agronomes en France au XVIIIe siècle*, 3 vols. (Paris: S.E.V.P.E.N., 1967); Charles C. Gillispie, *Science and Polity in France at the End of the Old Regime* (Princeton: Princeton Univ. Press, 1980), 360–368; Norman Hampson, "The Enlightenment in France," in *The Enlightenment in National Context*, ed. Roy Porter and Mikulas Teich (Cambridge: Cambridge Univ. Press, 1981), 41–53.

3. Michael A. Osborne, "Zoos in the Family: The Saint-Hilaire Clan and the Three Zoos of Paris," in *The History and Evolution of the Modern Zoo*, ed. Robert A. Hoague (Washington, D.C.: Smithsonian Institution Press, forthcoming).

4. Pietro Corsi, *The Age of Lamarck: Evolutionary Theories in France, 1790–1830* (Berkeley: Univ. of California Press, 1988), 1–39.

5. Isidore Geoffroy Saint-Hilaire, *Acclimatation et domestication des animaux utiles*, 4th ed. (1861; reprint, Paris: Librairie Agricole de la Maison Rustique, 1986), 470–486.

6. Keith Thomas, *Man and the Natural World: A History of Modern Sensibility* (New York: Pantheon Books, 1983), 173–181, 277. The influence of England on France is detailed in André J. Bourde, *The Influence of England on the French Agronomes* (Cambridge: Cambridge Univ. Press, 1953).

7. Roger Hahn, *The Anatomy of a Scientific Institution: The Paris Academy of Sciences, 1666–1803* (Berkeley: Univ. of California Press, 1971), 104.

8. Yves Laissus, "Le Jardin du Roi," in *Enseignement et diffusion des sciences en France au XVIIIe siècle*, ed. René Taton (Paris: Hermann, 1965), 287–341, esp. 297, n. 3.

9. Louis Roule, *Daubenton et l'exploration de la nature* (Paris: E. Flammarion, 1925), 110.

10. Gustave Loisel, *Histoire des ménageries de l'antiquité à nos jours*, 3 vols. (Paris: Octave Doin, 1912), 2:321–334.

11. Roule, *Daubenton*, 109–133.

12. J. H. Clapham, *The Economic Development of France and Germany, 1815–1914*, 4th ed. (Cambridge: Cambridge Univ. Press, 1961), 328, 352.

13. Camille Limoges, "Daubenton, Louis-Jean-Marie," *Dictionary of Scientific Biography*, 15:111–114, esp. 113.

14. B.-G.-E. Lacépède in Lacépède, [G.] Cuvier, and [E.] Geoffroy [Saint-Hilaire], *La Ménagerie du Muséum d'histoire naturelle*, 2 vols. (Paris: Tardieu Duesle, 1817), 1:12.

15. For a general discussion of social utility, see Jean Belin, *La Logique d'une idée-force: L'Idée d'utilité sociale et la Révolution française* (Paris: Hermann, 1939). For a discussion of the relationship between utility and science, see Jean and Nicole Dhombres, "Popularité de la science autour de 1800: Une Science 'utile,' " *Sciences et techniques en perspective* 1 (1982): 1–26; idem, *Naissance d'un pouvoir: Sciences*

et savants en France, 1793–1824 (Paris: Editions Payot, 1989), 394–413. Contrary to Leora Auslander, who argues in the present volume (144–174) that utility is *not* a useful concept when thinking about collecting, I maintain that utility is an essential construct for the history of menageries and natural history cabinets.

16. Charles C. Gillispie, "The *Encyclopédie* and the Jacobin Philosophy of Science: A Study in Ideas and Consequences," in *Critical Problems in the History of Science,* ed. Marshall Clagett (Madison: Univ. of Wisconsin Press, 1959), 255–289, esp. 277.

17. Corsi, *Age of Lamarck,* 7–11. Corsi also gives a bibliography of the historiography of French revolutionary science in "Models and Analogies for the Reform of Natural History: Features of the French Debate, 1790–1800," in *Lazzaro spallanzani,* 381–396. Hahn refers to the "legend" and "myth of Jacobin vandalism" of science (*Anatomy of a Scientific Institution,* 289–290).

18. Corsi discusses how chemical nomenclature and crystallography provided models for reform ("Models and Analogies"). At best it was a reflexive relationship. Natural history was so enmeshed in the larger fabric of science that chemistry borrowed much from it. See James W. Llana, "A Contribution of Natural History to the Chemical Revolution in France," *Ambix* 32 (1985): 71–91.

19. Michael A. Osborne, "The *Société zoologique d'acclimatation,*" 15–19; Ernest T. Hamy, "Les Derniers Jours du jardin du roi et la formation du Muséum d'histoire naturelle," in Muséum national d'histoire naturelle, *Centenaire de la fondation du Muséum national d'histoire naturelle, 10 juin 1793–10 juin 1893* (Paris: Imprimerie nationale, 1893), 3–162, esp. 56, n. 1.

20. "Première adresse des officiers du Jardin des plantes et du Cabinet d'histoire naturelle, lu à l'Assemblée Nationale le 20 août 1790," in *Adresses et projet de règlemens presentés à l'Assemblée Nationale par les officiers du Jardin des plantes et du Cabinet d'histoire naturelle, d'après le décret de l'Assemblée Nationale, du 20 août 1790* (Paris: Buisson, 1790), 1–12, esp. 1–2.

21. "Première adresse des officiers," 3–4.

22. "Projet de règlemens," titre premier, ii, 32–33.

23. Jacques-Bernardin-Henri de Saint-Pierre, *Mémoire sur la nécessité de joindre une ménagerie au Jardin national des plantes de Paris* (Paris: Didot le jeune, 1792), 5.

24. *Ibid.*

25. *Ibid.,* 24.

26. *Ibid.*

27. Hamy cites *Rapport fait à la Société d'histoire naturelle de Paris sur la nécessité d'établir une ménagerie: Par A. L. Millin, Pinel et Alex. Brongniart* (Paris: Boileau, n.d.) in "Les Derniers Jours," 58.

28. *Ibid.,* 60, no. 1; Isidore Geoffroy Saint-Hilaire, *Vie, travaux et doctrine scientifique d'Etienne Geoffroy Saint-Hilaire* (Paris: P. Bertrand, 1847), 47–54.

29. Toby A. Appel, *The Cuvier-Geoffroy Debate: French Biology in the Decades Before Darwin* (New York: Oxford Univ. Press, 1987); Goulven Laurent, *Paléontologie et évolution en France de 1800 à 1860: Une Histoire des idées de Cuvier*

et de Lamarck à Darwin (Paris: Comité des travaux historiques et scientifiques, 1987).

30. Loisel, *Histoire des ménageries*, 3:133, 138.

31. In the biography he wrote of his father, Isidore Geoffroy Saint-Hilaire barely mentions practical zoology. See I. Geoffroy Saint-Hilaire, *Vie.*

32. Bibliothèque centrale du Muséum, MSS 2737,ii,3.

33. I. Geoffroy Saint-Hilaire, "Ménagerie," in *Encyclopédie moderne* (Paris: Mongie aîné, 1823–1832), 16:59–64.

34. Laurent, *Paléontologie et évolution*, 470–472; I. Geoffroy Saint-Hilaire, *Acclimatation et domestication*, ix.

35. I. Geoffroy Saint-Hilaire, *Acclimatation et domestication*, ix.

36. Paul L. Farber, *The Emergence of Ornithology as a Scientific Discipline: 1760–1850* (Dordrecht: D. Reidel, 1982).

37. Michael A. Osborne, *The Société Zoologique d'Acclimatation and the New French Empire: Science and Political Economy during the Second Empire and Third Republic* (Bloomington: Indiana Univ. Press, forthcoming); Philip D. Curtin, *Death by Migration: Europe's Encounter with the Tropical World in the Nineteenth Century* (Cambridge: Cambridge Univ. Press, 1989), 42–47; David N. Livingston, "Human Acclimatization: Perspectives On a Contested Field of Inquiry in Science, Medicine, and Geography," *History of Science* 25 (1987): 359–394.

38. I. Geoffroy Saint-Hilaire, *Note sur la ménagerie, et sur l'utilité d'une succursale ou annexe aux environs de Paris* (Paris: n.p., 1860).

39. I. Geoffroy Saint-Hilaire, *Acclimatation et domestication*, 518.

40. AN F[10]1733, Acclimatement-Commission pour l'introduction en France de nouvelles espèces animales et végétales, 16 March 1848.

41. AN AJ[15]678, Liste des mammifères et des oiseaux en doubles à la ménagerie, meeting of Muséum professors, 2 October 1849; Loisel, *Histoire des ménageries*, 3:92.

42. Camille Limoges, "The Development of the Muséum d'Histoire Naturelle of Paris, c. 1800–1914," in *The Organization of Science and Technology in France, 1808–1914*, ed. Robert Fox and George Weisz (Cambridge: Cambridge Univ. Press, 1980), 211–240, esp. 229.

43. AN F[17]3982–3983, A. Brongniart to Minister of Public Instruction, 10 November 1868.

44. Dorinda Outram, "Politics and Vocation: French Science, 1793–1830," *British Journal for the History of Science* 13 (1980): 27–43, 39–40; Limoges, "The Development of the Muséum," 230–233.

45. See Leora Auslander's essay in this volume. On the construction of the exotic and its conjuncture with consumerism in the Third Republic, see Rosalind H. Williams, *Dream Worlds: Mass Consumption in Late Nineteenth-Century France* (Berkeley: Univ. of California Press, 1982).

46. I. Geoffroy Saint-Hilaire, *Acclimatation et domestication*, 508.

47. *Ibid.*, 518.

48. Quoted in Guerin-Méneville, "Faits divers," *Bulletin de la Société zoologique d'acclimatation* 6 (1859): 228–232, esp. 231.

49. AN F[17]3980, 10, H. Milne-Edwards, Rapport sur une collection d'animaux vivants offerts à S. M. l'Empéreur pour le Muséum d'histoire naturelle par les Rois de Siam, 9 November 1862.

50. AN F[17]3883, Meeting from 16 April 1861 [for Hamlin], 26 April 1859 [for others]. Cf. Muséum MSS 2739, L. Rydagad to I. Geoffroy Saint-Hilaire, 20 August 1860.

51. AN AJ[15]545, I. Geoffroy Saint-Hilaire to F. Prévost, 22 August 1852.

52. AN F[17]3883, Meeting of Muséum professors, 12 July 1859.

53. AN F[17]3883, Meeting of Muséum professors, 2 October 1859.

54. AN F[17]3980, H. Milne-Edwards to Roulin, n.d. [9 or 10 November 1862].

55. H. Milne-Edwards, "Rapport sur une collection," 11.

56. Charles C. Gillispie, "Science in the French Revolution," *Behavioral Science* 4 (1959): 67–73, esp. 69; *idem*, "The *Encyclopédie* and the Jacobin Philosophy of Science," 267. Gillispie partially revises the earlier distinction he made between pure science, i.e., mathematical physics, and science applied to the arts, i.e., the Jacobins' antitheoretical natural history (*Science and Polity*, 551).

57. H. Milne-Edwards, "Rapport sur une collection," 11.

58. AN 65 AQ R3157–3158, Arthur Porte, *La Vie financière*, 1903. On scientific societies, see Robert Fox, "The *Savant* Confronts his Peers: Scientific Societies in Nineteenth-Century France," in *Organization*, 241–282; Harry W. Paul, *From Knowledge to Power: The Rise of the Science Empire in France, 1860–1939* (Cambridge: Cambridge Univ. Press, 1985), 267–285.

7. After the Revolution

I would like to express my thanks to Caroline Ford, Michael Geyer, Jan Goldstein, Anne Higonnet, Colin Lucas, Joan Scott, Martha Ward, and especially Tom Holt for their assistance in thinking through this essay. Karl Bahm, Alex Dracobly, and Carol Scherer are to be thanked for their indispensable research assistance. Versions of this paper were presented at the Minda de Gunzberg Center for European Studies at Harvard University and to the Committee on Critical Practice at the University of Chicago; I am grateful to both audiences for their comments. The research for this project was funded by the Social Science Research Council and Tocqueville, Chateaubriand, and Fulbright fellowships.

1. Henri Fourdinois, "De l'Etat actuel de l'industrie mobiliaire," *Revue des arts décoratifs* 5 (1884–1885): 537.

2. See Charles Blanc, "Etude sur les arts décoratifs: Les Meubles," *Journal de menuiserie* 12 (1875): 22–48. This article describes the variety of ancien régime styles available to the producer and consumer as offering opportunities to make precisely the appropriate object for the particular consumer. For the relative failure of *art nouveau* and *style moderne*, see Madeleine Deschamps, "Domestic Elegance: The French at Home," in *L'Art de Vivre: Decorative Arts and Design in France, 1789–1989*, ed. Catherine Armijon (London: Thames and Hudson, 1989), 125. For the difficulties in marketing bentwood furniture, see Alexander von Vergesack, *L'Industrie Thonet: De la Création artisanale à la production en série: Le Mobilier en bois courbé* (Paris: Editions de la Réunion des Musées Nationaux, 1986).

3. This is a conclusion arrived at after many hours spent comparing original ancien régime furniture and drawings with their nineteenth-century descendants. That comparison makes clear that these pieces could not have been understood by their makers to be copies. The variation with the original "ideal" is too systematic. Witold Rybczynski uses the terms (borrowed from William Searle) of "creative" and "historical" revivals instead of historicist pastiche. William Searle, *The Tasteful Interlude: American Interiors Through the Camera's Eye, 1860–1917* (Nashville: American Association for State and Local History, 1982), cited in Witold Rybczynski, *Home: A Short History of an Idea* (New York: Penguin, 1986), 175. I think that the distinction between historicist pastiche and reproduction is more exact, at least in the French case. Names of historicist pastiche furniture styles are enclosed within quotation marks. For (incompatible) theoretical discussions of the complexity of pastiche as a form, see Fredric Jameson, "Postmodernism and Consumer Society," in *The Anti-Aesthetic: Essays on Postmodern Culture*, ed. Hal Foster (Port Townsend, Washington: Bay Press, 1983); Judith Butler, *Gender Trouble: Feminism and the Subversion of Identity* (New York: Routledge, 1990), conclusion.

4. For a contemporary discussion by woodworkers of the role of old techniques and old forms in the creation of new work, see, for example, "Planche 3: Porte Louis XV," *Journal de menuiserie* 3 (1865): 28–29.

5. For a very early statement of the power of the consumer to determine production, see "Sur la tyrannie de la mode," *Journal des dames et des modes* 23 (25 August 1811): 226–230. This popular magazine obviously had an interest in asserting the power of the consumer, but the overall tone of the article is very critical. For the refusal of consumers in the later nineteenth century to buy new designs, see the bitter statement by Henri Fourdinois (a furniture manufacturer) in "Quelques réflexions sur le mobilier à propos de l'Union Centrale," *Revue des arts décoratifs* 3 (1882–1883): 162–165. For additional critiques of the conservatism of consumers, see Alfred Picard, *Exposition universelle internationale de 1889 à Paris: Rapports du jury international*, 19 vols. (Paris: Imprimerie Nationale, 1891–1892), 3:6–7; Victor Champier, "La Maison modèle: Etudes et types d'ameublement," *Revue des arts décoratifs* 5 (1884–1885): 20. See also "Le Goût du vieux en art," *Revue des arts décoratifs* 5 (1884–1885): 592–594. For a discussion of the evil

effects of mechanization, see Henri de Noussane, *Le Goût de l'ameublement* (Paris: Firmin-Didot, 1896), 16. For an attack on artisans' abilities, see Georges Duplessis, "Le Département des Estampes à la Bibliothèque Nationale: Indications sommaires sur les documents utiles aux artistes industriels," *Revue des arts décoratifs* 6 (1885–1886): 334–341, esp. 336. For a historian's point of view, see among many others Bernard Deloche's *Le Meuble: Introduction à l'ésthetique des arts mineurs*, which in its radical argument for the creativity of eighteenth-century furniture reiterates the supposed imitativeness of nineteenth-century style (Lyon: Editions l'Hermès, 1985). David R. McFadden also critiqued the style of interior decor under the Second Empire and Third Republic ("Two Centuries of French Style," *L'Art de Vivre*, 28). Adrian Forty argues that contemporaries criticized taste in part at least as a way of avoiding criticizing industrial capitalism (*Objects of Desire: Design and Society from Wedgwood to IBM* [New York: Pantheon, 1986], 61). The contemporary attack on historical painting, however, complicates the story; see Patricia Mainardi, *Art and Politics of the Second Empire: The Universal Expositions of 1855 and 1867* (New Haven: Yale Univ. Press, 1987), 160–169.

6. Emile Bayard, *Le Style Empire* (Paris: Garnier, n.d. [c. 1914]), 56–57. See also Jacqueline Viaux, *Le Meuble en France* (Paris: Presses Univ. de France, 1962), 129.

7. On the fondness for the Renaissance under the Second Empire, see Gerald Reitlinger, *The Economics of Taste*, vol. 2 of *The Rise and Fall of the Objets d'Art Prices since 1750* (London: Barrie and Rockliff, 1961), 130–131.

8. An extraordinary fin-de-siècle statement of this position may be found in an anonymous, untitled article on Félix Aubert in *L'Art décoratif* 4 (January 1899): 157–158.

9. On the gender, class, and age meanings of wood, see Auguste Luchet, *L'Art industriel à l'exposition universelle de 1867: Mobilier* (Paris: Librairie Internationale, 1868), 134. For the point of view of etiquette-book writers, see Mme. de l'Alq, *Le Maître et la maîtresse de la maison* (Paris: Bureaux des Causeries Familières, n.d. [c. 1885]), 62. See also Mme. de Bassanville, *L'Art de bien tenir une maison* (Paris: Victor-Havard, 1892), 26. See also Mme. la comtesse Drohojowska, *Conseils à une jeune fille sur les devoirs à remplir dans le monde comme maîtresse de maison à Paris* (Paris: Perisse Frères, n.d. [c. 1875]), 206. It is noted that the work is approved by Monseigneur, the bishop of Rodez. For fashions in woods earlier in the century, see M. Blanqui, "Section VI—Ebénisterie et tabletterie," in *Exposition des produits de l'industrie française en 1839, Rapport du jury central*, 3 vols. (Paris: L. Bouchard-Huzard, 1839), 3:175–176.

10. For examples of the specific requirements of a Catholic woman's home, see the characterization in the following etiquette books: Drohojowska, *Conseils à une jeune fille*, 206; Bassanville, *L'Art de bien tenir une maison*.

11. On the importance of individual expression, see Mme. Hennequin, *L'Art et le goût au foyer* (Paris: Armand Colin, 1912), 7.

12. These competing discourses are accessible through a variety of sources. Al-

though the bibliographic and primary source base is too large to be discussed in detail here, a brief sketch is possible. A number of new decorating magazines from varied standpoints that targeted different publics came into existence in this period. I have read through the *Revue des arts décoratifs* (1880–1902), *L'Art décoratif: Revue internationale d'art industriel et de décoration* (1898–1914), *L'Art et l'industrie: Organe du progrès dans toutes les branches de l'industrie artistique* (1877–1889), *Art pour tous: Encyclopédie de l'art industriel et décoratif* (1861–1905), *Journal de menuiserie.* Less weighty were (among others): *Moniteur de l'ameublement: Journal des modes et du confort* (1863–1868), and *Album de l'ameublement: Journal de la décoration intérieur* (1882–1892). Decorating books intended to guide consumers and pattern books for the use of producers also number in the hundreds. The collection at the Bibliothèque Forney in Paris is quite complete, and I have surveyed all of it. Etiquette books were an older genre that expanded greatly in the late nineteenth century. Of the perhaps two hundred French works published between 1860 and 1914, I have read approximately fifty. For a fascinating discussion of the shift from courtesy to etiquette books in England as the culture shifted from aristocratic to bourgeois, see Michael Curtin, "A Question of Manners: Status and Gender in Etiquette and Courtesy," *Journal of Modern History* 57 (1985): 395–423. The World's Fairs of 1855, 1862, 1867, and 1889 produced voluminous documentation, including reports written up by "worker delegates" to the fairs as well as by state officials, social commentators, sociologists, and art critics. The nineteenth-century advertising materials held in the Bibliothèque Historique de la Ville de Paris in the series Ameublement-120, in the Archives Nationales in the series 65 AQ T (Documentation Imprimée Concernant les Sociétés: Sociétés commerciales, grands magasins), and in the Archives de la Seine in the series D12 Z 1–3, D17 Z 1–4, D18 Z6 and Z9, D19 Z1, D39 Z are quite large (although often undated), and I have thoroughly surveyed them. Lastly, sociologists and other social commentators from Frédéric Le Play to Edgar Allan Poe were preoccupied with decoration, and I have read widely in those literatures as well.

13. The archival materials on the institutions of taste production—including the Union Centrale des Arts Décoratifs, the Bibliothèque Forney, and the Ecole Boulle—at the AN and AD Seine are extensive and informative concerning the interests and preoccupations of the founders of these institutions. AN F^{17}, F^{21} (concerning schools), and F^{12} (on institutions involved in the arts) are crucial, as is AD Seine VR 216–219 on the Bibliothèque Forney.

14. The sources on the actual use of furniture, as opposed to the discourses around it, are predictably more problematic. However, the sociologists' investigations, family account books, furniture distributors' archives, memoirs, auction records, and secondary work is rich enough to allow one to make arguments concerning what people owned and how they used it.

15. For Britain, see Alastair Service, *Edwardian Interiors* (London: Barrie and Jenkins, 1982); Bernard Denvir, *The Late Victorians: Art, Design, and Society*

1852–1910 (London: Longman, 1986); Lyndel Saunders King, *The Industrialization of Taste: Victorian England and the Art Union of London* (Ann Arbor: UMI Research, 1985); John Grant Rhodes, "Ornament and Technology: A Study of Mid-Nineteenth Century British Design" (Ph.D. diss., Harvard Univ., 1983). For Germany and Central Europe, see Gertrud Benker, *Bürgerliches Wohnen: Stadtische Wohnkultur in Mitteleuropa von der Gotik bis zum Jugendstil* (Munich: Callwey, 1984); Sonja Günther, *Das Deutsche Heim* (Werkbund-Archiv 12) (Berlin: Anabas, 1984); Gert Selle, *Die Geschichte des Design in Deutschland von 1870 bis heute* (Cologne: DuMont, 1978).

16. For additional evidence of this temporal gendering, see, among many others, [Etincelle], *Carnet d'un mondain: Gazette Parisienne, anecdotique, et curieuse* (Paris: Edouard Rouveyre, 1881), 50–51; La Comtesse Jean de Pange, *Comment j'ai vu 1900* (Paris: Grasset, 1962), 247; Judith Gautier, *Le Second rang du collier* (Paris: Juven, 1909), 35; Gustave Droz, *Monsieur, Madame et Bébé* (Paris: Victor-Havard, 1884), 135–136. Another kind of evidence is to be found in the private archives of the furniture manufacturer and distributor, Maison Rinck. In their account books of 1901 to 1905 and their earlier photographic documentation of their production, one can clearly see the pattern of earlier styles being used for public rooms and later styles being used for private rooms (the private archives of the Maison Rinck, passage de la Bonne graine, 75012 Paris). For confirmation by one of the leading historians of design, see Forty, *Objects of Desire*, 65.

17. Vicomtesse Nacla, *Le Boudoir: Conseils d'élégance* (Paris: Flammarion, 1895), 219–220.

18. See the discussion of Mme. Pompadour's desk in Rioux De Maillou, "Causerie sur le mobilier: Le Bureau," *Revue des arts décoratifs* 6 (1885–1886): 138–142, 234–255. The taste professionals included architects interested in interior decor; the owners of the largest and most prestigious furniture companies (men who had typically built furniture in their youth); the most successful of interior decorators and designers; the members of the Union Central des Arts Décoratifs, and other such organizations; writers concerned with tastefulness and beauty, including the writers of etiquette books; and, lastly, legislators preoccupied with aesthetics and working-class dwellings. In general, they earned their living through their role as taste professionals, although not through the sale of particular objects. The taste professionals often disagreed with each other and engaged in fierce debate, although they did systematically, if individually, assert their legitimacy in the face of new claims to aesthetic authority on the part of the distributors. They were not an entirely new group in the late nineteenth century; there had been individuals working in these professions and expert amateurs since the eighteenth century, but the taste professionals, as an identifiable assemblage of subgroups, increased greatly in importance in the 1870s. They were very active from the early days of the Third Republic in trying to resuscitate—primarily through schools, museums, world's fairs, libraries, books, and magazines—the taste of both the producers and the consumers of furniture.

19. Nacla, *Le Boudoir: Conseils d'élégance*, 201.

20. Georges de Landemer, *Le Carnet des fiançailles* (Paris: Fédérlé, [c. 1910]), preface.

21. *Ibid.*

22. Few have been brave or foolhardy enough to try to correlate politics and furniture style in any direct way. An interesting discussion of the issue in the American context is found in Edward O. Laumann and James S. House, "Living Room Styles and Social Attributes: The Patterning of Material Artifacts in a Modern Urban Community," *Sociology and Social Research* 54 (1970): 321–342. The authors found that they could correlate consistency of style with consistency and extremity of political position, but that they could not correlate a certain style with a particular political party (335).

23. There is a wide variety of evidence for this claim. Many etiquette books and decorating magazines discuss what one ought to put in each room, novels provide descriptions of imagined rooms, memoirs provide other kinds of evidence of the meanings given ancien régime styles in the nineteenth century.

24. For an interesting discussion of the trans-historical association of femininity with decoration and especially makeup, see Jacqueline Lichtenstein, "Making Up Representation: The Risks of Femininity," *Representations* 20 (1987): 77–87.

25. Artisans in the trade understood (and understand) sculpting to be the most masculine of the wood trades. In fact, it was an enduring belief that having women working in a shop would "blunt the tools."

26. *Rapports des délégations ouvrières contenant l'origine et l'histoire des diverses professions*, ed. Arnould Desvernay (Paris: A. Morel, 1867), 5:86–87. For another, similar quote that explictly identifies Louis XVI furniture as feminine, see Paul Mantz, "Les Meubles du XVIIIᵉ siècle," *Revue des arts décoratifs* 4 (1883–1884): 183, 381.

27. Victor Champier, "La Maison modèle: Etudes et types d'ameublement," *Révue des arts décoratifs* 3 (1882–1883), 57.

28. The strongest version of this argument is Bonnie Smith, *Ladies of the Leisure Class: The Bourgeoises of Northern France in the Nineteenth Century* (Princeton: Princeton Univ. Press, 1981).

29. AN, series AB XIX "Account Books of Parisian Families, 1863–1937." AN AB XIX 3496 72G, "Livres de compte de la famille Bernard."

30. See, for example, Edouard Bajot, *Du Choix et de la disposition des ameublements* (Paris: E. Rouveyre, 1898). The only dining rooms shown are "Louis XI," "Henri II," and "Louis XIII." All of the "Louis XIV" and later furniture is for the more private spaces (salons, boudoirs, and bedrooms, with the exception of a "Louis XV" library). Evidence from decorating guides, advertising materials, company archives, and death inventories confirms this. One major source for this assertion is the collection of family accounts in AN AB XIX 3496–3503, "Livres de compte des familles parisiennes, 1863–1937." The series includes the private account books of

five Parisian families, all of which cover many years in multiple volumes, two of which traverse two generations.

31. Bedrooms were furnished with a double bed, often a canopy bed with curtains, a wardrobe, a dressing table, a chaise longue, a couple of other comfortable chairs, a small writing table, and a dresser or two. The boudoir would be furnished with a sewing table, a vanity, a chaise longue, a wardrobe, a few decorative small tables, some delicate shelves, and perhaps a couch. The public rooms of the house were even more thoroughly furnished than the private. A medium-sized living room had a couch or love seat, six armchairs, four chairs, a screen in front of the fireplace, a few *tabourets*, a firewood chest, a *table/guéridon*, and a piano. The assortment was adjusted for larger or smaller rooms, but a piano was an absolute requirement whether or not anyone played. Dining rooms generally contained a table, with leaves for larger dinners, six chairs, a sideboard, and sometimes a *dessert* or a *pannetier*. To these pieces of furniture must be added carpets, curtains, tablecloths, doilies, photographs, paintings, sculptures, clocks, small statues, vases, crucifixes, souvenirs, mirrors, ashtrays, silver tea services, decorative plates, dried flower arrangements, and assorted other objects. See, for example, Gautier, *Le Second Rang du collier*, 181–182; de Pange, *Comment j'ai vu 1900*, 189; Edmée Renaudin, *Edmée au bout de la table* (Paris: Stock, 1973), 13.

32. Valerie Feuillet, *Quelques années de ma vie* (Paris: Calmann-Lévy, 1894), 138–139.

33. AN AB XIX 3503, "Livres de compte des familles parisiennes, 1863–1937: Comptes de la famille Pariset, 1887–1914."

34. See also the record of Victor and Clélie Dujardin. Clélie Bernard and her future husband, Victor Dujardin, each brought into the marriage precisely the sum of 35,484 francs and 55 centimes. This sum represented Clélie's dowry and the liquid assets of both parties but did not count personal goods, which included furniture. Victor brought 1500 worth of personal goods, Clelie 3000. They also noted precisely all wedding presents received, whether given by a relation of Clélie or Bernard, and their worth (AN AB XIX 3496 72G).

35. Camille Marbo, *A Travers deux siècles, souvenirs, rencontres, 1883–1967* (Paris: Grasset, 1967), 364; Renaudin, *Edmée au bout de la table*, 115.

36. See, for example, Feuillet, *Quelques années de ma vie*, 39–40.

37. The records of auction houses provide detailed evidence for the tendency of family members to sell off inherited furniture. See the collection of auction catalogues at the Bibliothèque Forney in Paris.

38. See, for example, AN AB XIX 3498, "Décès de Mme. A. Allotte de la Fuye, 3 janvier 1898: Partage, Georges et Maurice." Georges and Maurice were her sons.

39. On the cost of furniture during the ancien régime and the difficulties the poor had in acquiring it, see Daniel Roche, *The People of Paris: An Essay in Popular Culture in the 18th Century*, trans. Marie Evans and Gwynne Lewis (Berkeley: Univ. of California Press, 1987); Annik Pardailhé-Galabrun, *La Naissance de l'intime:*

3000 foyers parisiens XVIIe-XVIIIe siècles (Paris: Presses Univ. de France, 1988), chap. 6; David Garrioch, *Neighborhood and Community in Paris, 1740–90* (Cambridge: Cambridge Univ. Press, 1986).

40. For the impact of mechanization on making ancien régime style veneered furniture available at a low price, see Alphonse Baude and A. Loizel, "Ebénistes," in *Exposition universelle de 1867 à Paris: Rapports de délégations ouvrières*, ed. M. F. Devinck (Paris: A. Morel, 1868), 16; Auguste Van Doren, *L'Ebénisterie à Bruxelles et à Paris* (Bruxelles: E. M. Devroye, 1860), 42; Tresca and Lecœuvre, "Machines-outils servant spécialement au travail des bois," in *Exposition universelle de 1867, Rapports du jury international*, ed. Michel Chevalier (Paris: Imprimerie Administrative de Paul Dupont, 1868), 9:133–134, 142–144. For the effects of the division of labor, see, for example, Descamps and Beaujean, "Tourneurs en chaises," in Devinck, *Exposition universelle de 1867 à Paris*, 2. For examples of the availability of furniture rental and credit, see BHVP, 120-Ameublement Bellot, undated advertising flyer, probably c. 1900; BHVP, 120-Ameublement, BE-BU, Berger, flyer 1903; BHVP, 120-Ameublement, V, Ville d'Aboukir, 1880s—from A la Ville d'Aboukir, 143 rue d'Aboukir, 2d arrondissement; AD Seine D 18 Z 9, Advertisement from "Le Comptoir français du meuble, 158 rue Lafayette (Paris, 1925). See also J. Boucher, *De la Vente à tempérament dans des meubles corporels au point de vue économique* (Paris: A. Pédone, 1906); Ismael Chaveau, *De la Vente à tempérament des objets mobiliers* (Paris: A. Pédone, 1909).

41. BHVP Ameublement-120, which contains advertising materials from approximately two hundred twenty Parisian stores, supports this claim. See, for example, BHVP 120-Ameublement, C, Advertisement for Au Confortable Moderne, 1902, 57 bis, ave. de la Motte-Picquet; BHVP 120-Ameublement, V, Ville d'Aboukir.

42. On socialist commentary on the arts, see Gaston-Louis Marchal, *Jean Jaurès et les arts plastiques* (Castres: chez l'auteur, 1984); Benoît Malon, *Le Socialisme intégral, 2e partie: Des Réformes possibles et des moyens pratiques* (Paris: Librairie de la Revue socialiste, 1894). The conservative sociologist Frédéric Le Play also expressed his views on style and the working class. See, among other texts, *Les Ouvriers des deux mondes* (Paris: A l'Enseigne de l'Arbre verdoyant, 1983). See also Octave Du Mesnil, *L'Hygiène à Paris: L'Habitation du pauvre* (Paris: J. B. Baillière, 1890).

43. Adrienne Cambry, *Fiançailles et fiancés* (Paris: Armand Colin, 1913).

44. For the critique of bourgeois taste, see Fourdinois, "Quelques réflexions sur le mobilier," 164–165.

45. On this aspect of the problem, see *Rapports des délégations ouvrières contenant l'origine et l'histoire des diverses professions* (Paris: Imprimerie Nationale, 1868) 5:67–68.

46. *Exposition universelle (de 1855): Galerie de l'économie doméstique* (Paris: J. Claye, 1855), 44.

47. Cambry, *Fiançailles et fiancés*; M. A. Cochin, "Classe 91: Meubles, vêtements et

aliments de toute origine, distingués par les qualités utiles, unies au bon marché," in *Exposition universelle de 1867 Paris*, 13:775–776. See also *Exposition universelle de 1855: Rapports du jury mixte internationale, publiés sous la direction de SAI le prince Napoléon* (Paris: Imprimerie Impériale, 1856), 1402–1403.

48. On this issue, see Lion Murard and Patrick Zylberberg, *Disciplines à domicile* (Paris: Recherches, 1977) and *L'Haleine des faubourgs: Ville, habitat, et santé au XIXe siècle* (Fontenay-sous-bois: Recherches, 1978). For another reading of the forms of planned dwellings for the working class, see Anne Louise Shapiro, "Paris," in *Housing the Workers, 1850–1914*, ed. M. J. Daunton (London: Leicester Univ. Press, 1990), 33–66.

49. *Exposition universelle (de 1855)*, 44.

50. For the earlier history of this image of the working class, see Louis Chevalier, *Laboring Classes and Dangerous Classes in Paris during the First Half of the Nineteenth Century*, trans. Frank Jellinek (New York: H. Fertig, 1873).

51. Luchet, *L'Art industriel*, 134.

52. For documentation of this, see *Exposition universelle (de 1855)*.

53. *Ibid.*, 13.

54. M. A. Cochin, "Classe 91: Meubles," 13:776.

55. *Ibid.*, 13:775–776.

56. Elisabeth de Gramont, *Mémoires: Les Marronniers en fleurs* (Paris: Grasset, 1925), 189.

57. *Exposition universelle de 1855: Rapports du jury mixte internationale*, 1402–1403; M. A. Cochin, "Classe 91: Meubles," 13:777; Picard, *Exposition universelle internationale de 1889 à Paris*, 3:6–7

58. See Lenard Berlanstein, *The Working People of Paris, 1871–1914* (Baltimore: Johns Hopkins Univ. Press, 1984); Eugène Atget, *Intérieurs parisiens du début du XXe siècle: Artistiques, pittoresques et bourgeois* (Paris: Musée Carnavalet, 1982). For the difficulties and possibilities of using Atget as a historical source, see the introduction to that catalogue, Margaret Nesbit, "Atget's *Intérieurs parisiens*, the Point of Difference," 25–28.

59. The advertisements in BHVP 120-Ameublement include detailed flyers from twenty stores serving popular consumers. Much of this furniture was given an ancien régime attribution.

60. Emile Zola, *Son Excellence Eugène Rougon* (Paris: Fasquelle, Livre de Poche, 1962), 151–152.

61. Paul Nizan, *Antoine Bloyé* (Paris: B. Grasset, 1930), 161–162.

62. *Ibid.*, 162.

63. For this understanding of the invention of the social, see Denise Riley, *"Am I That Name?" Feminism and the Category of 'Women' in History* (Minneapolis: Univ. of Minnesota Press, 1988). On the exclusion of women from history in the nineteenth century, see Christina Crosby, *The Ends of History: Victorians and 'the Woman Question'* (New York: Routledge, 1991).

64. On this point, see Pierre Verlet, *The Eighteenth Century in France: Society, Decoration, Furniture* (Rutland, Vt.: Charles E. Tuttle, 1967), and his *L'Art du meuble à Paris au XVIIIᵉ siècle* (Paris: Presses Univ. de France, 1958). For the use of furniture as a means for newly enriched bourgeois to accede to noble status, see Elinor Barber, *The Bourgeoisie in Eighteenth Century France* (Princeton: Princeton Univ. Press, 1955).

65. For a discussion of courtly consumption, see Norbert Elias, *The History of Manners*, vol. 1 of *The Civilizing Process*, trans. Edmund Jephcott (New York: Pantheon, 1978 [first published in German in 1939], esp. chaps. 3–5. More recent is Michael Stürmer, "An Economy of Delight: Court Artisans of the Eighteenth Century," *Business History Review* 53, no. 4 (Winter 1979): 496–528, esp. 500–514.

66. This is not, obviously, to imply that political power, or history, went uncontested during the ancien régime, but that such struggles over memory and the past did not play themselves out in decoration. See Keith Michael Baker, "Memory and Practice: Politics and the Representation of the Past in Eighteenth-Century France," *Representations* 11 (Summer 1985): 134–164.

67. There is a vast debate on the timing and importance of consumer demand in England. The literature on this aspect of industrial expansion and cultural transformation on the Continent, especially in the ancien régime, is still very thin. Although this debate is far from resolved, it does appear—not surprisingly—that consumer goods were first available to bourgeois consumers in Britain with the Continent following more slowly. It would also seem that the first goods to be widely available were small nondurables—pins, thread, small household goods—with durable, expensive goods like furniture following much later, even in Britain. Clothing occupied an intermediate position. Thus it does not appear that goods useful for social differentiation were widely available even in Britain before the second half of the eighteenth century, and on the Continent they were not widely available until well into the nineteenth. It also appears that France was far more court-dominated in the ancien régime than were Britain and the German lands. Among the central works for understanding the dynamic of consumer culture in Britain are D.E.C. Eversley, "The Home Market and Economic Growth in England, 1750–1780," in *Land, Labour, and Population in the Industrial Revolution*, ed. E. L. Jones and G. E. Mingay (New York: Barnes and Noble, 1967); W. A. Cole, "Factors in Demand, 1700–1780," in *The Economic History of Britain since 1700*, vol. 1, ed. Roderick Floud and Donald McCloskey (Cambridge: Cambridge Univ. Press, 1981), 36–65. The classic (and false, I think) argument for the strength of working-class demand in the eighteenth century is found in Neil McKendrick's "Home Demand and Economic Growth: A New View on the Role of Women and Children in the Industrial Revolution," in *Historical Perspectives: Studies in English Thought and Society*, ed. Neil McKendrick, (London: Europa, 1974). A stronger version appears in Neil McKendrick, John Brewer, and J. H. Plumb, *The Birth of a Consumer Society* (Bloomington: Indiana Univ. Press, 1982). For a recent and powerful argument on the relative

nonimportance of consumer durables and the greater importance of the well-to-do in creating consumer society, an argument that many of these authors will not accept, see Carole Shammas, *The Pre-industrial Consumer in England and America* (Oxford: Clarendon Press, 1990). For a demonstration of the notion that consumerism first emerged among the small things of everyday life, see Joan Thirsk, *Economic Policy and Projects: The Development of a Consumer Society in Early Modern England* (Oxford: Clarendon Press, 1974). On the role of cities in generating demand, see M. J. Daunton, "Towns and Economic Growth in Eighteenth-Century England," in *Towns in Societies: Essays in Economic History and Historical Sociology*, ed. Philip Abrams and E. A. Wrigley (Cambridge: Cambridge Univ. Press, 1982). (I am grateful to Alexander Dracobly for his help in establishing this argument.) On the German lands, see Ulrich-Christian Pallach, *Materielle Kultur und Mentalitäten im 18. Jahrhundert* (Munich: R. Oldenbourg Verlag, 1987). For additional references on French consumption, see the preceeding and following notes.

68. For the now classic formulation of the idea that the Revolution created the bourgeoisie rather than being created by the bourgeoisie, see Colin Lucas, "Nobles, Bourgeois, and the Origins of the French Revolution," *Past and Present* 60 (1973): 122, 130.

69. Although I have used the work of Norbert Elias to think through the distinction between courtly and bourgeois consumption, I am obviously here disagreeing with the argument he makes in *The History of Manners*. In that work Elias argues that courtly manners, having permeated bourgeois milieux in the eighteenth century, continued essentially unchanged into the nineteenth century (see esp. 49).

70. This is not to imply that those outside the courtly society did not own goods, but before the commodity consumer regime of the late nineteenth century, the primary sphere for the construction of representation and memory was not the possession and deployment of objects of style. For discussions of popular consumption under the ancien régime, see Roche, *The People of Paris*; Arlette Farge, *La Vie fragile: Violences, pouvoirs et solidarités á Paris au XVIIIe siècle* (Paris: Hachette, 1986), as well as the texts cited above.

71. For one of the most useful works on neoclassicism in interior decoration, see Svend Eriksen, *Early Neo-Classicism in France*, trans. Peter Thornton (London: Faber and Faber, 1974). For discussion of Greek aesthetics from within the trade, see André-Jacob Roubo, *L'Art du menuisier*, 5 vols. (Paris: Saillant et Nyon, 1769–1770), and from the nineteenth century, Agricol Perdiguier, *Le Livre du compagnonnage* (Paris: Pagnier, 1841).

72. The most extraordinary example is the pillaging of Chinese furniture for its lacquer surfaces that were then simply built into French forms. For additional discussion of the thoroughness with which Chinese forms and materials were de-exoticized in the seventeenth and eighteenth centuries, see, for example, Hugh Honor, *Chinoiserie* (London: John Murray, 1961), esp. chaps. 3–4.

73. Even seemingly "private" forms like clothing were, because they were worn in

public, of more central concern than the symbolic representations located behind walls.

74. See Mona Ozouf, *Festivals and the French Revolution*, trans. Alan Sheridan (Cambridge: Harvard Univ. Press, 1988); Lynn Hunt, *Politics, Culture, and Class in the French Revolution* (Berkeley: Univ. of California Press, 1984); Dorinda Outram, *The Body and the French Revolution: Sex, Class, and Political Culture* (New Haven: Yale Univ. Press, 1989).

75. Although it is often asserted that the economic impact of the Revolution was minimal because a considerable amount of production happened outside the guild and royal workshop structure, I would argue that the shift from a court to a market culture in the domain of consumption had critical implications for the development of artisanal production. The best and most recent discussions of eighteenth-century French artisanal production are Michael Sonenscher, *Work and Wages: Natural Law, Politics, and the Eighteenth-Century French Trades* (Cambridge: Cambridge Univ. Press, 1989); William Reddy, *The Rise of Market Culture: The Textile Trade and French Society, 1750–1900* (Cambridge: Cambridge Univ. Press, 1984). For the powerful impact of the Revolution on the furniture trades see, among others, Michael Stürmer, *Herbst des Alten Handwerks: Quellen zur Sozialgeschichte des 18. Jahrhunderts* (Munich: Deutscher Taschenbuch Verlag, 1979), 237, and *Handwerk und höfische Kultur* (Munich: C. H. Beck, 1982).

76. This notion of cultural forms, even seemingly hegemonic cultural forms, expressing societal contradictions has been elegantly developed by Thomas Crow in "Modernism and Mass Culture in the Visual Arts," in *Pollock and After: The Critical Debate*, ed. Francis Frascina (New York: Harper and Row, 1985), esp. 248–252, 255–256.

77. For a related, but somewhat different, argument on the importance of the absence of a monarch in creating style, see Deschamps, "Domestic Elegance," 118.

78. The only historical work of much use here is Philippe Perrot, *Les Dessus et les dessous de la bourgeoisie* (Paris: Fayard, 1981). For an interesting recent sociological study on fashion that is attentive to the ambiguity of women as self-constructed and women as manipulated by a fashion industry, see Elizabeth Wilson, *Adorned in Dreams: Fashion and Modernity* (Berkeley: Univ. of California Press, 1987). Dick Hebdige's book on style is also useful (*Subculture: The Meaning of Style* [London: Methuen, 1979]). Rosalind Coward and Stuart Ewen's analyses are both marred by their tendency to see consumers and especially women consumers as simply manipulated (Coward, *Female Desires* [New York: Grove Press, 1985]; Ewen, *All Consuming Images: The Politics of Style in Contemporary Culture* [New York: Basic Books, 1988]).

List of Contributors

LEORA AUSLANDER teaches European social history at the University of Chicago. Before becoming a historian, she built furniture for a living and has been obsessed by matters of taste ever since. She hopes her book resulting from that obsession, *The Production of Good Taste: The Social Life of Furniture in Paris, 1860–1914*, will come out in 1993.

SUZANNE DESAN is an associate professor of history at the University of Wisconsin, Madison. She has recently published *Reclaiming the Sacred: Lay Religion and Popular Politics in Revolutionary France* and is now working on urban culture and society during the Directory.

JAMES H. JOHNSON is an assistant professor at Boston University, where he teaches European intellectual history and humanities. His Ph.D. is from the University of Chicago (1988), where he studied with Keith Michael Baker and Jan Goldstein. His research includes work in the cultural history of listening among opera and concert audiences in France during the Old Regime, the Revolution, and the first half of the nineteenth century.

CATHERINE J. KUDLICK is an assistant professor of history at the University of California, Davis. She received her Ph.D. from the University of California, Berkeley (1988) and is currently completing a manuscript on social and cultural responses to the cholera epidemics of 1832 and 1849 in Paris.

MICHAEL A. OSBORNE teaches history of science and history at the University of California, Santa Barbara. He completed his Ph.D. in the history of science at the University of Wisconsin, Madison, where he studied under the itinerant historian and amateur naturalist William Coleman. A historian of the life sciences, Osborne is currently engaged in a study of French tropical medicine at Val-de-Grâce Hospital in the nineteenth and twentieth centuries. His *The Société Zoologique d'Acclimatation and the New French Empire: Science and Political Economy during the Second Empire and Third Republic* is forthcoming from Indiana University Press.

BRYANT T. RAGAN, JR., teaches French history at Fordham University. He received his doctorate from the University of California, Berkeley (1988) under the supervision of Lynn Hunt. He has published several articles on village politics in the late eighteenth century and is currently at work on a book manuscript, "Rural Political Culture during the French Revolution."

ELIZABETH A. WILLIAMS is an associate professor of history at Oklahoma State University. Her *The Physical and the Moral: Anthropology, Physiology, and Philosophical Medicine in France, 1750–1850* is forthcoming from Cambridge University Press. She has recently begun research on the vitalist tradition in Montpellier with the aid of a Scholar's Award from the National Science Foundation.

Index